NO POPE OF ROME

NO POPE OF ROME

ANTI-CATHOLICISM IN MODERN SCOTLAND
STEVE BRUCE

MAINSTREAM
PUBLISHING·EDINBURGH

First published in 1985 by
MAINSTREAM PUBLISHING COMPANY (EDINBURGH) LTD.
7 Albany Street
Edinburgh EH1 3UG

The publisher gratefully acknowledges the financial assistance of the
Scottish Arts Council in the publication of this volume.

ISBN 0 906391 78 4

Typeset in 11 point Garamond by Studioscope in conjunction with
Mainstream Publishing.
Printed by Billing & Sons, Worcester.

Contents

No Pope of Rome
No chapel to sadden my eyes
No nuns and no priest
No rosary beads
Every day is the Twelfth of July

(sung to the tune of *Home on the Range* by supporters of Glasgow Rangers FC, March 1983)

Preface

THIS book was written to fill an embarrassingly large gap in the literature on Scotland and Protestantism. While Protestant politics in Ulster, South Africa and the United States of America have been well researched and documented, the Scottish case has been almost entirely neglected. Few people now living know that there were anti-catholic political parties in Glasgow and Edinburgh in the nineteen-thirties that won more popular support than Mosley's fascists and yet British fascism has been the subject of much scholarly writing. That this book is innovative means that it will contain inaccuracies and misunderstandings. I am well aware that parts of the analysis are speculative. Despite my best endeavours some obviously important sources of material could not be found; an example: Protestant Action in Edinburgh produced a broadsheet between 1933 and 1936 which had a print run of more than a thousand copies but I am unable to find any. Hence the appeal: I would appreciate hearing from anyone who has any material on modern Scottish Protestantism which has not been referred to in the text.

It could be argued that Scottish anti-catholicism has been ignored because it is unimportant and uninteresting. I cannot accept this. Militant Protestantism was an important force in the development of modern Scottish religious, political and social life. And in the wider context, it offers an important contrast to the Ulster setting. An understanding of why anti-catholicism has declined in Scotland might help us to understand why it remains such a potent force in another part of the British Isles. It is my hope that, far from being the final word on the subject, this book will stimulate interest in anti-catholicism in Scotland. If it quickly becomes superseded by better informed analyses it will have been successful.

Finally in this preface I wish to acknowledge my debts. Professor Roy Wallis of The Queen's University of Belfast taught me when I was an undergraduate and supervised my doctoral research. Since then it has been my privilege to work with him in teaching and research. His influence on me has been considerable and can be clearly seen in the good bits of this book. The bad parts are almost certainly the result of my ignoring his advice. The British Academy, the Nuffield Foundation and Queen's University have all at various times supported my research and, most recently, the Social Science Research Council has funded a number of interviewing expeditions to Scotland. Without that financial assistance this research could not have been completed. However, none of these bodies is responsible for my analysis of the material. A large number of leaders and ordinary members of Scottish churches and other Protestant organisations have gone to great lengths to help me and the knowledge that I did not share their beliefs has never prevented them being extremely kind and helpful. There is not the space here to acknowledge them all and some would prefer to remain anonymous but Pastor Jack Glass and James Macdonald Morris deserve to be publicly thanked.

A number of my friends and colleagues have allowed themselves to be bored with many hours of "Did you know . . . ?" presentations of snippets of this work. Others have been as useful by refusing to feign the slightest interest. I am grateful to all of them, and to my wife. Finally, I would like to thank Angela Smartt and everyone in the Queen's University Secretarial Centre for their assistance in the production of this book.

Steve Bruce
The Queen's University of Belfast, January 1985

1

Protestants and Catholics
in the Nineteenth Century

SINCE the Reformation Scotland has been a Protestant country. It is true that the influence of Knox and his fellow reformers was hardly felt above the highland line but, despite the tourist trade image of clans and tartans, the highlands have never been the essence of Scotland. Political and economic power, and hence social and cultural influence, lay in the lowlands, the part nearest to England. The lowlands were Protestant, Hanoverian and Whig. That the highlands were not owed a great deal to the geology. One traveller to the North offered the following description of the glens:

> In this country one mountain is rudely piled upon another, with vast hollows between them, that are filled with snow . . . The ridge runs east and west and if they are viewed in that direction, they form the most dreadful prospect that can be conceived . . . The eye then penetrates far among them, and sees more particularly their stupendous bulk, frightful irregularity and horrid gloom which becomes more striking by the shades . . . Among these scenes of desolation, which look either like the embryo or ruins of the world, a few firs and small oaks are sometimes discovered.[1]

The physical inaccessibility of the glens was mainly responsible for the continuation of the feudal social structure of the highlands. The people were organised on familial lines. Below the chief were a number of chieftains and below them the "tacksmen": tenant farmers who maintained a large number of subtenants. The terrain discouraged travel and there was considerable inter-marriage. Whether or not the majority of any one clan was actually the chief's kin is debatable but that myth was a crucial part of the sense of social solidarity in the clan, which was not only an extended family and a large economic organisation; it was also a fighting unit. Intense solidarity within each clan had its counterpart in hostility between clans. Stealing the cattle of other clans (and from the farms of bordering lowland counties) was a major part of economic activity and the animosity it caused was added to by long-standing feuds over seemingly trivial insults to clan honour. The general lawlessness made it vital that a chief was thus measured not by the productivity or the rent value of his lands but by the size of the army he could raise. In areas where judicial machinery of the state could not penetrate, the clan chief was also the source of law.

There were small pockets of Roman Catholicism left in the highlands but generally the highlanders followed the religion of the established church: the Kirk. This alternated between Presbyterian and Episcopal forms of Protestantism with changes in the fortunes of governments. Or, to be more precise, it *should have alternated*.[2] In practice, there was very little fondness for Presbyterianism in the highlands. When the Williamite Revolution of 1647 that replaced the Jacobite Stewarts with William of Orange also removed the Bishops, the lowlands rejoiced. The highlanders did not.

> There were a few among the people who had hailed the Revolution with delight, and who, still more, rejoiced in the restoration of the Gospel to their land; but the number of such was small. In several parishes the first presentees had much opposition to encounter. In 1716 the minister of Gairloch was compelled to leave his parish, owing to the ill-treatment he received at the hands of both the laird and the people. His crops were destroyed, his home robbed and he and his family reduced to starvation. In 1720, the presentee to Lochalsh was not allowed to preach at all in the parish, and for several years after he was first driven out of it, he could not venture to return to his charge.[3]

The Presbyterian Duke of Argyll's nominee for the charge of Glenorchy was forced to leave the parish by armed men who first made him "swear on the Bible that he would not return".[4] The previous Episcopal incumbent remained for a further thirty years. Another example of the tenacity of Episcopalianism was offered by the people of Daviot. The Episcopal incumbent, Michael Frazer, was a pleasant but hardly conscientious cleric. At the Revolution his Presbyterian predecessor was still alive and re-claimed the incumbency. The Commissioners of the Assembly declared the parish vacant in 1694 but Frazer retained the support of the congregation. When the Presbytery visited Daviot in 1721 they were stoned. The unfortunate Minister of Croy, who agreed to "supply" the officially vacant church and took some of his own congregation with him when he went to preach, received similar treatment:

> With some difficulty I got access to the church and had no sooner begun worships than by stones thrown in, the pulpit was broken about me, and some of my parishioners wounded. Being obliged to remove for our safety, we were assaulted by a multitude of men and women, with swords, staves and stones, some of our number wounded and others barbarously beaten.[5]

Nor was the opposition entirely local and spontaneous. A group of Macraes took it upon themselves to travel from one parish to another threatening the Presbyterian appointees.

Even where there was no active opposition from the people, it was still not possible to remove the Episcopalian ministers quickly because there was a shortage of Gaelic speaking replacements. It was this shortage of provision that explains the inroads made by Catholic missionaries. The peasants' religion was sufficiently superstitious for them to believe in the absolute necessity of certain rituals. If there were no Presbyterian ministers to baptise their children, then they would make use of the services of a Roman Catholic rather than have no baptism. For this reason, the religion of the people had little to do with deliberate choice between competing alternatives and a lot to do with simple supply. In the seventeenth and early eighteenth century, people tended to accept the religion that was provided. As will become clear below, when there was a deliberate choice, it was based more on political than theological preference. Catholicism and Episcopalianism were associated with the Jacobite cause; the Presbyterians were by and large Whigs.

The lack of provision is a major feature of the Church in the highlands and islands until the middle of the nineteenth century. The financial support of the parish minister was the responsibility of those who owned the land — the heritors — and many of them were not too

keen to be put to considerable expense. They therefore supported the
union of parishes. Before the Reformation the Hebrides had almost
fifty parishes. By the beginning of the seventeenth century the process
of amalgamation had turned the whole of Lewis into one parish.[6]
Where there was no formal union, a lack of manpower created *de facto*
united parishes. It was not until the 1720s, when the threat of
"popery" loomed large, that the structure of the Church was reformed:
but centuries of neglect could not be annulled easily. Anyway, there
was a world of difference between the Church instructing heritors to
build churches and provide manses and glebes, and anything actually
happening. Jacobite chiefs were not keen to spend money on the
Protestant cause and the state was not in a position to force them to
accept their legal responsibilities.

Education

The provision of schools and teachers was almost as thin as that of
churches and ministers. The Scottish Privy Council had in 1616
ordained the planting of a school in every parish but fifty years later
many lowland parishes were still without one and the position in the
highlands was considerably worse. A number of grammar schools
were established in the burghs and some rural parishes would combine
resources to provide one such school, where the teaching of Latin and
Greek were obligatory and not optional. These institutions were
responsible for the literacy and culture of the gentry but they did little
to educate the mass of the people. Even if the ideal of one school for
every parish had been attained this would still have been woefully
inadequate. Leaving aside the already mentioned "united" parishes,
one can simply note that the parish of Ardnamurchan was ninety
miles in length! Furthermore, the dissemination of elementary
education was not assisted by the stated policy of the Church, which
was the eradication of Gaelic. Even enlightened observers of the mid-
eighteenth century, such as John Walker, believed that Gaelic could
not become a written language. The consequence was that the
highlands were some 70 years behind the lowlands. By 1700 the
problem in the south was, as McInnes put it, not quantity of schools,
but quality. The same could not have been said about the highlands; in
1758 there were still 157 highland parishes that had no school.[7]

The Civilisation of the Highlands and Islands

One can suppose that the Scottish periphery would have gradually been assimilated into the economy and society of Britain. The demand for meat in the south was increasing and the highlands were becoming more involved in grazing and fattening animals reared in the lowlands. Economic ties would have strengthened and gradually drawn the people of the north into greater contact with the rest of the country but the process was considerably hastened by the two great political adventures of the Jacobite Risings. In 1715 and again in 1745, leading highland chiefs and their followers fought in the interest of the Stewart monarchy. These rebellions convinced the Whig government and its lowland supporters of the need to destroy the traditional culture of the north.

The Whigs were sensitive enough to see that the willingness of the highlanders to engage in such adventures could only be diminished if their whole way of life was undermined. Civilisation of the north required military conquest, economic reform, increased physical accessibility and a cultural revolution. Although the progress was halting and uneven, affecting some parts of the highlands and islands long before others, one can picture the changes in the north in the eighteenth century as being a result of a general process of externally stimulated social change.

One of the first sources of change was the Royal Bounty. George I presented the General Assembly of the Church of Scotland with £1000 in 1723 (it became an annual gift in 1725). The money was used to pay lay catechists; itinerants who taught the peasants the basics of the Shorter Catechism. Many of the catechists also worked as teachers for the Society for the Propagation of Christian Knowledge (SPCK). The SPCK had been given its Royal Charter in 1709. It was a charity, founded to "eradicate error and to sow truth, to teach true religion and loyalty and to strengthen the British Empire by the addition of useful subjects and firm Protestants".[8] In 1711, five SPCK schools were built in the highlands. By 1732 that number had risen to 109 and by 1795 there were 229 SPCK schools in the north of Scotland. The schools, while they later played a major part in the reformation of the highlands, were not immediately great agents of change. Although some were bravely planted in Catholic areas, these had little initial impact. A report to the General Assembly in the 1730s said:

When the Papists send their children to the SPCK schools, Priests do
threaten the parents with excommunication, and they are laid under the
displeasure of their Popish landlords: yea Popish schools and
Seminaries are kept in place yet, and Popish Bishops have their
meetings with Clergy, and send Youth abroad to Popish Colleges, and
many of them when returned are put in orders, and sent to their
respective pretended functions, and many marry and Baptise Papists
and Protestants, and Intrude themselves on Sick persons, whereby
some few have been brought over to Popery.[9]

Similarly, enclaves of Episcopalianism survived where the chiefs
supported it.

The early attempts at education had their greatest impact when
combined with more direct and forceful methods of dislocating the
society. After the 1715 Rising, General Wade constructed 250 miles of
metalled road. After the 1745, another 800 miles were added.[10] Many
chiefs, realising the destitution of the Jacobite cause, became
Protestants. In 1748 the power of chiefs to act as judges was removed.
It was declared illegal for highlanders to wear the tartan or to carry
arms. Cumberland's army systematically destroyed Catholic and
Episcopalian chapels.

The failure of the second Jacobite rising opened the way for
modernisation in one direct fashion. In a rather enlightened act,
George decided to use the assets of the estates of the rebels for general
social and economic improvement rather than for his own use. The
Scottish Court of the Exchequer was authorised to take charge of the
forfeited estates:

For the Purposes of civilising the Inhabitants upon the said Estates, and
other Parts of the Highlands and Islands of Scotland, and promoting
amongst them the Protestant religion, good Government, Industry and
Manufactures, and Principles of Duty and Loyalty to his Majesty, his
Heirs and Successors, and to no other use or Purpose whatsoever.[11]

The Estates were administered by a group of the "good and true" from
the "Enlightenment" circles of Edinburgh, which included Lord
Kames, the great agricultural improver. Improvements were
introduced and attempts were made to introduce manufactures to the
highlands. Those reforms tend, however, to be overshadowed by the

costly and in the end pointless construction of the Caledonian Canal.

The Clearances

Major economic transformation did come to the highlands and islands but it was not in the form promoted by John Walker in his report to the Commissioners for Annexed Estates. Walker was alert to the problem of surplus population that would arise from any attempt to get away from the unproductive subsistence economy of the region and he suggested a variety of ways in which arable farming could be made efficient. In the event, what came to pass was precisely what he feared; massive enclosure of the land for increased pastoral farming.

This phase of social change followed the pattern common to most European societies. A complex social structure, based on customary rights and obligations, was simplified and traditional rights and obligations were replaced by relations based on cash exchange and contracts. The highland chiefs had long enjoyed a double life. Many of them were as much at home in the courts of London and Paris as they were in their glens. While they still had a military role to play there was some purpose in keeping the land over-stocked with people. Once the clan system had been undermined it better served their interests to become simple landlords. To keep up their status in London they required increased income from rents and that could not be produced while the land was let out to tacksmen and sub-tenants for minimal rents in return for military services. Tenants had to become efficient farmers; peasants had to become labourers.[12]

Although the time-scale varied from place to place — usually in relation to the wealth of the chief with the wealthiest, such as the Duke of Argyll, being the slowest to act — the general principal of change was that which had been seen all over Europe: enclosure. For a short period the lords of the Hebrides and the west coast turned to kelping.[13] Seaweed when burnt produces an alkaline resin which was used in a variety of industries such as glass and soap making. The peasants cleared from the land were encouraged to work as kelping labourers and it was the desire to keep a large (and hence cheap) labour force that explains why the highland lairds were initially opposed to emigration. The great kelp boom was, however, short-lived. Cheaper substitutes were found. One might add, as a sad footnote, that while kelping provided large profits for the owners of the estates for a short period, it further reduced the ability of the peasants to survive on their subsistence farming because, as Walker noted in his tour of Lewis, seaweed was the most common fertiliser. When it was diverted to kelping, the fertility of the land, already disastrously low, was further reduced.

The clearing of the land for large sheep walks was not planned in an entirely heartless manner. Even in the most criticised clearances — those on the Sutherland estates in the 1820s — efforts were made to resettle the population and provide new forms of more productive employment. Often they were moved to newly cleared settlements on the coast and encouraged to fish. Sometimes this "encouragement" took the form of barring alternatives. In writing to one of his aides, the Duchess of Sutherland's agent said:

> I am particularly anxious that their lots should be so small as to prevent their massing any considerable part of their rent by selling a beast, rent must not depend on that. In short I wish them to become fishers only, but if you give them any extent of land or of Commonality they will never embark heartily in that pursuit.[14]

At this distance from the clearances it is easy to be so impressed by the physical and practical hardship forced on the highlanders that one misses the more serious psychological loss. The clansmen, while certainly poor, had a considerable independence and a deep commitment to the ancestral land. Whether or not the chief actually "owned" the clan lands, the people regarded that land as theirs, the property of the whole community. Subsistence farming, while inefficient in modern terms, afforded both independence and security. The chiefs' replacement of custom by contract was devastating, not just because it caused financial hardship, but because it removed from the peasants something they had always taken for granted: their possession of the land. This can be seen clearly in the background to the Kildonan riot of 1813.[15] When the people of the Strath found that they were being moved to make way for sheep walks, they offered to match any rent that might be paid by the incoming sheep farmers. They failed to recognise that the Duchess of Sutherland and her agent were not simply interested in the highest short-term rent but in "improvement", almost as if it were a virtue in its own right.

The second half of the eighteenth century and first part of the nineteenth century saw the destruction of a society. Its social structure, its economy and its culture were changed beyond recognition.

The Evangelical Revival

The economic and social transformation of the highlands and islands was accompanied by the conversion of the highlanders from a folk religion which combined pagan elements with Catholicism and Episcopalianism to Calvinist Protestantism. Ironically this change took place at a time when Calvinism was being eroded within the Church of Scotland in the lowlands. At the same time as the peasants of the north were becoming evangelicals, the city dwellers of the south were developing a rational Protestantism that tended towards a univeralism and an emphasis on good works and morality rather than salvation and piety. This is a good measure of the degree to which the two parts of Scotland were out of step. At the start of the eighteenth century the lowlanders decried the highlanders for their paganism and popery; at the end of the century they attacked them for their evangelical enthusiasm.

It is not uncommon for religious revivals to accompany large-scale social change. Changes in the economy of medieval Europe produced a large pool of dispossessed and insecure individuals and many of these joined religious movements that preached the imminent end of the world. Similar millenialist movements — the cargo cults — have been a common feature of Polynesia and Melanesia since the disruption of the Polynesian way of life by modern culture.[16] Certainly contemporary commentators saw the evangelical revival as a response, a reaction, to social change: "It is well-known that no itinerant preacher ever gained a footing among the highlanders, till recent changes in their situations and circumstances made way to fanaticism."[17] Although that author was a Jacobite romantic who mourned the passing of the highlanders' quaint superstitions, his view is supported by a Whig observer who said it was well-known that "the recent degradation and misery of the people have predisposed their minds to imbibe these pestiferous delusions to which they fly for consolation under their sufferings."[18]

Ministers and Men

The dominant feature of the religious revival was its lay character. Far from being a social movement led by the clergy of the Church, it was a movement that very often took the form of opposition to the ministers. The reason for this is not hard to find; the clergy of the highlands were in a fairly parlous condition. The difficulties of serving a people scattered across enormous areas of difficult terrain cannot be exaggerated but it has to be said that many clergymen "regarded the difficulties of their situation not as spurs to action but as convenient excuses for doing nothing".[19] Most ministers had to farm to survive but some farmed as a career rather than a necessity. John Skeldoch of Farr (1732-1751) held three tacks and in the opinion of the Synod of Caithness, "seems to be obstinately determined to entangle himself with worldly affairs and to have no regard to the command of the judicatories".[20] The later point refers to Skeldoch's neglect of earlier injunctions from the Presbytery of Tongue to attend more to his spiritual concerns. Skeldoch played the role of "pastor" in a literal rather than figurative sense. The minister of Applecross only celebrated communion four times in twenty years, kept a boat for his fishing, and "has a considerable land property and money stocked otherwise".[21] It is said of the minister of Duthil that he had only two sermons but for variety changed the passages of scripture that were the pretext for them.

Such laxity was, of course, not confined to the highland clergy nor even to the ministers of the Scottish Church. A similarly minimalist view of the degree of piety and of the amount of attention to the flock required was common in the Anglican church and among the Scots ministers of the lowlands. John Walker, whose report on the highlands and islands of 1764 showed considerably more sympathy for, and understanding of, the peasants than was common, was an archetypal "moderate" minister of the south. He took holy orders because the ministry seemed a good occupation for a man of bookish tastes and he devoted himself to geology and natural history. He was far more at home in the drawing rooms of the Edinburgh bourgeoisie than he was in his pulpit. Although he abhorred popery, this dislike had more to do with what he saw as the social and economic consequences of that religion:

> Even the progress of the arts of Industry will be prevented, as Popery prevails. For the Baleful influence of the Popish religion, wherever it is generally professed in the Highlands is visible, even in the face of the country. There, not only the morals and manners of the people but the very Soil, is more rude and uncultivated. The Popish inhabitants . . .

become peculiarly averse to every innovation, that tends to promote industry, or improve the country.[22]

Protestantism was a matter of the correct moral and social values, not a set of beliefs and practices necessary for salvation. Walker absented himself from his parish for months on end while he went in search of botanic specimens. A parishioner said: "he spent the week hunting butterflies and made the cure of the souls of his parishioners a bye-job on Sundays".[23]

Whether the "moderates" of the north were any more lax than their southern counterparts is difficult to judge. From what was said of them, it seems likely that they were.[24] Alexander Simpson of Lochs (1793-1833) was reputed to be a serious drunk and "the gospel which he was ordained to serve at, he seemed ignorant of, and it was a strange substitute he preached".[25] Such condemnations could be multiplied but Kennedy's succinct judgement of the ministers of Ross-shire can stand for many of the highland clergy: they "cared not to affect much Godliness and were not suspected of any".[26]

The cast of the minister depended largely on the character of the landlord. Although the Restoration Settlement had guaranteed the future of Presbyterianism in the Scottish Church, it was not long before the government saw the value of removing the right to choose the minister from the congregation and investing it in the principal landowners. The patrons could then choose ministers whose views agreed with their own.

> It thus happened that the west coast and the islands generally, where the patrons were not noted for their Protestantism or their piety, had ministers presented to the livings who were in all respects like their patrons; while in Sutherland, Easter Ross, and Moray, where the gentry were, on the whole, zealous and pious Protestants, evangelical and zealous ministers were settled among the people.[27]

The Men

"The Men" were so called, not because they were not women, but because they were not ministers. Many of the Men were catechists and school-teachers in the employ of either the SPCK, the Gaelic School Society or the Royal Bounty Committee of the General Assembly.

Poorly paid, these individuals worked in difficult conditions to impart the rudiments of education and religion to the peasants. Their humble status was undoubtedly an aid to this endeavour. Almost all of them had been peasants and their small salaries did nothing to separate them from the mass of the people. Macfarlane's collection of biographies of the Men of Lewis records the occupation of forty-one.[28] Twenty-two of these were catechists, teachers or both; seven were crofters; two were joiners; and there were two weavers. One of the Men was an itinerant evangelist. There was one cartwright and one boat builder. The final five with recorded occupations were respectively a tacksman, a chemist, a pair of merchants, and one manufacturing business man. It is interesting to note that this group belonged to the later generation of 1850-1900; they were the upwardly mobile offspring of the teachers and catechists. In Kennedy's account of the Ross-shire men the only named occupations are crofter and teacher/catechist. Unlike many ministers, the Men were never in the position of being landlords.

Although many of them had some formal status as purveyors of religion, it was not this status that made them "Men". The recognition that a certain individual was especially pious and "useful" as an expositor, public prayer, or preacher came mainly through his performance at either the regular fellowship meeting or the "speaking to the question" on the Friday of a communion season. The fellowship meeting was an evening gathering, usually weekly, for prayer and discussion of some text of scripture and the morals that could be drawn from it. Such loose associations meeting outside the formal ministry of the church were common in the lowlands in the days of Covenanters when persecution and a lack of ordained clergy forced the people to make their own provision. Some praying societies were known in the north and evangelical ministers, such as Thomas Hog of Kiltearn, revived them as an additional part of their missionary activity.[29]

In the highlands, some communions were "private": that is, attendance was restricted to people of that parish. But many were public events. Believers from all over the highlands would gather on one parish and four or five ministers would be required to perform all the services. The "season" began with a fast day on Thursday. There were preparatory services on the Saturday, the communion service on the Sunday and a thanksgiving service on the Monday. To this programme was added the fellowship meeting on the Friday. Here the

Men came into their own. One person at the meeting, originally an "anxious enquirer", would read a piece of scripture and then ask what were the "marks of the true believer" that could be discerned from the text. This was "the question". The presiding minister would normally offer a short homily and then invite various members of the audience to "speak to the question". It was the ability to deliver suitable, arresting evangelical addresses that was the main criterion for becoming one of the Men. A chief characteristic of the homilies was the homely illustration. One of the Men of Lewis was John Macleod, Gaelic teacher in Maravaig, in Lochs. One of his illustrations was: "The Christian is known by his tastes in the matter of food. I know a Uist man at once by how he goes for Barley scones. I know a real child of God by what he delights to feed his soul on".[30]

McInnes, in listing the typical characteristics of the Men, begins by noting their retentive memories.[31] Like many members of non-literate cultures, the Men could recall large amounts of text and many of them could recite, without prompt, any passage of scripture. One of the leaders of the first generation of the Men of Skye, Donald Munro, was blind and yet his knowledge of the Bible was second to none. The Men were also great prayers. Eight hour prayer meetings were not unknown and some of the highland divines were so given to prayer that they could do no work. Donald Kennedy of Balallan, was such a case:

> He was much in communion with God, and often found his way to a quiet hillock where he entered the cloud and the glory. He withdrew from earthly concerns into the serener themes of the spiritual world. He was a crofter, but his wife and family toiled at the croft and did not ask him to condescend from his kingdom of thought. There was an air of calm about him which impressed the village.[32]

Interestingly, like many other religious enthusiasts, Donald Kennedy alternated serenity with deep depressions as his sense of sinfulness overwhelmed him.

Many of the Men were credited with the powers of prophecy and second sight. Murdo Macdonald of Lewis once:

> lifted up his voice in an earnest cry that God would remove by death or otherwise, those feather-bed shepherds who fed not their flocks. It was a startling prayer. The minister of Uig died that year, and the

minister of Stornoway was drowned the following year while crossing
the Minch in the mail packet. It raised a storm against Murdo
Macdonald.[33]

Stories are frequently told of Men sensing that someone, not present,
had died. It was said of Malcolm Campbell, a Lewis joiner, that his
coffin-making tools rattled together when somone died. It was
certainly the case that the peasants had a superstititous fear of some of
the Men. A farmer who threw the itinerant evangelist Finlay Munro
out of his kitchen is reputed to have simply faded away and died.
Malcolm Maclean was of a later generation but was also reputed to
have second sight. The local people turned to him to enquire about the
fate of missing or delayed boats. His reputation had one fortunate
consequence for the Free Church after its formation in 1843. Malcolm
Maclean became the local collector of donations for the Sustentation
Fund and people usually gave generously for fear that the dire fates he
predicted for the ungenerous might be realised.[34]

Another distinguishing feature of the Men was their staunch
sabbatarianism. One Lewisman had to walk thirty miles to church in
Stornoway. He considered taking his pension slip with him so that he
could draw the money on Monday but this offended against the
sanctity of the Lord's day. So he walked to Stornoway and back on the
sabbath and then repeated the journey to collect his pension on
Monday.[35]

A final point to make about the Men was that they were conscious
of their identity as part of a movement. They were not simply isolated
individuals who shared the common characteristic of an enthusiastic
evangelical Protestantism. They were part of an organised social
movement. They met regularly at different communion seasons;
touring from one communion to another was common among the
devout. When they travelled, they lodged with each other. They quoted
each other and exchanged ideas and epithets. Like all such movements,
there were internal divisions. At one time the Men of Ross-shire were
set against the Men of Lewis because they doubted the validity of the
Lewis revival. Such sectional divisions sometimes surfaced at
fellowship meetings when one of the Men from one area might rise to
criticise what a previous speaker had said. (The question of why
conservative Protestantism is particularly susceptible to schism will be
discussed later.) Although the Men had their own quarrels, they did
form a distinctive social movement with their own beliefs, practices,

and a social network that kept them in touch with each other. Finally, their identity was signalled to the world by their dress. They often wore long blue cloaks, a spotted handkerchief over their hands, and kept their hair longer than was the fashion. This style seems to have been more of a uniform in Ross-shire and other parts of the mainland than it was in Lewis where many of the Men wore hats. Of the Ross-shire Men, Kennedy said, "if their dress seemed peculiar, it was only because it was old-fashioned even for the highlands".[36]

Reactions to the Men varied considerably. The moderate ministers naturally disliked them intensely. They accused them of fanaticism, heresy, and even sexual licence. In 1737, the Synod of Caithness and Sutherland officially suppressed the great public fellowship meetings which were the key element in the movement. The controversy continued for twenty years and the Men won. Relations between the Men and the clergy varied from one region to another. Kenneth Ross, of Lochs and Carloway in Lewis, although only a catachist and lay missionary, acted as "minister" in Carloway for fourteen years and was not harassed; presumably because he was in an area which had no clerical provision. Another Lewisman, John MacLeod of Galson was not so fortunate. A teacher for the Gaelic Schools Society, he fell foul of Reverend William Macrae of Barvas, a moderate who was keen on education but not evangelicalism. Macrae had Macleod dismissed by the Society. The people of Galson and Dell reacted by building Macleod a school-house and paying his salary. Macrae then had most of Macleod's supporters barred from the church and they stayed out until the evangelical Finlay Cook was presented to the newly erected parliamentary church at nearby Cross.[37]

In these two cases, the Men confined their challenge to offering an alternative. Some lay evengelicals preferred more direct confrontation. Four of the Men of Lewis were arrested and imprisoned after they interrupted their minister's sermon to accuse him of being a "murderer of souls".[38] A mid-nineteenth century source reports a case of a minister having to listen to one of his members, at a congregational fellowship meeting, praying that it might be revealed to the people "for which of their sins God had allowed *him* to be their pastor".[39]

The story of Macrae and Macleod is illustrative of the ambiguity of the Men, and of their followers, towards the national Church. They objected strenuously to moderate ministers and frequently withdrew from one particular parish church. But even those Men who preached

regularly in competition with their ministers would travel to hear
evangelical ministers such as John Porteous, Lachlan Mackenzie, John
Macdonald and John Kennedy. A few of the Men — Alexander
Campbell, Norman Macleod, John Grant — became out and out separatists, arguing that the sins of the moderates were so great as to defile
the whole national Church and all in it, but the dominant mood was
one of considerable attachment to the Church as an idea.[40]

Macrae's explanation for the failure of the separatists is that the
conflict between Catholics, Episcopalians and Presbyterians had
forced the latter to close ranks and created a sense of identity that
continued even once the others had ceased to offer significant
competition.[41] There is much merit in this notion but one should also
add the influence of the fact the movement led by the Men was a
highland, rather than merely local movement. Although they rarely
travelled outside the highlands, the Men thought nothing of going
considerable distances. And what they usually travelled for was to
attend a communion season and to hear their favourite ministers
preach. Although considerable crowds might gather to hear one of the
Men preach, it was only at a communion season that multitudes
gathered, that numbers of the Men and evangelical ministers from
distant places could be heard. The separatists could not with any
conviction hold communion services. The changes in the religious
climate of the north had certainly been away from beliefs in the
authority and necessity of an ordained clergy (that is, from Catholic to
Episcopalian to Presbyterian) but the people had not broken so far
away from their past as to accept communion without ministers. Thus,
although the religious revival was predominantly a lay movement in
which the Men played a greater part than the evangelical ministers,
the church still had a vital institutional part to play in providing the
occasion for the main meeting point for those involved in the revival.
Hence the residual attachment to the idea of the Church even amongst
those who were alienated from their own ministers.

There is no need here to offer a detailed explanation of the
highland revival. There is no doubt that it was a reaction to the social
dislocation of the clearances and "modernisation".[42] It was also a
reaction to the toadying moderate ministers who cared more for the
gentry who paid them than for the people they were supposed to
serve. What is important for this book is not the cause but the
consequence of the revival.

The ironic effect of the revival, forged largely in opposition to the clergy of the established Church, was to save the highlands for the Church. In the lowlands, the moderate domination had caused not one popular opposition movement but a number of isolated schisms. Those who were not prepared to abandon their Calvinism and stop being "religious overmuch" left and formed various "Seceder" churches. Here again one returns to the time delay between lowland and highland change. The disputes between the moderates and evangelicals in the lowlands occurred in the middle of the eighteenth century and by the time similar arguments were being fought in the highlands the lowland Seceders had developed into a well established denominational organisation.

Moderate domination of the Kirk began to wane in the 1830s. Over a ten year period, the evangelicals gradually increased their power and influence but they were prevented from achieving domination by the institution of patronage. The senior heritor or heritors, who as the major landowners supported the minister and the church, were given the right to call a minister against the expressed wishes of the people. Patronage was the source of many disputes, although fewer than one might have expected because many absentee landowners were happy to leave their local representative to settle the matter in consultation with the people. Still, disputes were frequent enough to keep a steady trickle of congregations leaving the Kirk for one of the Seceder groups because they had been "intruded" upon with an unpopular minister. Patronage was not only a permanent sore on the church body; it was also an insurmountable obstacle for the evangelicals. Few patrons were supporters of the evangelical cause and so the evangelicals would be constantly under-represented unless the law could be changed. This the evangelicals tried to do without success. Gradually the whole question of proper church and state relationships came to dominate General Assemblies and Presbyteries. In 1843, the evangelicals walked out of the Church of Scotland and formed what became the Free Church of Scotland.

The Free Church men were not "voluntaries". Unlike the earlier Seceders, they did not reject the idea that the state should support a national established church; they just thought that the actual terms of the present arrangement were one-sided. They were prepared to come back to an established church once the state stopped meddling in the church's affairs. In all about one-third of the Church of Scotland walked out into the Free Church but this third was made up of two quite different constituencies. The lowlanders of the new Free Church were, like the Seceders, the new rising bourgeosie.[43] This is not surprising. Separation from the state church required two types of independence: the financial independence to be able to support a minister and a building programme, and the intellectual independence to make up one's own mind. The people who had most of these two forms of independence were the new middle classes.

In the highlands, however, it was the peasantry, the ordinary crofters and labourers who followed the Men, who moved into the Free Church. This split nature of the Free Church explains the rapid change in its theology and character. In the space of forty years, the Free Church in the lowlands changed from being considerably more conservative than the Kirk to being more liberal. This was the result of modernising influences on the urban middle class. They were acquiring wealth, status, position and with them, travel, education and considerable opportunities to indulge the senses. They quickly found (usually in German rationalism) new theologies that would justify their accommodation to the ways of the world. The peasants of the highlands, however, remained socially and culturally isolated and attached to the Calvinism which they had only recently acquired with such gusto. The result was a further division with the highland element coming out of the Free Church. The liberals united with the Seceders (who had divided into liberals and conservatives) to form the United Free Church. Thus there were at the start of this century three main Presbyterian Churches: the established Church, the United Free Church and the mostly highland Free Church.[44]

The arcane mysteries of Scottish church history have not been introduced here to demonstrate erudition but to give enough background to the religious situation in Scotland to set the scene for the other element in anti-catholicism: the arrival of some Roman Catholics.

The Irish in Scotland

As already noted, the incomplete nature of the Reformation left small pockets of Scottish Catholicism and the poor provision of Presbyterian clergy left a demand that was exploited by Catholic missionaries. The result was small groups of Catholics in the north-east — Banff, Angus, the Mearns and Kincardine — and in some of the Hebridean islands; Barra and South Uist, for example. In the lowlands as a whole the

Reformation was complete. Bishop Hay's 1780 census mentions only 6,600 Roman Catholics below the highland line.[45]

In this period Protestants and Catholics generally enjoyed harmonious relations. Whether this was due to the numerical insignificance of Catholicism, or to the greater attention that was given to the fight between the Whig Presbyterians and the Jacobite Episcopalians is not clear but there are many recorded instances of positive co-operation and few records of active anti-catholicism. To give an example, parts of the inner Hebrides were so poorly supplied with religious offices that one island had no resident minister. The seas were often so rough that both the Presbyterian and the Roman Catholic ministers had trouble getting to the island. The people arrived at the happily indiscriminatory system of attending the services of whichever minister managed to get to the island, irrespective of their supposed affiliations.[46]

Anti-catholicism was essentially anti-Irish. The proximity of Scotland and the north-east of Ireland had meant a constant two-way traffic. The Protestants of Ulster were descended from Scots settlers. The Irish had long been coming to Scotland, either *en route* to America, or as seasonal labour. But after the middle of the eighteenth century the patterns of migration changed and a large number of Irish people came to Scotland to settle. The causes of this migration can be readily listed. The poverty of much of Ireland meant that wages were better in Scotland. The growth of industry in the western and central lowlands was the "pull" factor, offering work in the new industries and in filling the gaps in the agricultural work-force left by the move of native Scots into the new industries. The failure of the 1798 rebellion in Ireland was another major "push" factor, as were the famines of the early nineteenth century.

In 1795 there were only 50 Roman Catholics in Glasgow. By 1829 there were 25,000 and by 1843 there were almost twice that number. Edinburgh in 1829 had about 14,000 Catholics where thirty years earlier there had been no more than a thousand.[47] Almost all of these would have been Irish immigrants or the children of Irish migrants. Handley offers the following figures from the 1841 census for the proportion of the population that was Irish born.

Counties	Total Population	Born in Ireland Males	Females	Percentage Irish-born
Aberdeen	192,387	455	582	.5
Argyll	97,371	506	456	1.0
Ayr	164,356	6,411	5,624	7.3
Banff	49,679	50	38	.2
Berwick	34,438	101	53	.5
Bute	15,740	139	149	1.8
Caithness	36,343	28	37	.2
Clackmannan	19,155	96	54	.8
Dumbarton	44,296	2,885	2,006	11.0
Dumfries	72,830	580	452	1.4
Edinburgh	225,454	3,971	3,129	3.2
Elgin or Moray	35,012	52	33	.2
Fife	140,140	413	391	.6
Forfar	170,520	3,024	3,450	3.8
Haddington	35,886	212	156	1.0
Inverness	97,799	134	134	.3
Kincardine	33,075	49	24	.2
Kinross	8,763	8	11	.2
Kirkcudbright	41,119	860	644	3.7
Lanark	426,972	29,343	26,572	13.1
Linlithgow	26,872	976	346	4.9
Nairn	9,217	3	7	.1
Orkney & Shetland	61,065	19	11	.5
Peebles	10,499	59	35	.9
Perth	137,390	322	334	.5
Renfrew	155,072	9,894	10,523	13.2
Ross & Cromarty	78,685	40	41	.1
Roxburgh	46,025	193	123	.7
Selkirk	7,990	20	11	.4
Stirling	82,057	2,686	1,570	5.2
Sutherland	24,782	9	15	.1
Wigton	39,195	2,964	2,808	14.7
Scotland	2,620,184	66,502	58,819	4.8

The following are the proportions for the major cities.

	Population	Irish-born	Percentage Irish-born
Glasgow (and suburbs)	274,533	44,345	16.2
Edinburgh (and suburbs)	166,450	6,187	3.7
Aberdeen	64,767	841	1.3
Dundee	62,794	5,672	9.0
Paisley	48,416	5,231	10.8
Greenock	36,936	4,307	11.7
Kilmarnock	19,956	1,624	8.1
Airdrie & New Monkland	20,511	2,074	10.1
Perth	19,293	217	1.1
Montrose	15,096	108	.7
Dumfries	11,409	417	3.7

Such figures are always dubious. What is sure is that they seriously underestimate the extent of Irish immigration. They only record those who were born in Ireland and yet by 1840 "immigration into the industrial areas had persisted long enough to establish a second and even third generation among a race of manual workers who soon attained their maximum wages and married young".[48] Handley estimates the real figure to be about twice that given by the census: about 10% of the population of Scotland in 1840 were either Irish or of recent Irish descent and, most importantly, they were heavily concentrated in specific areas.

The Native Reaction

The difference between the religion of the native Scots and that of the newly arrived Irish could not have been greater. The worship of the Scots was dominated by preaching. The life of the Roman Catholic church centred on devotion and ritual; an emphasis that led the Scots to suppose that Catholics did not care much about the morals of their people. The relationship between the Catholic priest and his people was also strange to the Scots. The domination of the congregation by the priest may have seemed normal in rural Ireland where a college

trained priest ministered to illiterate peasants but in the newly
industrialised Scottish lowlands with Kirk sessions choosing their
own ministers the authority of the Catholic clergy looked like authoritarianism. Such religious and cultural divisions between Protestant
and Catholic were novel in Scotland. The old Scots Catholics had
absorbed much of the spirit of the Calvinists who surrounded them
and they were as revolted by the ritualism and vulgarity of the Irish
Catholics as were the Presbyterians.

Reinforcing these religious and cultural divisions were language
differences and crucial differences of status. The native Scots felt that
the Irish Catholics were undercutting their wages, and it is certainly
the case that the Irish came in at the bottom of the Scottish labour
market, taking jobs that the native Scots were themselves loath to fill.
The Irish were also used by Ayrshire mine owners as scab labour to
break strikes. In addition, the Scots operated on a very simple model of
the economy which supposed that any increase in the size of the
labouring population reduced the chances of the natives keeping or
getting jobs. The possibility that increased population could cause
increased demand, hence increased production, hence an increase in
the possibility of work did not occur to them, just as it does not occur to
those who currently suggest repatriating British Blacks.

The coincidence of the arrival of the Irish and the appearance of
the social problems of industrialisation led the Scots to suppose that
the one caused the other. The long hours of work in appalling
conditions, the increase in crime and vice, the bad housing conditions,
the masters' almost complete lack of any sense of obligation to their
work-force, the easy availability of alcohol and the frequent recourse to
it as the only way to blunt the effects of all the other problems; these
were problems found in every growing industrialising city in Europe,
whether or not it had Catholic immigrants. They were as characteristic
of Sheffield as they were of Glasgow and Liverpool, yet this
comparative material was either not available or it made no impact.
The Irish and the problems of a newly industrialised society arrived at
the same time; so the Irish must be the cause of the problems.

There was thus a situation primed for ethnic conflict. The fuse was
provided from the same source as the dynamite. Not all of the Irish
who settled in Scotland were Roman Catholics. Some were Protestants
from Ulster and they brought to Scotland their own Orange anti-
catholic traditions.

The native reaction to the Irish Catholics was one of hostility in various degrees and forms. A year before the 1798 Gordon riots in London, the Scots rioted against the Catholic Relief Bill. An anonymous note was circulated around Edinburgh calling all Protestants to meet to destroy a Catholic chapel.

> On Tuesday, February 2, the building in Chalmer's Close, Leith Wynd, used as a Catholic chapel, was attacked by a mob. After a preliminary onslaught with hatchets and stones, the rabble distributed straw and barrels of tar over the floors and set the house alight. A Popish cat, which was making a tardy escape from the building, was thrown back by the mob into the flames.[49]

Shops owned by Catholics were looted and burned. Small scale violence against Irish Catholics was commonplace. They were likely to be assaulted and their property destroyed. Many newspapers provided implicit legitimation for this ruffianism by keeping up attacks on the intelligence, honesty, hygiene and loyalty of the immigrants. The fact that their economic position forced many on to the poor relief was constantly used to advocate the forced repartriation of Catholics. The following snippets are from the *North British Daily Mail:* "Yesterday, at the Central Police Court, an ape-faced, small-headed Irishman . . . An impudent Irish ruffian . . . Pat O'Shannan, a startled looking Irish tailor . . . Two surly-looking sons of the Emerald Isle . . ."[50]

The scale of anti-catholic violence varied from district to district and also with the wider political considerations. Any acts of the government to extend political and citizenship rights to the immigrants, or to Catholics in Ireland, caused an increase in violence. One particular agitation is worth looking at in detail.

On the 5th February 1829, George IV bowed to pressure from his ministers and asked parliament: "that you should review the laws which impose civil disabilities on His Majesty's Roman Catholic subjects. You will consider whether the removal of these disabilities can be effected consistently with the full and permanent security of our establishments in church and state . . ."[51] The *Glasgow Courier* wrote: "The extraordinary sensation increases with every passing hour. Doubt increases. Fear spreads".[52] A joint meeting of all the Church of Scotland ministers and elders in the city of Glasgow resolved to petition against the proposed emancipation of Catholics. The Incorporation of Hammermen declared that the legislation would "subvert the Protestant Constitution in Church and State Established at the glorious era of the Revolution". Twelve of the fourteen incorporated unions similarly petitioned the government. Nor was the Church of Scotland alone among the churches. The various Seceder churches in the west and central lowlands joined in, with the Original Burgher Presbytery of Stirling and the Associate Synod of Kirkcaldy adding their petitions to the hundreds already on their way.

What is interesting about the Protestant opposition to emancipation is the narrow geographical area and narrow class base from which it was drawn.

> Hammermen, coopers, tailors, gardeners, cordiners, maltmen, skinners, wrights, weavers, bakers, and barbers opposed emancipation unanimously or with few dissentients. The seven incorporated trades of Dumfries, the six incorporated trades of Kirkudbright, and trade guilds at Lochmaben, Inverkeithing, Perth and Inverness were all of the same mind.[53]

But the same social class on the east coast took a different view. Aberdeen produced two petitions; one for and one against emancipation. The guilds of Arbroath were for the changes. The guildsmen of Edinburgh either took no action or cooly supported the changes. Part of the unanimity of the guilds and the Church of Scotland in Glasgow may be explained by the fact that the two groups overlapped considerably. The General Session in Glasgow's petition was moved and seconded by two elders, John Alston and John Robertson, and the Glasgow weavers petition was also moved by two men with identical names![54] The New Light Seceders are thought to have been generally in favour of the proposals; a position that would have been consistent with their generally enlightened views not only on religious matters but also on social and political questions. The Old Light Seceders supported the Church of Scotland's opposition but even their support was confined to the west coast. The Church of Scotland in Edinburgh was either neutral or pro-emancipation. In a presbytery vote the 14 elders divided exactly but of 17 ministers only four wished to petition against the changes and 13 voted to take no action, which was *de facto* a pro-emancipation stance.

The main blow against anti-catholicism in the Kirk came from Thomas Chalmers. Chalmers was already emerging as the leading spokesman for the evangelicals; he was to become the effective leader of the Free Church after the 1843 split. Chalmers was the main speaker at a pro-emancipation rally in Edinburgh and although the petition launched at that meeting only gained 8,000 signatures (as against 18,000 for continued oppression), the names represented the intelligentsia of Edinburgh.

Interestingly, the only area outside the western lowlands that produced considerable opposition was Inverness and the east highland coast. Here the fervent Calvinism produced by the highland revival was at its height, and (unlike the western highlands and islands) there was contact with Irish Catholics who had been labouring on the Caledonian canal. While the western highlands had the right theology for anti-catholicism, they do not seem to have developed the racist anti-Irish attitudes that were common in other parts of Scotland because they had no history of contact with the immigrants.

To summarise the nature of the opposition; the Church of Scotland was only actively anti-catholic in the western lowlands, Dundee and the Inverness area: the places that had a history of conflict between the Protestant working class and Irish immigrants. The other presby-terian churches divided along the obvious lines: the conservative Old Light Seceders were against emancipation while the liberal New Light Seceders were in favour. In class terms, the strongest opposition came from the skilled manual working class in those areas where it competed with Irish Catholics. But what is most significant, and what underlies the whole subsequent development of anti-catholicism in Scotland, is the absence of any active anti-catholicism from a large part of the leadership of the Churches.

This is not to say that the Churches did not produce militant Protestant leaders or that they did not offer some legitimation to ruffianism. But as will become clear when we look closely at the various leaders and organisations, such legitimation was coming more and more from people who were marginal to the churches.

Anti-Popery in the Free Church: James Begg

When the evangelicals walked out of the Established Church of Scotland in 1843 James Begg went with them. Begg had been born in 1808 in the small town (if that is not too grand a term for it) of Monklands in the central lowlands of Scotland. His father was the parish minister and Begg decided to follow him into the ministry. He served as an assistant in various churches, including Lady Glenorchy's

Chapel in Edinburgh; a curious institution which, because it was not a fully assimilated parish church, did not have its minister in the church courts, but which nonetheless had considerable prestige. In this post Begg was close to the political and intellectual heart of the church. He then moved to Paisley where his first recorded remarks on Roman Catholicism were made.

Before looking at some of the examples of Begg's anti-popery, it is worth noting a few things about his concerns that often go unnoticed and unremarked. There is no doubt that he was a convinced Tory; something that separated him from some of his colleagues who were active supporters of the Liberal Party. His biographer says that Begg's political ideal was "that of a contented, industrious, and religious peasantry living in happy concord with a genial and kindly aristocracy".[56] But this desire for a contented peasantry led him to become active in a number of causes which, no matter how paternalistic and patronising they may now seem, were then progressive. He was horrified by the general standard of farm labourers' accommodation and agitated on the issue. He produced schemes for the financing of model apartment blocks in Edinburgh. He helped workmen to campaign for a shorter working week and played a major part in having the West Gardens in Edinburgh opened to the general public. Like the better known English evangelical philanthropists such as Shaftesbury and Wilberforce, Begg's basic concern was with people's religious state but he was sufficiently sensible (when many of his contemporaries were not) to realise that people who lived and worked in filthy and degrading conditions could not be expected to be overly concerned about the state of their souls.

However, it is for his role as the Free Church's main voice on popery that Begg is best known. He spoke against the changes in the government's grant to the Roman Catholic college at Maynooth, arguing that it was "a mere concession to the turbulence of Ireland; and it occurs to me that if the Government saw a sufficient amount of popular agitation on the other side, they would be disposed to give way after all".[57] Begg, along with Candlish, Cunningham and other Free Church leaders, did his best to provide the sort of pressure that might make the government "give way after all", but failed. The Assembly unanimously agreed to petition the Lords and sent a memorial to the Queen, but it had no impact. Begg and Candlish were instrumental in setting up the Protestant Institute of Scotland as an educational centre to repel the "papal aggression". For Begg, Roman Catholicism was not a religion with which he disagreed: it was "a studied and diabolical attempt to stamp out religion ... everything which would lead the soul to Christ was either completely denied or destructively perverted.[58] The Protestant Institute would form a centre for equipping the people of Scotland with the defence against the re-establishment of Romanism. Lectures on the evils of Rome would be given and a library of anti-catholic literature would be collected. The Institute clearly met a demand:

> The fifth of the series of lectures on popery being at present delivered in Edinburgh . . . was redelivered on Monday evening by the Rev Dr Begg, the subject of the lecture being Purgatory and Indulgences. Long before the hour of commencing the large chapel was crowded to overflowing, upwards of 2,400 pennies having been collected at the door (the price for admission being a penny), whilst nearly 1,000 persons were obliged to leave, unable to obtain admission. The Reverend Doctor was listened to with breathless attention for nearly two hours and was frequently applauded rapturously during the course of his lecture.[59]

In addition to his many speeches on popery, Begg was a frequent contributor to *The Witness* and he edited *The Bulwark*, a monthly magazine devoted entirely to "the Romanish controversy", founded in 1851 and still in print. Today it is bi-monthly and has a very small circulation, almost entirely confined to ministers, but in the 1850s it was widely read in Scotland.

The essence of Begg's view of Rome is contained in the following; a report of the opening section of one of his speeches:

> He need not say a single word in reference to what Popery was, for he supposed all here present were at one in thinking that, considered theologically, it was the Antichrist of Scripture, the deadly enemy of the Gospel of Christ — that, considered politically, it was a great gigantic system of despotism, and the right arm of all the despotisms of Europe — that, considered socially, it was a most complicated curse to any country or neighbourhood in which it prevailed — and that, considered historically, it presented a series of the most fearful degradations of man, and insults to God, which history had ever exhibited. It was more to the purpose at present to reflect on the fact that Popery was not only aggressive, but that it was assuming that attitude avowedly with the determination not to cease until either Protestantism in every form was

extinguished over the whole earth, or until Popery was overthrown, which they believed it would be, and that ere long, by the Spirit of God's mouth, and the brightness of His coming.[60]

It is hard to gauge to what extent Begg was representative of the Free Church at large. A large and comprehensive collection of sketches of the leaders of the Free Church is notable for the lack of mention of anti-popery agitation.[61] Only in the cases of Begg and two others is this aspect of their ministry mentioned, but this may well signify not the absence but the normality of anti-catholicism. Perhaps it was so much a part of Free Church thinking that it was not note-worthy. Certainly, the Assembly had a special committee on popery and Begg's Presbytery — the Presbytery of Edinburgh — frequently passed, unanimously, anti-catholic motions. Nonetheless, a certain amount of caution is needed here. It costs very little to pass motions and setting up a committee is often a very simple way of sidetracking an enthusiast who threatens to disrupt the organisation's routine business with his magnificent obsession. I have already mentioned Chalmers' refusal to oppose the Catholic Emancipation Act of 1829, and it may be that the clergy of the Free Church were not as vigorously anti-catholic as the motions they unanimously passed now suggest. What is certainly the case is that the Free Church of the last quarter of the century, the generation after Begg, did not share his enthusiasm for combatting "papal aggression".

One element in that change may have been Begg himself. There are conflicting views of the man. His biographer, naturally enough, admires him greatly but another gives the following account:

> He was . . . a man of mean intellect and little culture. Some good qualities he had — courage, tenacity, a shrewd business head and a rough clownish humour that enabled his sorely tried obituary writers to describe him as "genial withal". He also had some pulpit gifts, and was a forceful, though not acute debater. But he was a truculent and vindictive bully whose influence in the councils of the Church was won and maintained by a system of terrorism and coarse intrigue. His callous contempt for the ordinary decencies was shocking even to those who shared his bigotry. He had been Moderator in 1865, when he achieved the distinction of being rebuked by the Assembly for profanity in his address from the chair. As a pushful, money-making Lanark farmer Begg would have done well and might have passed for a useful member

of society; but as an ecclesiastic it does not appear that he ever in all his ministry of fifty odd years devised or did anything but mischief.[62]

A caustic portrait but one that is supported by the evident lack of sympathy for Begg among his colleagues. He might have been admired by some but he does not appear to have been greatly loved.

But it was not his profanity or his rudeness which damaged his anti-popery cause so much as his gullibility. His own intense dislike for Rome led him to naively accept as honest and decent all others who shared his obsession, and he was very publicly conned by one Peter MacMenemy.

MacMenemy appeared in Edinburgh, some think from Ulster, representing himself as an ex-priest, now in the ministry of the Presbyterian Church of Ireland. He developed the Edinburgh Irish Mission, which sent out Gaelic-speaking evangelists to the hovels of the Irish slums. His favourite turn was the public debate. At his Gayfield Square hall, he demolished the arguments of weak opponents billed as Catholic priests, Maynooth students and so on. MacMenemy joined Begg's church and became an elder there. The violence that often accompanied his meetings brought him considerable notoriety and public attention (but Handley seems to slightly exaggerate when he calls him "a leading member of the Free Church Presbytery of Edinburgh").[63] Rumour began to spread that the so-called Maynooth students were, in fact, friends of MacMenemy, paid by him to offer poor opposition to his irresistible arguments. There was suspicion of drunkenness. The Presbytery decide to withdraw its support for the Irish Mission but it did so without publicly denouncing MacMenemy and thus allowed him to continue his work.

> A non-denominational committee was formed, of which Dr Begg was a leading member. Ere long it appeared that the expenditure had not been duly checked, and that a considerable debt had been incurred. Still it was not supposed that MacMenemy was chargeable with aught worse than an excess of Irish generosity, and an ignorance of affairs, and a lack of business habits. But an inquiry behoved to be made ... it was in the course of this investigation that the real character of the work appeared. One of MacMenemy's chief agents made a clean breast of it, acknowledging that the major part of the disputants and the converts were men of straw, paid and dressed to perform their several parts in the scene. Of course these statements were strenuously denied ... But

enough of them were substantiated to make it manifest that
MacMenemy was an imposter, and the committee dismissed him from
their service.[64]

But even now Begg continued to believe in him, a belief that endured
until MacMenemy decided to abandon his wife and emigrate to
America. He was charged in Liverpool with resisting arrest and
assaulting a constable in a fight in a brothel. A deputation of Free
Churchmen, sent to investigate, reported that "the charge was of a
very distinct character, involving drunkenness, being found in a house
of ill-fame, continuing there for a time and being guilty of violent
outrage, and also of direct falsehood".[65]

Anti-catholicism in the Church of Scotland: John Hope

Many movements owe considerably more to an unknown organiser
than they do to the public figures who spread their new faith through
oratory. The British Student Christian Movement, which laid the
foundations for the ecumenical movement in the British churches, was
very much the product of its general secretary, a man who rarely
graced its platforms, but who created and maintained its organisation.
Similarly, the Inter-Varsity Fellowship, the conservative secession
from the SCM, owes more than is generally known to its general
secretary, Douglas Johnson. John Hope was the quiet bureaucrat
behind the anti-popery movements in the Scotland of the last half of
the nineteenth century.

Hope was born in Dalry House, Midlothian, in May 1807, to a well-
to-do Edinburgh family. In his youth he showed no great religious
enthusiasms and his education was conventional. The Royal High
School was followed by university and reading law. In 1828 he was
admitted to the Society of Writers to the Signet and, following the
conventional pattern, embarked on the grand tour of Europe. Eleven
months of finding little of interest on the continent — he thought
Naples less attractive than Edinburgh — was followed by seven years
of building up a profitable legal practice. He joined the Junior
Conservatives in Edinburgh and immediately began to display the
devotion to rational organisation that characterised all his later enthusiasms. In planning for a municipal election, he updated the registration of
Tory voters and played a major part in getting out the Tory vote.

His biographer says nothing of their source, but in 1838, Hope "came to have serious religious impressions",[66] which he expressed by organising schemes. Many of these involved re-ordering the lives of individuals in his employment. He was fond of taking up people and offering them an apprenticeship which went well beyond office-skills and deep into their personal character. Where a parent was willing to give over the rearing of their son to Hope, and agreed to adopt total abstinence principles, Hope was a generous patron, but most of his schemes fell through, with the supposed beneficiaries reacting against his authoritarian guidance.

His favourite campaigning method was to arrange a large public meeting on, say, temperance, and arrange for some articulate advocate of the cause to write a pamphlet. Hope then paid for the production of hundreds of copies of the pamphlet which would be handed out at the meeting. He continued a massive correspondence with ministers and other influential figures who might be able to promote his causes, subvented temperance and Protestant publications, and frequently arranged and funded meetings. Letters to the press on this or that cause were almost a weekly part of his output.

One of Hope's major successes — the British League of Juvenile Abstainers — developed an interesting side-line. Following the example of the Edinburgh Apprentice School Association, Hope started a number of evening schools which were open to all comers on the following conditions: "That one night in the week be scrupulously held as the abstinence night. That the monthly prayer-meetings be observed. That none have at the meetings the smell of intoxicating liquor or tobacco. That pupils provide their school materials at the reduced price intimated. That the fee of 6d per month be paid in advance." Demand for subjects such as Latin, French and Mathematics soon fell away but "there was a great and continued demand for instruction in the ordinary branches, including book-keeping, drawing, music, and sewing".[67] In the years 1850 and 1851 there were seventeen such schools in the city.

Hope's success in promoting the temperance cause re-awakened his interest in the anti-popery campaign. He funded a prize essay competition for the best written answers to questions on the "Popish controversy". A later chapter will take up in detail the constant internal squabbling and bickering that characterises militant Protestantism but one may note here that Hope was firmly in the "independent" tradition. He always preferred to run his own enterprises and was noticeably absent from a number of anti-catholic organisations. He stayed out of the Scottish Reformation Society because he thought the Free Church men (who included Begg) were "very active and talked much, yet they did not come down with money, proposing to make everything pay for itself, and to publish tracts at 2d each — a price beyond the working classes".[68] Instead of working with the SRS, Hope followed the methods of his temperance work: public meetings, distributing cheap and free literature and organising evening classes.

It is easy to suppose from the fact that a Church of Scotland layman was actively campaigning against popery that the Church as a whole shared his enthusiasms. This would be a mistake. Of course, because the Scottish Presbyterian churches were Protestant and Reformed no ministers would have been in *favour* of Roman Catholicism but only a small number were active in supporting Hope's campaigns. One of his schemes involved promoting a monthly tract called the *Banner of Truth* and he circulated all the Edinburgh churches on behalf of this publication. "The churches at first made to the circular a creditable response but they did not long continue their cooperation. The kirk-session of St Andrews intimated they had given a favourable decision in haste, and now begged to withdraw it. St George's would no longer have the papers in the pew. St Mary's declined taking charge of their circulation."[69]

Many other initiatives were similarly rebuffed and Hope worked largely without the support of the Church. But he was more in tune with the spirit of the Kirk than was his successor Jacob Primmer. Hope was ignored; Primmer was attacked. His most successful ventures were the result of his own independently organised and funded work. His success with the British League and its evening classes convinced him that anti-popery was best served by a similar emphasis on education. Like most zealots he saw, not two divergent perspectives, but truth and error. Protestantism was, for Hope, self-evidently superior to Rome. All one had to do was to present people with the facts, the evidence, and they would come to that conclusion. Hence the key to defeating Romanism was to *educate* people. This he did by establishing courses of lectures and training in debate with Romanists. In one of his schools there was enrolled in the first six months of 1873, 451 men and 46 women, of whom four-fifths were between the ages of fourteen and twenty-four. And it was in one of these schools that Jacob Primmer learnt the skills of a Protestant controversialist.

Two events demonstrate the increasing marginality of Hope and his anti-popery. The first was a minor administrative change in the structure of the Kirk that symbolised a much deeper change in attitudes. In 1859, the General Assembly's Committee on Popery was merged with the Home Missions Board. Now the fight against Rome was to be treated as only one part of the general fight against the erosion of the position of the Church. The second event was the contest of Hope's will. Hope was an abstemious man with a successful law practice. Despite his generous support of his various causes, he died wealthy, with no dependants. His will brought into operation a trust deed which clearly stated Hope's wishes for the use of his money. Between £1,000 and £1,500 a year was to be used to promote total abstinence and the use of unfermented wine at the Lord's Supper. The rest was to be used to combat the evils of popery, to convert Roman Catholics and "in exposing and opposing all attempts to introduce a liturgy, or prelacy, or sacerdotalism, or ritualism in any form or degree into or among any of the Presbyterian churches of Scotland".[70] The will made no provision for his relatives; Hope said that his relatives were all well off and would only use the money to increase their indulgences in material things.

There was no doubt about Hope's sanity. No one had ever expressed any suspicion that he was not in possession of his faculties and yet his relatives decided to contest the will on the grounds that being so concerned about temperance and popery as to leave all one's money to such causes was itself evidence of insanity. Fifty years earlier, or even in the lifetime of James Begg, such an argument would have been implausible, but the trustees were sufficiently unsure of their ground to make an out-of-court settlement. Although Primmer and other trustees could not have believed of Hope that "especially in regard to matters connected with temperance and total abstinence and with the Church of Rome, he was subject to hallucinations and delusions",[71] they paid the relatives £15,000 to discontinue their suit. In the Edinburgh of 1893 they could not rely on a jury to find sympathy with Hope's causes.

Jacob Primmer and the Margins of the Kirk

Jacob Primmer was the *fin de siècle* church man of anti-catholicism. His career bridges the two worlds of Victorian Presbyterian anti-catholicism and the extra-church movements of Alexander Ratcliffe and John Cormack that are the subject of the next two chapters. Primmer was born in 1842, the year before the Disruption, in Leith, the son of a merchant seaman. After his father's death by drowning, his mother married a God-fearing evangelical joiner. He entered first the drapery trade and then became a printer: "Soon after I began my apprenticeship as a compositor I was induced to go to the Anti-Popery classes, instituted by Mr John Hope".[72] Primmer became an active participant in the classes in which the students were instructed in the evils of popery and trained in argument against Catholics, often by debating with actual Roman Catholics, or if none were available, with fellow-students playing "devil's advocate." Primmer soon met John Hope and so impressed him that Hope gave him a reference when he applied for better jobs. Reports of the 1859 revival in Ireland had a great impact on Primmer and he decided to enter Edinburgh University to train for the ministry. During the summer holidays Primmer was employed as a subscription agent for the Scottish Reformation Society. With a lantern slide show he toured England lecturing on the errors of Rome. In an interesting personal example of a wider political trend, Primmer offended liberals by exhibiting a poster that accused radicals of being pro-Rome. A number of leading liberals withdrew their subscriptions from the Reformation Society so, in Primmer's own words: "I obtained the names of the chief conservatives, and told them the Radicals had withdrawn their subscriptions from the Society because of its exposure of the support of Popery by Gladstone's government, with the result that I received contributions of ten shillings and one pound in place of the half-crowns I had lost".[73] Primmer was so successful as a fund-raiser that he made enough in commission to support himself at university.

After graduation Primmer went as a missionary to a small town in Banff where he was popular and successful but "being anxious to fight Popery, Ritualism and Rationalism, I decided to leave Gardens-town".[74] He went next to Townhill in Dunfermline where he entered into a thirty years war with his own congregation, his Presbytery and the General Assembly.

Primmer had absorbed Hope's other principle, temperance crusading, and his total abstinence offended most of his congregation. His constant preaching on popery alienated his church managers (as a mission church, Townhill had managers rather than a properly constituted kirk session of elders). The two wealthiest patrons left because of his frequent voicing of anti-Irish sentiments and the Presbytery again summoned him, this time to complain about the notoriety he had acquired by writing constantly to newspapers about the evils of popery, the Irish, drink and rationalism.

The most public part of Primmer's ministry was his series of Covenanter meetings. On 22 July 1888, with two other ministers and a banner reading "Christ our King and Covenant", he ascended a hill at Beath. Some six thousand people attended that meeting and so begun a tour that took in Edinburgh (where there were fights with papists), Aberdeen, Inverness, Dundee and all the major Scottish towns.

For the rest of his career Primmer was in trouble with the authorities of the Church of Scotland. His own Presbytery frequently complained about his activities. His reputation prevented him being called to a regular parish and this meant that throughout his career he never acquired the security of a settled charge. He was thus vulnerable to such coarse attempts at censorship as the Home Mission Committee's withholding £45 from his annual income. Annually he protested against this at the General Assembly and annually his protest was rejected.

Primmer's interests and concerns are perfectly representative of classic anti-catholicism. He lectured on the evils of the convent, and the drunkenness of the Irish, Roman Catholics, and especially priests. He taught that Catholics were rebellious and disloyal subjects, ever on the look-out for ways to undermine the British Empire and Constitution, and essentially criminal as well. His addresses were popular entertainments in a culture that appreciated the controversial public meeting and the constant threat of minor violence added an attractive touch of danger but Primmer was already working in a declining market. Fewer and fewer people cared a great deal about religion and the onset of the first world war made "the threat of papal aggression" seem a little remote compared to more immediate problems. Although the decline had set in before the war, the five years of social upheaval and disruption finished the movement that Primmer had led.

2

Ratcliffe and the
Scottish Protestant League

ONE of Jacob Primmer's many speaking engagements was for the Scottish Coast Mission in Bo'ness, a small town near Edinburgh on the Forth. He had been invited by George Ratcliffe, the father of the man who was to emerge as the leading Protestant politician of the thirties. Alexander Ratcliffe was raised on evangelical Protestantism. When his father moved to Leith he attended the Young Men's Class at the Carrubers Close Mission, one of the main "greenhouses" for militant Protestantism in Edinburgh. On leaving school he went to work for the Caledonian Railway Company (later part of the London, Midland and Scottish group) as a clerk and thus joined that social class from which John Hope had recruited most of his followers twenty-five years earlier.

Ratcliffe's first entrepreneurial act was to launch the "Leith Protestant and Bible Union" while he was a deacon and secretary of the Madeira Street Baptist Church. His first meetings were held in halls lent by the Hope Trust and, as if the links in the chain of tradition were not strong enough, he persuaded Primmer to chair one of the meetings.

The Scottish Protestant League was formed at a poorly attended meeting in 1920 and had little impact until Ratcliffe began to publish the *Protestant Advocate* two years later. The first issue is classically anti-catholic. Ratcliffe was a convinced militant: "A Protestant is really one who protests against the errors of the Church of Rome, and no person who is not protesting against Rome, one way or another, has any legitimate right to the name Protestant".[1] Like other Ratcliffe periodicals the *Advocate* was almost entirely written by Ratcliffe himself and all of his concerns were represented. There were features on Roman Catholics and crime, the lewdness of 16th century Scottish nuns, the treachery of the IRA, and criticisms of the Labour Party for being dominated by the Roman Catholic Church. But quickly, education emerged as a major issue.

Education had traditionally been the business of the church. John Knox had been a strong advocate of the national church's responsibility to maintain a national education system. The "heritors" (basically the wealthy members of any community) had an obligation to finance the minister, maintain the manse and the church, *and* support a school teacher. In the lowlands of Scotland the system had worked tolerably well but the split in the Scottish Church in 1843 had created two major parallel systems: one run by the established Church and paid for by what was in effect a local rate, and an alternative "voluntary" system supported by the Free Church. Roman Catholics and Episcopalians ran their own schools. While the country had one national church, to which everyone belonged, and which had its resources evenly distributed in some parish system, it made sense for that organisation to provide services such as poor relief and education. But by the middle of the nineteenth century both of these functions were collapsing. More and more people were outside the established Church and many people were outside any church. The result was a gradual increase in the operations of the secular state.

The first stage in the secularisation of education came in 1872 when the Presbyterian Churches handed over their schools to the state. The Roman Catholic and Episcopalian Churches refused to co-operate and continued to run their own schools, largely on a voluntary basis but with sporadic *ad hoc* state assistance. Many attempts were made to produce one national system and this was finally achieved with the 1918 Education Act. Under the terms of this act, Catholic and Episcopalian schools were incorporated into the state system but the state had in effect to buy the schools and conceded considerable autonomy in teacher selection and course content to the incorporated schools. It was these concessions, the price for Catholic and Episcopalian support, which so offended Presbyterians. They had handed their schools over for nothing. In the case of the Kirk this might have been appropriate. If one regards the heritors' obligations to support the Kirk as an early form of taxation then one could argue that the schools had been paid for by "public" money. But the Free

Church's schools had been built with voluntary contributions and that Church got nothing in return for handing them to the state. The state paid the salaries of all the teachers but many of the teachers in the Roman Catholic schools were members of religious orders and would not keep their salary but rather pass it on to the Church. Thus the state was indirectly subsidising its general operations.

The other major imbalance was in the status of religious instruction. The Act allowed the Roman and Episcopalian schools the right to veto teacher appointments and made religious instruction mandatory. Thus the religious character of these schools was guaranteed. The Presbyterian schools had no such safeguards. Although ministers were involved in the governing boards no one Church had control over appointments and religious instruction was subject to the wishes of the governing bodies. The difference between the state's control of the Presbyterian schools and its control of Roman Catholic and Episcopalian schools can be clearly seen in the fact that the former no longer exist. The schools that were once Presbyterian are now secular state schools; those that were once Roman Catholic remain Roman Catholic in culture and ethos.

These then were the main grievances. But militant Protestant resentment of the 1918 Education Act went beyond their belief that it meant "Rome on the rates" and included a sense of treacherous betrayal:

> When the Protestants of Scotland were fighting for their country and their Empire, and when those who were left at home were "carrying on" to keep the "home fires burning", the Roman Catholics were busy with the time-serving politicians framing an Act of Parliament that was to put the clock of the Reformation back and reduce Scotland to another Ireland.[2]

In the depressed economy with unemployment problems control over hiring was a major grievance. The existence of two parallel systems meant that people denied work in one could see themselves as being victimised in favour of less well qualified candidates who were employed in the other sector because they had the appropriate religious qualification. In the *Advocate*, Ratcliffe published a long letter from an unemployed Protestant sewing teacher who complained that her rivals in the RC sector were less well qualified and then attacked the appointment of a Roman Catholic as a janitor in an "ex-protestant" school:

> I know Protestant ex-soldiers who are still unemployed and would
> willingly have accepted such a post. But the priest sees to it that none of
> his "flock" is out of work so that their collections won't suffer . . . why
> can't this be made public? and it would be interesting to know if a
> Protestant janitor has been installed in the (RC) Slateford Road School.
> I doubt not.[3]

It was another local education dispute that increased the visibility of
the SPL. The Edinburgh Education Authority had agreed to transfer
an "ex-Protestant" school to the Roman Catholics because they were
convinced that Causewayside School was by its location better suited to
serving the local Catholic community. Ratcliffe took a prominent part
in the campaign to resist the transfer, wrote and circulated a pamphlet
on the issue and used that campaign as a stepping stone to his first
public office. In March 1924 he and six others stood as Independent
Protestant candidates for the Education Authority; the main
Presbyterian Churches already had their own candidates. The other six
were defeated but Alexander Ratcliffe was elected for South
Edinburgh.

This success had a curiously contradictory effect on Ratcliffe's
career. It brought him public prominence and gave him a platform for
his policies. It brought him invitations to speak from other militant
Protestants such as H. D. Longbottom of Liverpool. But it also
demonstrated the weakness of militant Protestantism, even with as
good an issue as Section 18 of the Education Act. In retrospect it was a
good issue. Whether or not the generous terms offered to the Catholic
and Episcopal Churches were justified as a measure of what would now
be called "positive discrimination" is a moral question. Certainly the
Act was discriminatory in creating two education systems on different
terms and it was easy to present those terms as favouring Roman
Catholics at the expense of the Protestants. In the context of Scotland
it was probably hard to find a better cause for a Protestant movement,
a source of grievance more likely to galvanise anti-catholic feeling.
And yet Ratcliffe (and others)[4] had little or no success in using
education to create a popular mass movement. To put it like that,
however, is to move ahead of the story. The main moral of Ratcliffe's
sojourn on the Education Authority is not concerned with mass
support but with lack of élite support. As the only militant Protestant

voice on the Authority Ratcliffe was entirely powerless. One of his motions to prevent building further schools for Roman Catholics did not even gain a seconder! He completely failed to persuade the Authority to campaign against the Education Act. Caithness, the small traditionally conservative Protestant county in the north, had resolved to petition the government for the rewriting of Section 18 and the establishment of a uniform national education system. Caithness on its own was insignificant but had the larger metropolitan authorities taken up the initiative it might have succeeded. Ratcliffe proposed that Edinburgh endorse the Caithness motion. The rest of the Authority rejected the motion.

After that failure Ratcliffe lost interest in the Education Authority. References to its proceedings in the *Advocate* became fewer and shorter and when his three-year term expired, he chose not to stand again. Particularly galling for Ratcliffe had been the refusal of Protestant ministers to support him. The majority of the ministers of the main Presbyterian Churches were not anti-catholic. This is a point sometimes missed by those who pick out the report to the General Assembly of the Kirk in 1923 which expressed plainly racist attitudes towards the Irish. Similar material can be found in a report to the 1924 Synod of the United Original Seceders (a very conservative remnant of early Presbyterian schisms):

> Besides being inaccessible to the healthy influence of our Scottish national life, the vast preponderance of the non-Scottish element of our population is of a type that threatens to water-log our civilisation. In Temperance Reform they are an obstacle of a formidable kind. In crime they have an easy alarming pre-eminence.[5]

The mistake is to suppose that the Assemblies and Synods receiving a report means that even a majority of the members agree with the sentiments expressed. It is misleading to quote at length from the 1923 report on *The Menance of the Irish Race to our Scottish Nationality* and not note that the 1924 Assembly made no mention of the Irish at all! It is obvious from the actions of the Church of Scotland ministers in positions of power (such as membership of the Education Authority) that the overt racialism of the authors of *The Menace* was restricted to only a small group, and more than that, a small group confined to certain parts of Scotland. The ministers of Edinburgh were not prepared to support the League. In 1922, Ratcliffe had written to twenty-two Edinburgh ministers offering to supply their pulpit for one Sunday in return for a collection for the League. Only three ministers replied, all in the negative. And that was the response from the ones Ratcliffe had selected as most sympathetic! Three years later he wrote to all the Protestant clergy in Edinburgh asking them their position on the verbal inspiration of the Bible, the uniqueness of Christ and the truth of the Genesis account of creation. Of seventy ministers, only seventeen bothered to reply and half of those were critical of the League. Typical of the responses from conservative evangelicals who rejected the aggressive anti-popery of the SPL was the reply from W. L. Fraser of Portobello: "While I give place to no one in my zeal for Protestantism and evangelical truth I do not admire the attitude of the Scottish Protestant League so that I find myself unable to share, either personally or through distribution of literature among my people, in any demonstration under its auspices".[6] Even the clergy of the west coast were less than enthusiastic. When Ratcliffe was refused the use of Dunoon Town Hall, he wrote to all five local Protestant ministers asking for their support. None replied.

If Ratcliffe was less than popular with the clergy, he was also having problems with the Orange Order. The first issue of the *Advocate* had made a serious attempt to court Orange readers. In addition to an article on the virtues of Orangeism there was a special "Orangeman's Page" given over to Orange Lodge news and short features on the history of Orangeism. Issue No. 3 has an appeal for funds directed at the Lodges and signed "Bro Alexander Ratcliffe L.O.L. No. 52". But four months later a new note appears in the second half of a long editorial on the Order. The first half praises the lofty Christian principles of the Order but Ratcliffe goes on to argue:

> Reformation within the Brotherhood is urgently required, and what honest member of the Order can deny it? We hold Orangeism itself to be a Christian and desirable force, and we are second to none in our admiration of its Christian constitution, lofty ideas and noble aims, but is it at present an effective fighting force on behalf of Protestantism and righteousness?[7]

In particular, too many Orangemen were ignorant of the positive values of Protestantism. They knew what was wrong with Catholicism but had nothing to offer in its place because they were not evangelical

Christians. Worse than that, they drank. The leaders must be "aware
of the deplorable fact that at demonstrations Orangemen enter public
houses with their regalia on and in consequence are seen in an
intoxicated state by their old friend the enemy (sic), the priest of the
parish!"⁸

This was the first example of criticism of the Order which was to
become routine in later issues of the *Advocate*, and its successor, the
Protestant Vanguard. One of the main proofs of the degenerate state
of the Orange Order was the failure of its members to buy the
Advocate! Ratcliffe estimated that there were some 50,000
Orangemen in Scotland but only 1,000 bought his paper. His scheme
to have the magazine distributed within the Order by sending bulk
orders to Lodge secretaries for distribution failed miserably and even
the small number circulated in that fashion did not produce the
expected income because some secretaries did not send in the money.
The collapse of this scheme combined with a general lack of sales to
the general public (part of the problem was that few ordinary
newsagents would stock it for fear of being boycotted by their Catholic
customers) to cause the temporary suspension of publication at the
end of 1926. The situation was saved by a large gift from an "exiled
Protestant" in India who offered £100 on the condition that Ratcliffe
raised a matching sum from his readers. He did.

The re-launch of the magazine seems to have brought a new
confidence to Ratcliffe. He had often previously argued that religion
should be put before politics and had been a keen supporter of the
short-lived Orange and Protestant Party which had been founded in
the autumn of 1922 to support Protestant candidates. The OPP had
one MP elected — Hugh Ferguson for Motherwell — but Ferguson
only lasted one term and the party was re-absorbed by the Unionists.
Ratcliffe started to toy with the idea of standing for Parliament. In
April 1927, in response to the Catholic Relief Bill, he said: "What is
wanted today is a real Protestant Party in the House of Commons. A
party of Christian Protestant Men and Women to do battle for the
cause of Christ and Protestantism against the forces of political
corruption and Roman Catholic plot".⁹ Given his criticisms of
mainstream Unionists and the Orange Order, and the failure of the
Protestant churches, there was really only one organisation prepared
to take on the task of providing principled Protestant leadership: his
own Scottish Protestant League!

When he first floated the notion, Ratcliffe mentioned looking for a suitable Glasgow constituency with a sitting Roman Catholic member but in the event he chose to contest the seat for Stirling and Falkirk Burghs in the 1929 Westminster election. Describing himself as "independent and Protestant" he campaigned for control of Irish immigration, revision of the Education Act, withdrawal of the British envoy from the Vatican and legislation to "do away with the marriage laws of the Church of Rome, and for the inspection of convents".[10] To control the Irish he suggested that none be allowed to enter unless they had a firm offer of a permanent job, that those who lost their jobs be expelled, that a seven-year residency be required to qualify for the dole, and that those with criminal records or "criminal tendencies" be refused entry. He did not say how people with a tendency to crime were to be identified!

It is not known why Ratcliffe chose that particular seat, although he was limited in his choice. The rationale of standing at all required him to contest a seat held by a Roman Catholic and there were very few Roman Catholic MP's in Scotland. Some of them, such as Wheatley and Maxton, must have seemed invulnerable and perhaps Stirling and Falkirk Burghs was the most likely seat but it was never going to be easy. The sitting MP was a Roman Catholic socialist — Hugh Murnin — but he had an array of characteristics that gave him broad appeal. For 25 years he had been the agent for the Stirlingshire County Miner's Union and he had been President of the Scottish Mine Worker's Union but he was also a "moderate" socialist — so moderate that in 1911 he had seriously suggested forming a centrist Catholic Party — and a Justice of the Peace. Thus while he had good labour credentials as a miner's leader, it was hard for Ratcliffe to depict him as a dangerous extremist. The third candidate, the Unionist, was a lawyer with military service and the support of the Orange establishment.

Ratcliffe's candidacy raised public interest and his meetings were well attended and reported. There was some rowdiness and minor disturbances but the main attacks were verbal and they came from both the socialists and the Unionists. Ramsay Macdonald came to Stirling to defend himself against the charge that he, and his party, were under the thumb of Rome. He rejected specific charges about his appointing Catholics to senior offices in government but carefully refrained from suggesting that he accepted there was anything wrong with doing just that if he wanted to. With a Catholic candidate, he had a tight-rope to walk but this he did, describing himself as a "Presbyterian of Presbyterians" but suggesting that people should leave their religion at home during the election.[11]

On the Unionist side Ratcliffe was faced with a team performance from the candidate, Douglas Jamieson, and the Grand Master of the Orange Order and MP for Renfrewshire, Lt.-Col. McInnes Shaw. Shaw accused Ratcliffe of vote-splitting and used his own known opposition to Roman Catholics — he had seconded an amendment to the Catholic Relief Bill which tried to exempt Scotland from its provisions — to court the Orange vote. At the same time, Jamieson soft-peddled his Orangeism in the hope of collecting some of the Catholic vote. While Ratcliffe was addressing a meeting on the ground floor of the Albert Hall in Stirling, Jamieson was upstairs telling his meeting:

> The gentleman downstairs has, I understand, hinted that I am pro-Roman. That is untrue (applause). I am a Protestant who holds pretty strong views on religion (applause). But I do hold this view, that the question of religion is a question for the conscience of each man and woman, and while I hold my own views I am averse to anything in the nature of religious persecution.

At one meeting about 500 people heard the Protestant and Progressive candidate — as Ratcliffe styled himself — being asked the question which ruthlessly exposed the weakness in the political posture of the SPL. Ratcliffe had mentioned his own working-class background and said he was in favour of "fair play" for the miners. A voice from the crowd asked if he was aware that Lord Scone, the Honorary President of the SPL, was standing as the Unionist candidate in Lanark, and was opposed to the miner's interests and how did he reconcile this with his own position?

> Mr Ratcliffe replied to the effect that although a man might be a member of the Scottish Protestant League he could hold his own political views, but if both he and Lord Scone were returned to Parliament he would oppose Lord Scone on this matter. Lord Scone was not standing in the interests of the League. If he were a voter in Lanark, said Mr Ratcliffe, he would vote for Lord Scone not because of his party but because he was a consistent Protestant. He would vote for Protestantism before Politics.[12]

Unfortunately for Ratcliffe, Lord Scone did not feel the same way about it. He resigned from the SPL because Ratcliffe had stood against an official Unionist candidate and the news of that resignation was spread by Ratcliffe's opponents.

That question had neatly revealed the central problem for the SPL. In a world that had already become largely secularised, the League wanted to replace secular politics by the politics of religious identity and religious principle. But the guardians of religion — the churches — refused to support the League. One United Free Church minister, James Barr, was actually the socialist MP for Motherwell, having displaced the Orange Party's only representative. The voters of Stirling and Falkirk gave their verdict on the League by returning Murnin with 47.5% of the poll (an increase of almost 3,000 votes on his previous majority). The Unionist polled 31.3% and Ratcliffe came home with a decent 21.3%.

There are two interesting footnotes to the campaign. The first is that Ratcliffe offered to stand down if the Unionist would agree to take up his positions on immigration and education. The Unionist would not accept the deal; a decision that in the light of the result looks foolish. If all or almost all of Ratcliffe's vote had gone to the Unionist, Murnin would have lost. The second footnote concerns Ratcliffe's reaction to Lord Scone's resignation. Ratcliffe was typically vindictive. Many examples will be given later of Ratcliffe's controversial style but he was usually quick to criticise those who slighted him and he was nothing if not cruel in his attacks on his opponents but he took Scone's resignation with a timidity that was surprising given that it certainly cost him votes. His response was to print a short, polite expression of gratitude for all that Scone had done for the SPL in his time as Honorary President and wish him all the best for the future. It is tempting to speculate whether that meekness stems from Ratcliffe's own snobbishness or whether it comes from an awareness of the esteem in which the Orange aristocracy (what little of it was left) was held by working-class Protestants.

Glasgow and Populist Politics

It is not the case that we are neglecting Edinburgh for Glasgow, so if the rumour gets your way, deny it. We go to Glasgow and address meetings there because they are organised for us. In Edinburgh the organisation of everything is left to the Editor and as indicated opposite, having only one pair of hands and legs, the impossible is impossible.[13]

Thus wrote Ratcliffe in 1927. Three years later he moved to Glasgow.
His meetings in the Christian Institute and later in the Grand Central
Picture House were well attended. He was being actively promoted by
a number of Glasgow ministers, one of whom offered him the use of St
James Parish Church at Glasgow Cross. This venue was used for a few
months until a member of the congregation set fire to it. The purpose
seems to have been to dramatically illustrate the idea that Ratcliffe's
anti-popery meant trouble. The fire-raiser was imprisoned but the
arson worked. Under pressure from the elders, the minister asked
Ratcliffe to go elsewhere. He was then offered another church, in
Campbellfield Street, which was the home of the League until an
empty church building in the town centre was rented and re-named
the Forum.

The *Advocate* was relaunched as the *Protestant Vanguard;* a full-
size weekly newspaper.

Ratcliffe's first political act as a Glasgow resident was to stand for
the council in Dennistoun Ward. At the same election, a full-time
worker for the League, Charlie Forrester, stood in Dalmarnock. To the
considerable surprise of the local papers, both men were elected. The
move from the east to the west coast had been vindicated.

Those who were surprised by Ratcliffe's success were ignorant of
both the persistence of anti-catholic feeling in the west coast of
Scotland, and of the other element to Ratcliffe's appeal: its populism.
Populism has always been a difficult political philosophy to describe,
largely because one of its main characteristics is an anti-intellectualism
which prevents a coherent ideology being developed. Perhaps the best
description of populism is "non-ideological anti-élitism". The appeal
of Hitler in Germany, Peron in Argentina, Huey Long in Louisiana,
Paisley in Ulster, is to the little man, the honest hard-working
member of the masses who feels cheated by the élite, "the fur coat
brigade". Unlike socialism, populism does not have a refined ideology.
Rather it has a gut feeling, a sense of grudge. The core premise is that
the common people are good: the élite is corrupt.[14] Intellectualism is
dangerous; the uneducated instincts of the little people are a better
guide to action. Often this belief is given an added attraction for the
little man by increasing the hidden superiority inherent in it with the
addition of an inferior social group as contrast and enemy. The little
man is better than the Catholics. He is sandwiched between the
Catholics below him and the untrustworthy élite above who will sell

him out to the Catholics given half a chance.

One expression of Ratcliffe's distrust of élites was to accuse councillors of corruption and self-indulgence at the expense of the honest diligent rate-payer. He denounced the "free feeds" policy of the City Chambers which had a canteen to provide excellent meals free to councillors and committee members. Ratcliffe frequently used the *Vanguard* to attack those councillors who ate free in the Chambers even when their committees were not in session. Other "free feeds" included expenses-paid junkets to other cities for "fact finding missions" and conferences. Ratcliffe himself refused to attend any such events at council expense. Once, when he was persuaded of the value of a conference on public health he agreed to go provided he paid his own expenses. Unwilling to see such a dangerous precedent set, the rest of the council opposed his move.

In the depressed years of the thirties, such attacks on council corruption were popular and Ratcliffe was willing to emphasise the gulf that existed between the salaries of those who were supposed to be working for the people, and the incomes of many of those people. One of his few even slightly popular motions in the council was for the reduction of all council salaries to £500; sixteen members voted for it. Fifty-four (many of them Labour members) voted against it and Ratcliffe retaliated by printing a list of all officials who were paid more than £500. Later issues carried lists of councillors' expenses-paid trips. One reason for the popularity of Ratcliffe's accusations of council corruption was that there was considerable anecdotal evidence of corruption and a few years later Percy Sillitoe, the Chief Constable of the Glasgow Police, was able to bring a number of successful cases against councillors.[15]

Ratcliffe's populist streak combined with his temperance principles and his fundamental Protestantism to produce increasingly bitter assaults on the Orange and Unionist élites. He disagreed with Lord Carson's refusal to support plans for old age pensions. He was fond of pointing out that it was a Unionist government that passed the "Rome on the Rates" Education Act. In 1933 he wrote: "During the two years I have been in the Glasgow Town Council, the Orange members in the Council have been dumb on every question pertaining to the Protestantism and Orangeism of Scotland".[16] He was particularly critical of the two Church of Scotland ministers, both Orange Chaplains, on the Education Committee who refused to support his motions against the 1918 Education Act.

A popular part of his attack on the Orange establishment was its failure to exercise positive job discrimination for Protestants. In September 1933 the front page of the *Vanguard* carried a long article supporting the Ulster politician Sir Joseph Davison[17] who had coined the slogan "Protestants employ Protestants". Ratcliffe added in commentary:

> While Protestants in Glasgow cannot find work, there always seems to be work for imported "Free Staters" and we would like to see some of the big leading public men who employ labour taking a lead from Sir Joseph Davison . . . The only way to keep the Roman Catholic population down is to . . . prevent them from getting work . . . Ulster should have legislation making it an offence for a firm to give a Roman Catholic a job as long as there are decent Protestants looking for work.[18]

A fortnight later Ratcliffe returned to the question in an attack on Sir Edward Archdale, who had tried to defend himself against a charge of discrimination in the appointment of his civil servants: "he would only be doing his duty as an Orangeman and as a Britisher by being discriminate in the selection of his staff and by being so discriminate as to keep *Roman Catholics* entirely out of his staff".[19] Although he could sometimes find it in him to compliment a particular leading Orangeman on one action or speech (he was fond of Sir Basil Brooke's declaration that he would never employ a Catholic), Ratcliffe believed that the Protestant working man was only of interest to the Orange élite as vote fodder: "I left the Orange Order because I discovered that many of the leaders . . . were, and still are, betraying the cause of Protestantism and Orangeism . . . many have surrendered their Orange principles for a mess of political potage".[20] Naturally such criticism did nothing to make Ratcliffe acceptable to the Orange Order and, as we shall see, the Order helped kill the SPL as an electoral force.

Electoral Success and Failure

Ratcliffe had entered the council for Dennistoun in 1931 and at the same election Charlie Forrester, a full-time SPL organiser, had won the Dalmarnock seat. The following year the SPL took 11.7% of the total municipal vote and won one more seat: Kinning Park was taken by Crosbie. 1933 was the SPL's best year. The party managed to take one-third of the votes cast and acquired four more seats: a second in Dennistoun and seats in Govanhill, Camphill and Cathcart. Although four seats out of twenty-two contested might seem small beer, the totals and relative positions suggest a significant success.

Vote Totals in 22 seats contested by SPL

Scottish Protestant League	67,712
Labour	63,923
Moderate	53,073
Independent Labour Party and Communist	17,166
TOTAL	201,874

A number of interesting points emerge from an examination of the voting patterns in the 1933 elections. The first is that in the seats it fought the SPL gained *more votes than the other parties*. When taken as a percentage of total votes cast in the thirty-eight seats, the 33% drops to 22% but there is no reason to suppose that the SPL deliberately avoided the remaining seats because they were unlikely to poll well there. The main consideration seems to have been the availability of candidates and supporters who could nominate them. As a new party, the SPL was stretched at twenty-two.[21]

The SPL not only took votes, but it took them from both left and right. Ratcliffe seems to suppose that the SPL took votes mainly from the Moderates. This is what one would expect if all Catholics voted Labour and all Protestants voted Moderate (or Tory), but an examination of the results suggests that the SPL took votes from both sides. Certainly the SPL was more obviously conservative than it was socialist; at subsequent elections where there was no SPL candidate, Ratcliffe instructed his members to vote Moderate but they did not always do so, and it seems likely that Ratcliffe's populism took some disenchanted Labour votes. In some solid Labour seats (for example, Whitevale, where the Labour victor got more than twice as many votes as the Moderate) the SPL came second. Yet in some Moderate seats which Labour did not contest, the SPL won and one can only suppose that they did so with the backing of the Labour vote.

These results point to the chameleon nature of populism.[22] As with Peronism in Argentina, National Socialism in Germany, and Paisleyism in Ulster, there is constant doubt as to the political complexion of populism. Sometimes it appears to be radical and other times reactionary. It has a critique of the élites, the government, "the system" — what Ratcliffe called "the high heid yins" — yet it opposes the collectivism of socialist ideology. The populist product clearly had an appeal in the Glasgow of the thirties yet anyone who could add up should have been able to see the limits of populist Protestantism. The SPL had done well because of the confusion in socialist ranks. This was a period following a major Labour defeat. In many seats there were three candidates appealing to the socialist vote: Labour, Independent Labour and Communist. With the benefits of hindsight one can see that either reconciliation of all three or the elimination of any two of these parties would squeeze out the SPL but at the time Ratcliffe only saw a precursor of better things. When the results were announced he talked confidently of fielding thirty-eight candidates to fight every vacancy in 1934 and either winning power or taking enough seats to be able to form a coalition with either of the other parties.

In the event all of Ratcliffe's bluster and bravado produced only seven candidates for the 1934 elections, all of whom lost. Most of the defeats were serious with very poor second and third places but the most remarkable result was Ratcliffe's own fall.

Ratcliffe was framed. The man who stood against him was Matthew Armstrong, a well-known local figure and a JP who had been in the council before. Armstrong stood for no other reason than to defeat Ratcliffe and he was perfectly suited to the task. He had Orange and Protestant credentials and yet attended social functions to raise funds for Roman Catholic schools. He could thus play both sides of the field. At first Ratcliffe was not overly concerned about Armstrong. He had come to an agreement with the Moderates for an electoral pact. In return for not opposing him in Dennistoun, Ratcliffe would ask his members to vote Moderate in all the seats which had no League candidate. The local Moderate officials appeared to play reasonably fair and refused to endorse Armstrong as an official Moderate candidate. Armstrong stood as an "independent" Moderate but with the certainty of getting most of the Moderate vote.

The Orange Order played its part in defeating Ratcliffe. A questionnaire was circulated asking all the candidates for their views on the Education Act, the ban on loyalist processions then in force and the less than pressing issue of whether or not the right to say prayers at the opening of council meetings should be restricted to Church of Scotland ministers. Shortly before the election, the Order published its list of acceptable candidates. For the Dennistoun seat, both Ratcliffe *and* Armstrong were approved as Protestant candidates. Similarly for

Dalmarnock the list sanctioned both the SPL man *and* an independent Protestant candidate.

Thus Ratcliffe was faced by a candidate who had ceased to be an unimportant interloper and who was now looking every bit as acceptable to Protestants as Ratcliffe. What firmly sealed Ratcliffe's fate was the freeing of the socialist vote. The Labour Party and the ILP both stood down and left the election as a straight fight between Ratcliffe and Armstrong. The election was simplified to counting those who were for, and those who were against, the leader of the Scottish Protestant League. More people were against him than were for him. Guy Aldred — pacifist communist — got 650 votes. Ratcliffe gained 4,404 and Armstrong took 4,745.

The only difficulty in explaining why Ratcliffe lost is that one is spoiled for choice. There was obvious collusion between the various socialist parties to avoid splitting the anti-Ratcliffe vote. There is some reason to suppose that the Moderates encouraged Armstrong even though they had an electoral pact with Ratcliffe. The local churches united against the League and worked hard to undermine Ratcliffe's claim that he represented Protestantism. There was also the considerable damage done to the League's reputation by renegade Leaguers who stood as independent Protestants and in many places openly attacked Ratcliffe. His criticism of the Orange Order had ensured that the Orange leadership would do nothing to help him. Finally, there was an orchestrated campaign in the press to discourage "sectarian" voting.

Ironically, one of the leading spirits in this campaign was E. Rosslyn Mitchell, a Congregational lay preacher and socialist who had been Member of Parliament for Paisley from 1924 to 1929. In that office he had commended himself by his spirited attack on the proposed 1927 Prayer Book Act. Many conservative Protestants felt that the changes to the Prayer Book proposed in the Act were designed to erode the "Protestant" nature of the Church of England, and although neither Ratcliffe nor Mitchell were members of the Church of England, they saw the Act as a symbol of increasing Catholic power and influence, and hence as something that needed to be defeated. Mitchell's speech against the Act brought forth the following fulsome praises from Ratcliffe:

> Scotsmen rejoice that at least one Scotsman, Mr E Rosslyn Mitchell, the Labour MP for Paisley played the part of a true Protestant; Mr Mitchell

shamed the men of the Conservative Party who pose before
Orangemen as champions of the Protestant cause when elections come
round . . . the question that Protestants have to consider is this, are they
in future to give their votes to "Parties" or are they to vote for "men"
who have proved themselves true to their Protestant Constitution of
the country? . . . Better, far better, to vote for a Labour Member who has
proved his Protestantism, than to vote for a milk-and-water Unionist
who is ever ready to compromise and betray the Protestant cause.[23]

Four days before the 1933 election the *Daily Record* published an
article by Mitchell in which he attacked "sectarian values". In a moving
piece he asked people to separate religion and politics. On the 6th
November the *Record* ran a similar appeal on its front page and as a
footnote, it added:

> The *Daily Record* has no intention of publishing correspondence which
> would in any way inflame this terrible sectarian ill-feeling. On the other
> hand, it will have pleasure in publishing communications which
> sympathise with the necessity of dissociating politics with any form of
> religion.[24]

Defections and Bad Relations

It is not surprising that a socialist councillor wanted to defeat Ratcliffe.
But the opposition from his previous friends and allies is interesting.
After winning four seats in 1933, the SPL should have had seven seats
in the city council, a number that would have given it an audible voice.
Instead it only had five, and by the autumn of 1934, there were only
three. In the space of two years four SPL councillors defected. The first
to leave was Forrester, the full-time employee. Ratcliffe said he was
sacked for insubordination. He added that "the SPL has been very
unfortunate with its organisers all of whom have been men who were
more concerned about their own interests than they were with the
work of the SPL".[25] Crosbie resigned next. In reaction to these
defections, Ratcliffe composed a pledge for all SPL council candidates
in which they promised that they would resign their council seats and
face re-election if they ever left the SPL. The pledge made no
difference to Selby and McGee who resigned the SPL whip in 1934.
Neither resigned their seats!

Angelina Selby, the member for Cathcart, resigned on 18th May 1934. In her letter of resignation she said of Ratcliffe:

> Your influence in the council chamber is effete. I have not yet heard you give a reasoned and effective contribution on any matter brought before the council . . . Once before I tendered my resignation . . . but under great pressure from you and a pledge made before a witness that I would not be tied to any but the sectarian question, I decided to withdraw my resignation and stand as candidate.[26]

Ratcliffe denied that Selby ever tried to resign and asserted that her relationship with the SPL depended on whether or not she was picked to stand for a good seat. She had contested Parkhead in 1932 and lost before winning Cathcart.

It was not only SPL councillors who fell out with Ratcliffe. Although Lord Scone, the first Honorary President of the League, had given Ratcliffe's opposing a Unionist as his public reason for leaving the League, one member who was close to Ratcliffe believes that the election simply gave Scone the opportunity to do what he would have done anyway. Scone had agreed to be the organisation's figurehead when no one had heard of it and when it seemed destined to follow many other similar groups into oblivion. That it was becoming successful might not have bothered Scone if Ratcliffe had been at all responsive to his committee but the SPL's increasing notoriety was compounded for Scone by Ratcliffe's unwillingness to listen to advice. As Ratcliffe's confidante put it: "he was always a one man show".

Scone at least did not campaign against Ratcliffe. James Crawford, another defector, did. Crawford was a reasonably well known speaker in Orange circles who stood for the council in 1932 when he very nearly won Shettleston and Tollcross as an SPL candidate. In 1933 he chose to stand for the same seat but this time as an independent Protestant sponsored by the Shettleston Protestant Club, which had the gall to write to Ratcliffe asking for the SPL's support for its candidate! At that election Crawford was supported by Frederick E. Watson, a Church of Scotland minister who had been a patron of Ratcliffe and whose support had been influential in Ratcliffe's decision to move from Edinburgh to the west coast. By early 1934 a variety of people who had been members, officers or council candidates for the League were coming together in a coherent anti-Ratcliffe movement based around Watson's Protestant Vigilance

Society. One public meeting had on its platform Crosbie and Forrester (the two councillors who had deserted Ratcliffe), James Crawford and another ex-SPL candidate, one. ex-staff member and one former member of the League's executive committee. According to Ratcliffe's account, the meeting was broken up by loyal Leaguers but such divisions in Protestant ranks can hardly have gone unnoticed. When the League was facing such concerted opposition from institutions that also represented its natural constituency — the churches and the Orange Order — such internal divisions and defections could not have helped its chances of electoral success.

It is important in understanding the internal conflicts to appreciate the problems of a new party. The SPL did not have, as the major parties did, a large number of potential candidates to choose from. Ratcliffe had to "use any rusty tool that came to hand" (to quote a close friend) and some of the tools were pretty rusty. Councillor Crosbie had been found guilty of an assault with a broken bottle. Charlie Forrester was a drunk. The night of his election he arrived at a celebration meeting at Bridgeton Cross so drunk that he fell out of his taxi. Not only was he not sober, he was also not well informed. He had to be corrected at one public meeting for accusing Anthony Eden of being a Roman Catholic (he was in fact an Anglican; there was another Eden in the House who was a Catholic). In addition to their lack of competence, there was also a lack of commitment. Ratcliffe was a puritan, a fanatic in a cause, but he seemed unable to create a cadre which shared his commitment. Elected on an almost ascetic platform of criticism of "free feeds" and council junkets, no sooner were four SPL councillors inside the city chambers than they were gobbling down the free feeds and trotting off on the junkets.

Ratcliffe's own nature did not help produce internal cohesion. He was difficult. Those who knew him admit that he was dogmatic and convinced of his own correctness and virtue to a point approaching paranoia and megalomania. The following exchange gives ample evidence for this. In one of his customary attacks on other Protestant groups, Ratcliffe abused the Protestant Progressive Society which was reported in a West Lothian paper as having been launched in early 1935 in Broxburn. Alexander Young, claiming to be the leader of this group, wrote to Ratcliffe challenging his suggestion that the group was a recent organisation. In an apparently inoffensive letter Young claimed affinity with Ratcliffe and said: "I was reared in the controversy and love the name of Primmer the same way (Ratcliffe) does".[27] In an hysterical reaction, Ratcliffe printed the letter and then "replied" to it. He firstly insisted that the implication that the Progressive Society was new had come from the *West Lothian Courier* and was not his invention:

> Has he written to the *West Lothian Courier* and put that paper right? Why has he written to the *Vanguard?* Is it not to try to show that the *Vanguard* is wrong? Is this more anti-Scottish Protestant League propaganda?

Ratcliffe seems to have missed the obvious point that the *Courier*, being a normal secular paper, had an audience much wider than the membership and potential membership for the Protestant Progressive Society; hence there was no great point in putting it right. Given that the *Vanguard* served the militant Protestant constituency, it was obviously more important to set the record straight there. Later on in his letter Young, apparently to establish his own *bona fides,* said: "I am not out for money and while I have taken an active part in this society I have paid out but never received as I stand for the cause and not for what I can get out of it". Given the defections of the SPL councillors, such a point seems well worth making, but Ratcliffe chose to read it as an attack on his own motivation. At this distance it is hard to know whether Ratcliffe's reaction was appropriate but it seems unlikely. Coupled with the impressions one gets from reading vast quantities of his prose, it seems more likely that Ratcliffe was reacting hysterically to what he read as personal criticism, and his problem by 1935 was that he was reading almost everything as personal criticism and reacting in precisely the fashion to make people feel they ought to attack him. People who suppose that their friends are plotting against them in secret behave in precisely the suspicious manner that makes their friends talk about them behind their backs.

A common popular response to people whose ideas offend or outrage us is to assert that they are "mad". Such an accusation follows fairly reasonably from our own self-image. We like to suppose that we hold our beliefs because they are "true" or "obvious". If what we think is self-evidently true then it should be obvious to any reasonable person. Therefore, anyone who holds radically different views is not "a reasonable person". If such people are not too vociferous about their strange beliefs then we can tolerate them and offer a "they don't know any better" explanation for their deviance from normal standards. We could, for example, suppose that they were "just brought up that way". But *protagonists* for strange beliefs are clearly not just the passive uninformed dupes of some superior force. Their lapse from normality has been so great that it is very tempting to "explain" it by saying simply that they are crazy. Usually such explanations are nonsensical and completely unsupported by any symptomatology, but the case of Alexander Ratcliffe almost calls for an exception to that proposition. There is some evidence to suggest that Ratcliffe was not entirely stable. Of course, in one sense all leaders are "abnormal". Were they not driven by impulses unknown to the rest of us, they would not be leaders. But Ratcliffe's case goes beyond that observation. The first clue is provided by his lengthy absences from the movement with "illnesses". In 1931, three years later, and at various points until his death, Ratcliffe withdrew from the public for about a month. No reason beyond "ill health" was given but his daughter said: "It started when he caught scarlet fever. Then there were complications and the doctor did not seem to know what was wrong with him. For months he lay in bed and at times he was very weak and sometimes even delirious. In his work he had been driving himself beyond all limits of endurance". Only one other SPL member was able to cast light on Ratcliffe's illness and he said: "Brainstorms. Sometimes he worked too much and cracked up".

Given Ratcliffe's work schedule and his isolation it would not be surprising if he was the victim of periodic bouts of nervous exhaustion. At this distance, all that we can be sure of is that his writings show clear evidence of a state of mind that *could* readily be diagnosed as paranoia. Stating the case minimally, Ratcliffe was notoriously difficult and sometimes he had problems with himself. So the League had problems with both the character of its candidates and the personality of its leader, but both of these factors were compounded by the lack of political consensus in the League. "Putting Protestantism before politics", as Ratcliffe urged, may have sounded like the right thing to do but it did not itself produce a political platform. Beyond opposition to Rome, which meant wanting changes in education policy and the curtailment of Irish immigration (which had dwindled to a trickle anyway), the SPL had no politics. Ratcliffe tended to support the Labour party in the council. He had been a trade unionist when he was a railwayman and he sympathised with the working man. One other councillor, the faithful Miss Edith Fairbairn, also voted socialist on most issues, but the other three of the 1933 class voted with the Moderates. Tolerating such diversity of opinion might have fitted Ratcliffe's ideology but it was organisational suicide. It ensured that the party would be divided most of the time. It meant that outside of elections and the occasional vote on education or council prayers, the SPL councillors had to either hold their peace or publicly argue their case with each other. Given the small part of the town council's time that was devoted to issues that were sectarian, Ratcliffe's *laissez faire* policy almost encouraged internal conflict.

Where did the SPL vote go?

The rapid collapse of the League might be illuminated by a comparison of voting patterns for the 1933 and 1934 elections. Ratcliffe's account of the 1934 defeats supposes that the Protestants had heeded the *Daily Record's* appeal to leave religion out of the election. Wily Catholics were not so easily fooled. They had all turned out and voted socialist. He pursues this line so far as to calculate the number of "stay at home" Protestants by adding the 1933 totals for the SPL and the Moderate candidates and then subtracting the same total for 1934. There is a good deal of truth in it but something else can be discerned from the figures.

The contest in Ruchill in 1934 was a straight fight between SPL and Labour. There was no Moderate, as there had been in 1933, and yet the SPL vote was *down* on that year and the Labour vote doubled. This suggests that in Ruchill at least the SPL was unpopular in its own right and did not act as an alternative home for the Moderate vote. If the SPL took Moderate votes in Ruchill, it did not take many. The figures for the Sandyford ward are as follows:

	Sandyford Ward		
	1933		*1934*
Moderate	2,331	Labour	3,066
Labour	1,572	Moderate	2,583
SPL	1,436	Scottish Nationalist	188
2 Independents	614		
TOTAL	5,953		5,837

The turnout remained stable. In the absence of an SPL candidate, the

Moderate vote went up but only by 252. There are an "extra" 426 votes
(the difference between the combined totals of the two independents
in 1933 and the Scottish Nationalist in 1934) and yet the Labour vote
increased by 1,494 votes.

In Maryhill, in the absence of the League, the Moderate increased
his vote but only by 1,552 which was 823 votes short of the previous
year's League vote. The Labour vote increased by 812.

In Dalmarnock, there was division on all sides. The SPL was
opposed by an Independent Protestant and the Labour Party competed
with its Independent counterpart. Taking together the Protestant vote
and the socialist vote, the latter increased by 362 votes and the former
decreased by 365 votes. The Shettleston and Tollcross seat was one in
which two Protestant candidates competed in 1933; none stood in
1934.

	Shettleston and Tollcross Ward		
	1933		*1934*
ILP	5,102	ILP	6,072
Moderate	2,711	Moderate	5,381
Ind Prot	2,550	Labour	1,653
SPL	2,050		
TOTAL	12,413		13,106

The total poll went up by 600 votes. The ILP had increased its vote by
970. The Labour Party had created 1,653 votes and the Moderates had
gained 2,670 votes. Thus the total socialist vote and the Moderate vote
had increased by similar amounts and the net increase was 5,293.
Subtracting the "new" votes brings this down to 4,693 which is almost
exactly the same as the 1933 total Protestant vote. Of course, having
only numbers and not biographies we cannot do more than guess. But
unless we suppose that half of the 4,550 people who voted Protestant
in 1933 stayed at home in 1934 *and* that at the same time the socialists
found 2,623 new voters, then the obvious conclusion is that *half of the
people who voted for the Protestant candidates in 1933 voted socialist
in 1934.*

The problem with the voting figures is that they do not present the
changing biographies of individuals; only changing patterns of
aggregates. Thus it may be *possible* (if unlikely) that all the people
who voted Moderate in 1933 voted Labour in 1934 and a similar

number changed from Labour to Moderate. Fortunately we know from cases where individuals have been followed over a period of years that people have fairly stable voting habits. Our guesses about shifting votes can thus be based on the assumption that gradual movement and not constant alternation is the norm. Such an assumption would lead us to suppose that Ratcliffe was wrong in making the equation of "Protestant" with "Conservative". The figures suggest, and my interviews with the remaining small number of people who were in the League at the time support the proposition that the League's support divided into Conservative and Labour supporters in the ratio of about 2:1. That is, about one-third of those who voted for the League in 1933 voted for a socialist candidate the following year.

This is not altogether surprising. I have already mentioned the populist nature of Ratcliffe's positions. It is very likely that in its early years in Glasgow the League enjoyed the peripheral support of working-class Protestants who later became, or reverted to being, Labour supporters.

The 1934 elections were a considerable blow to Ratcliffe, who until then had seen his move from Edinburgh to Glasgow vindicated by support that increased each year. His reaction was embittered frustration and increasingly vicious attacks on other Protestant organisations. Through the following year he alternated between despondency and optimism. One week he threatened to contest every seat at the next election; the next he announced that the SPL was withdrawing from politics. In practice, the latter alternative was forced upon him. As the 1935 election approached it became obvious to Ratcliffe that the SPL did not have enough supporters or candidates to have any hope of electoral success. In addition, the independent Protestants — that loose coalition of ex-SPL people — were still active and so the Protestant vote would have been hopelessly divided. The 1936 elections were also passed over. In 1937 Ratcliffe seems to have had a change of heart, perhaps brought on by the success in the previous years of Protestant Action in Edinburgh. He contested the Camphill ward, a seat that had been won by the SPL in 1933. This time there was no deal with the Moderates, who by now regarded Ratcliffe as a spent force. Again the socialists withdrew in order not to divide the anti-Ratcliffe vote and the result was as follows:

Camphill Ward 1937

Moderate	4085	56.5%
Ratcliffe	2553	35.3%
Liberal	592	8.2%
TOTAL	7230	

This was the last election that the League contested.

The SPL and Ulster

Ulster was crucial to the Scottish Protestant League as it was, and still is, for all Protestant organisations. The north-eastern part of Ireland provided a physical home for Orangeism. Here the struggle against "Rome" took the vivid form of war and rumours of war. The Protestant reaction to the nationalist agitation had provided an actual "state" that could embody and symbolise anti-catholicism. To a large extent, anti-catholicism and Orangeism in Scotland was vicarious, feeding off the conflict in Ulster. Ratcliffe, like all other militant Protestants, was a unionist. He opposed the home rule movement, and after partition he supported the Stormont government. But his support was neither unconditional nor uncritical. Especially after the Stormont government had become firmly established and its existence was no longer an issue, Ratcliffe gave considerable space in the *Advocate* and the *Vanguard* to attacking the Unionist élite. His criticisms had two elements. The first was class based. As he had argued in the 1929 Westminster election when seeking miners' votes, the "high heid yins" of Orangeism were not interested in the common man. Secondly, they were weak on Protestantism. In the first place, this meant that they were not evangelical Christians. In the second place, this meant that they were not to be trusted with the future of Ulster (just as they were not to be trusted with the future of the Protestant heritage in the rest of the British Isles).

Ratcliffe made a number of trips to speak in Ulster and he formed the Ulster Protestant League as the local arm of the SPL. Like the Independent Orange Order,[28] the UPL had a curiously ambivalent character, seeming to be both radical (in its criticism of the Unionist leadership and their social policies) and reactionary (in the defence of Protestant ascendency) at the same time. Led by the Rev S. Hanna, the

UPL had no great impact on Ulster politics. Like many such organisations, it could produce a large audience for some suitably controversial talk but it never developed the deep roots in the community that the Orange Order had. And it was not long after its formation that the UPL fell into what was becoming a conventional pattern by rejecting Ratcliffe's leadership.

The split was the result of what Ratcliffe, with his usual lack of proportion, called "one of the outstanding events of the twentieth century"[29]: his wife's vandalism of a picture hung in Stormont. The picture had been a source of considerable unease since it was first hung. It showed King William of Orange being greeted by some citizens but it also had the Pope floating above King Billy, giving his blessing. A number of Protestants had demanded the removal of the painting. On the 1st May, 1933, Ratcliffe addressed a packed meeting in the Ulster Hall and to the unanimous approval of the house, proposed that the painting be removed. As on previous occasions, the government refused to comply. The next afternoon, Mrs Ratcliffe went to Stormont with Ratcliffe's secretary, Nan Dykes, and Charlie Forrester and assaulted the painting with a sharp knife. The Pope was too high up for her to reach but she did manage to cut out a Catholic priest from the foreground.

The Leaguers were arrested and spent a week in prison before being granted bail. When they came to trial they were found guilty and fined. Although the event gave the League a great deal of publicity, it alienated almost all Unionist and Orange opinion. The Ulster Protestant League refused to support Mrs Ratcliffe's action and of Ulster Protestants of any repute, only Alderman Nixon, an independent Orange politician, supported the action and called for the release of the three. The government refused to intervene and simply let the law run its course. Mrs Ratcliffe had no regrets:

> I have been very much abused by ignorant Protestants because of my action in destroying the picture. And more so have I been abused by the Political Orangemen of Belfast and other parts of Ulster. But the reason is simply because they are mad at a woman having the courage to do what they are afraid to do. They all wanted the picture down, and I had heard Orangemen say that they would take it down. But when it did come down many of these people turned against me and against my husband. But I have no regrets. I am proud to be able to say that I went to gaol in the cause of Protestantism. I have served my Master and I am satisfied.[30]

One Leaguer paid his tribute to Mrs Ratcliffe in the form of an appalling piece of doggerel of which the following is the last three verses:

> *But Leaguers went from Glasgow*
> *And when the picture they did see*
> *They soon made it their business*
> *To rip him to the knee*
>
> *Of course they were arrested*
> *And brought before a Papist Bum*
> *A fine and prison was their portion*
> *Yet they made the Papists run*
>
> *And now this narrative we close*
> *Of how the Papists fell*
> *And when the election date comes round*
> *Vote in the SPL*[31]

Ratcliffe's response to the imprisonment and fine was one of populist rage at the Unionist élite's refusal to intervene on his wife's behalf. In an editorial in the *Vanguard* he showed at tedious length that Carson and Craig had been willing to break the law in pursuit of some "higher good" when they formed the Ulster Volunteers:

> What is sauce for the goose must surely be sauce for the gander.
> But not in Protestant and Loyalist Ulster.
> The Public Prosecutor was not sent after Messrs Carson and Craig twenty years ago when *they* broke the King's laws.
> No Police arrested *them*!
> *They* were not cast into a prison and refused bail!
> *They* were not afterwards tried and fined and told by a judge of His Majesty's court that "in this country we expect our laws to be observed".
> Messrs Carson and Craig were not told *that*.
> All of which proves that in Ulster there is one law for the man with the pull and another for the man without any pull.[32]

Thus once again Ratcliffe had tried the Unionist and Orange élite and found it wanting. It had once again betrayed true Protestantism. As far as the Unionist élite was concerned Ratcliffe had once again shown himself to be a publicity-seeking trouble maker. In response to the perceived apostasy of the Ulster Protestant League, Ratcliffe formed a new Ulster group, the Ulster Protestant Society, but it achieved little. The UPL and the Ulster Orange Lodges took to rubbing salt in the wounds by inviting SPL defectors such as Forrester and Crawford to speak on their platforms. Ratcliffe responded in his usual bitter fashion with vicious editorials and lengthy criticisms of their speeches but he only returned to Ulster once or twice after that and the province rarely again figured in his programmes.

Routinisation

There is a well observed "career" for social and political movements. They tend to move from a loosely organised "enthusiastic" phase in which their goals seem likely to be rapidly achieved into a period of "institutionalisation".[33] Once it becomes clear that the new heaven, or whatever it is they are campaigning for, will not arrive this year, the initial enthusiasm fades as does a large part of the membership. The rump then settles down for the long haul and attempts to build an organisation that is stable enough to survive the long run. One generally sees a shift in the actual goals of the movement's members away from the stated aims of the movement and towards the various satisfactions of routine participation. *Being a member* becomes a source of satisfaction in its own right instead of being just a means to achieving some specified goals. One can see ample examples of this in the SPL of the late thirties.

Once the impetus of the 1933 political success had drained away other parts of the League's activities came to the fore. Not that these were late innovations. Far from it. Largely they were things that Ratcliffe had done in Edinburgh before the League moved to Glasgow and won its council seats, but with his council seat lost and further immediate political success unlikely, Ratcliffe could turn more of his energies to the various evangelistic and social elements of the League's life.

In a pre-television era, the public meeting was a major source of education and entertainment. Ratcliffe was an excellent debater and liked nothing better than to challenge leading Catholic or

socialist speakers to public debates. These were so popular with
audiences that tickets could be sold at a price that paid for the hall
and made a profit. There were further pay-offs. The speeches were
used to fill the pages of the *Vanguard* and were reproduced as
pamphlets. There were meetings twice every Sunday evening in the
Forum, the large church that served as the League's headquarters.
These were generally full with two thousand in each sitting. Special
topics were toured. One of his favourite campaigns — the old Begg
and Primmer staple of "goverment inspection of convents" —
packed the 5,000 seater Caird Hall in Dundee.

In 1878 there had been eight religious Orders for women in
Scotland running twenty-four houses. By 1914 this had grown to
twenty-two Orders with sixty-five houses and in the inter-war years
there was a small but steady increase in the number of convents.[34]
Any news item on the growth of convents was an opportunity for
Ratcliffe to revive the traditional claim that such institutions were
oppressive because they took in young girls when they were too
naive to make their own decisions and effectively imprisoned them.
Convents were also supposed to encourage sexual depravity (a topic
I will take up in a later chapter). Convent horror stories were very
popular with the mass of Protestants and lectures with titles such as
"The Life of a Carmelite Nun" packed the punters into the large
halls. Ratcliffe's star attraction was a genial old lady called Edith
O'Gorman Auffray, an American who had been a Carmelite nun for
a short period in her adolescence. By the standards of the genre her
"revelations" were very tame. She made no claims to having been
sexually abused and concentrated on the issues of authoritarianism
and freedom. Likewise, Ratcliffe's much advertised slide show was
hardly *risqué*. Most of the illustrations showed only very austere
living conditions, a few of the "degradation ceremonies" that
symbolised the death of the nun's previous self and her taking on a
new persona, and the odd horse hair shirt.[35] Nonetheless, Ratcliffe
made lurid claims for the content of his talks, advertising them with
a prose style well known to modern readers of papers such as the
News of the World; "shock", "horror" and "amazing revelations"
were the stock in trade of his copy and he thought some of his talks
so inflammatory that he spoke to single-sex audiences: men at one
sitting, women at the next!

As often happens when a movement is not prospering, such
meetings lose some of their point because they are consumed

mainly by people who are already confirmed believers. When the League was at its zenith, strangers would be attracted to hear Ratcliffe but for much of the League's career the activities took on the nature of an internal event. Ratcliffe would organise a meeting. In order to ensure that the League was not "let down" by a poor attendance, lots of League members would go and pack the meeting. Most modern evangelistic crusades have a similar character. Local evangelical Christians decide that it would be good to provide an opportunity for lots of people to be converted so they plan a series of crusade meetings. They then feel obliged to attend these meetings themselves in order to provide a respectable audience for the visiting evangelist.

Although such internal consumption seems on the face of it pointless, there is a value in such activity. Even if the immediate impact on people outside the movement was negligible the very fact of organising and taking part in League activities helped to create a sense of community and social solidarity *within* the League. Similarly, other activities such as fund-raising had a dual purpose. The money helped the organisation to pursue its stated aims but the very fact of working to raise the money allowed many people to feel involved in the movement; useful and part of some collective enterprise. When members of the League look back on their involvement it is the social side of the League that many best recall; it is the teas, the outings, and going to the Forum meetings with their friends that they speak of most fondly.

The SPL and Violence

For a period in the twenties, Ratcliffe had toured with a small trailer which served as a combination book store and podium. In the spring of 1934 he took possession of a purpose built caravan. Painted in covenanter dark blue, it had the SPL's triangular logo and "The John Knox Preachers" painted on the side. The van was used as the touring base for evangelistic meetings. One summer the young English minister who had accepted the post of assistant General Secretary of the League (he did not last long) toured the Ayrshire coast and Dumfries and Galloway. The reception was poor. Many towns banned the meetings. In some cases organised opposition to the ban forced it to be lifted but even then the

audiences were very poor. The audiences were better in the
Lothians but there the John Knox preachers were often met with
violence.

Minor skirmishes had always been a part of the SPL's reception.
Ratcliffe's Sunday afternoon meetings outside Bellahouston Park
in Glasgow were often attended by barracking and minor assaults.
On such occasions the League was well served by its women who
beat hecklers with their umbrellas! In the mining villages of West
Lothian, things sometimes became more serious. The son of John
Meacher, the Edinburgh secretary of League, said of one meeting in
Fauldhouse:

> My father had left the venue and was walking along a lonely road to
> the railway station when he was surrounded by angry men (Roman
> Catholics!) demanding to know what his business was at the
> meeting. Putting on a brave face my father light-heartedly said: "I'm
> from the *Edinburgh Dispatch* but there's nothing worth reporting at
> that meeting". At this a coarse intercepter grabbed my father by the
> collar and with faces nearly touching said: "It's a good job for you you
> are not involved with that lot. We'd have bashed your brains out
> against that wall".

Meacher may have improved the language of his assailant's threat
in reporting to his son but the truth of the basic message was
confirmed on the 9th July 1935 when the SPL caravan was attacked
in Fauldhouse and a member of the SPL Seafield branch seriously
injured. A few days later, the SPL returned to Fauldhouse, this time
with Ratcliffe as the main speaker and, in the words of the
Edinburgh Evening News, "there were several skirmishes and a
number of people were injured by stones".[36] Blackburn, West
Lothian, was another scene of minor violence when the SPL
campaigned there.

Six years earlier there had been a serious attack on League
members at a performance of *The Trials of Father Diamond*, a
Protestant play "revealing the evils and dangers of Protestants
marrying Roman Catholics" (to quote the sub-title). This Ratcliffe
composition, which featured himself and Mrs Ratcliffe along with
eleven other League stalwarts, was an interesting innovation in
Protestant propaganda which met with mixed reviews. It was given

tolerably pleasant mentions by a number of secular local papers. Some conservative Protestants criticised it because they were opposed to drama and some Roman Catholic hooligans attacked the players with stones, and on one occasion in Cambuslang, knives and bottles. Ratcliffe reacted by forming the Knights of Kaledonia Klan (KKK). The KKK was:

> A new organisation being formed for the purpose of vindicating free speech for all sections of the community. The organisation has no connection with the Scottish Protestant League. A full page advertisement appears in this issue and we commend it to our members. The KKK will be secret in its organisation in the sense that it will not permit its members to reveal the business of the organisation to those who are not members.[37]

Despite the claims about "no connection" with the League, prospective members were invited to apply "care of" the League. In fact, the KKK was intended as Ratcliffe's bodyguard and it was simply a faction within the League. For all the bluster in the original announcement with its stated intention of "putting down Roman Catholic influence and intimidation" the KKK did little and soon ceased to exist. In fact, it was not mentioned again until John Cormack in Edinburgh formed a similar grouping within his Protestant Action Society and then Ratcliffe "revived" his KKK in order to demonstrate the lack of originality in Cormack's movement.

But to put this violence, and Ratcliffe's response, in perspective one should compare it with sectarian violence in other places and at other times. In the nineteen-twenties in Belfast shootings and bombings were common. In Edinburgh in the thirties there were a number of very serious sectarian assaults involving members of Cormack's Protestant Action Society. That the SPL was not more often involved in violence probably owes a great deal to Ratcliffe's pacifism.

This was just one of the issues on which Ratcliffe was surprising. In the grand abstract stereotyping that is common to much political science, it is easy to suppose that movements which were reactionary on one issue were generally reactionary. This was certainly not the case with Ratcliffe who was original in his ideology if he was nothing else. In his rather convoluted

presentations on the question of war, he argued that there was
nothing in principle wrong with fighting. After all, God had
instructed his people to fight for the truth. But in practice, Ratcliffe
dismissed *all* contemporary wars as being distractions, at times
hinting that they were part of a Catholic plot, and at other times,
suggesting they were a device used by the élites to divide up the
working class. In his own speeches he often condemned
hooliganism, even when it was directed against the Catholics
(although he was always quick to add that, given working-class
Catholic attacks on the SPL, they had no right to complain). The
Protestant Actionists' willingness to disrupt Catholic and
ecumenical meetings was something that led to considerable
friction between the League and Protestant Action. Nor was
Ratcliffe unique in being a pacifist; at least one other core member
of the SPL was a conscientious objector in the second world war.

Ratcliffe believed in rational argument. He often argued that
everyone had a right to be heard and his favourite campaign device
was the public meeting. Whenever he disagreed with someone he
would challenge them to a public debate and these were often
highly staged affairs with complex protocols about chairman,
platform parties, distribution of tickets and recording of speeches.

This is an important part of the psychology of Ratcliffe and
other SPL members and it worth dwelling on. There are two
extreme ways of thinking about the world which can be called
"relativist" and "absolutist". The relativist view is the modern one.
We tend to suppose that, while there may be only one "real" world,
there are lots of different ways of looking at it. Different people and
different social groups have different perspectives. The very notion
of "perspectives" is itself a modern one which only appears when
societies cease to be made up of people who all share the same
beliefs and values. Most modern societies are pluralistic; they
include a variety of ethnic and class groupings who have markedly
different values. We tend to operate with a wide tolerance for
"different ways of seeing it". If there is a motto for the modern
world it must be "different strokes for different folks". It is
important to note that this relativism is not only found in the social
world at large (where it is a necessary condition for getting
anything done in a pluralistic world); it is also now found in science.
The old Victorian confidence in a world of "facts" that could be
collected until enough of them generated a "theory" has been

challenged by the relativist assumption that the theories come first and that the theories create the facts that are then claimed as the justification for the theory.

Ratcliffe was an absolutist. He believed in facts and in his possession of them. He was convinced that only other people's cupidity or stupidity stopped them appreciating the correctness of his views. Present the people with enough facts and, provided they can free themselves from domination by their clergy, they will accept the SPL's ideology. An SPL member who knew Ratcliffe well shared this approach and frequently followed his criticisms of Ratcliffe and others by saying: "you are allowed to be wrong in your opinions but not in your facts". There may well have been other sources for Ratcliffe's pacifism but his commitment to rational argument and to the presentation of "facts" played a major part in limiting the movement's encouragement of sectarian violence.

Another element is often overlooked. Ratcliffe was always sober. Like most theologically conservative Protestants, Ratcliffe was a total abstainer, as were many core members of the SPL. Naturally the fringes of the movement were not. This was a major source of friction between the core of the League with its evangelical piety and the periphery, attracted by its populist politics and its legitimation of conflict with Catholics. Ratcliffe often attacked Orangemen for drunkenness and that division still exists with Jack Glass constantly criticising the Orange Order for allowing Sunday opening in their social clubs. This aspect of Ratcliffe's behaviour fits in with the ethos of a certain social class. The self-educated clerk, attending evening classes and signing the pledge, was the foundation stone of John Hope's movement. This small fraction, the area where the *petit bourgeoisie* of the small shop-keeper and little businessman meets the old traditional labour élite, was the part of Scottish society to which Ratcliffe appealed. While the Labour movement was in flux and three Labour parties were competing, the SPL might have drawn some support from the unskilled working-class. So long as the Moderates could be painted as corrupt stealers of honest rate-payers' money, support might be drawn from the lower middle-class. But the character of the SPL spelt its own demise for it was too much a movement of a small social group that was fast disappearing. But whatever the social bases of temperance as a virtue, the sobriety of Ratcliffe and the core of the SPL did mean that League meetings, especially the more

evangelistic meetings that predominated after the failure of the
political initiative, were generally "dry" and orderly.

While one is discussing the unexpected aspects of the League, it
is worth mentioning that Ratcliffe could at times be surprisingly
fair and even-handed. On odd occasions he was prepared to concede
virtues to Roman Catholics and, more often, he was willing to point
out that Protestants were not beyond reproach; an attitude which
was absent from Cormack's pronouncements. Admittedly, Ratcliffe
was usually at his most "objective" when it allowed him to attack
other Protestant leaders and organisations. Part of the stock in
trade of the *Advocate* and later, the *Vanguard*, was the reprinting of
stories about Catholic crime. After one story about a priest being
fined for drunkenness, Ratcliffe added, "We have seen Orange
Chaplains the worse for drink, and some time ago we saw one in
Duke Street as drunk as any priest can be".[38] On another occasion he
criticised his old enemy, James Crawford, for false allegations
against "Free Staters" who were supposed to be pouring into
Glasgow to collect the dole: "No Free Staters who come over to
Glasgow get Public Assistance when they land . . . he must have
three to six months residence . . . Moreover, there is every reason to
believe that less Free Staters are coming to Glasgow these days than
in the past ten years".[39]

Thus the conflicts within anti-catholicism, by pitting militant
Protestants against each other, had the unintended consequences of
sometimes forcing the Protestants to be reasonable and even-
handed in their treatment of the old enemy.

The Decline into Fascism

The period from 1935 to 1939 was one of stable routine activity for
the League. The meetings were held, the paper appeared.
Pamphlets were sold and resolutions against this and that were
unanimously passed. The caravan toured. The League was probably
set to continue as a small Protestant society for the lifetime of its
members but three things hastened its demise. The first was the
running battle with Cormack's Protestant Action, which will be
examined in the next chapter. The second was the outbreak of war.
The third was related to the second: Ratcliffe's late conversion to
fascism and anti-semitism.

To some extent Ratcliffe was always game for right-wing authoritarian movements that had a populist complexion. His first issues of the *Protestant Advocate* contained articles sympathetic to the American Ku Klux Klan, including one which defended physical violence against the supporters of racial integration by arguing that one always shoots mad dogs and that anyone in favour of racial integration was obviously a mad dog. The fact that parts of the Klan were anti-catholic made it attractive. Ratcliffe's first known connection with fascism came through his membership of the very short-lived Scottish Fascist Democratic Party. This group circulated a draft constitution in the spring of 1933. Ratcliffe joined it because it shared his opposition to the "free feeds" policy of the council Moderates and, in clause 4, called for the expulsion from Scotland of all members of Catholic religious orders, the repeal of Section 18 of the Education Act, and the prohibition of Irish immigration to Scotland: "I am not a fascist at all in so far as political matters are concerned, and I never was ... I was a member of the SFDP because that constitution was consistent with clean political administration and with my own principles as a Protestant protagonist."[40] The SFDP issued a periodical, the *Commonwealth*, in June, July and August and then disappeared. It announced that it was re-thinking its religious views and withdrew from the Scottish Protestant League's annual parade. However, the SFDP band turned up for the march! The SFDP was never seen again, although in January 1934, a party called the Protestant Democratic Party distributed a charter which was very similar to that of the SFDP. This group came to nothing.

Ratcliffe's attitude to Jews was shifting and ambiguous. In 1923 he was quite willing to publish a speech by an American Klan leader which snidely attacked "a group of forty or more Jewish-Americans, some of whom could 'spik a little Englis'."[41] Yet in 1930 he attacked the Middlesborough and District Motor Club for barring Jews: "But was there ever such snobbery? And so *this* is England! The land of the free! Because a gentleman is a Jew he is not a fit companion for an English gentleman".[42] Three years later he criticised John Cormack for allowing the Jewess Esta Henry to stand as a Protestant Action candidate. He was careful in that case to make it clear that he had nothing against the Jews as such. He just objected to them being leading members of what was supposed to be a Protestant society. The reason for Ratcliffe's gradual conversion to outright support of Hitler was his hatred for popery. In 1934, he said: "We are not in any sense whatever defending Hitlerism. But we would prefer Hitlerism to Popeism".[43] He had great praise for Hitler after he had fired a German diplomat for bowing to a papal nuncio. Anyone who was against Rome was a potential friend for Ratcliffe. He gradually managed to combine Catholics and Jews. The *Vanguard* published a long article by Walter Allen which reported on the Protocols of the Elders of Zion, pronounced them to be genuine and then argued that the Jews were in fact incapable of such an efficient plot by themselves. Behind the Jews were the Jesuits. If the Jews were really Jesuits, then attacks on Jews were justified as attacks on Rome.[44] Incidentally, this technique of merging one's enemies by claiming that one group infiltrated another is common in extreme right-wing thinking. In contemporary America, where it is slightly more respectable to be anti-Jewish than anti-catholic, some ideologues on the lunatic right argue that it was the other way round: Catholics are too stupid to have been as successful as they have been and therefore they must have been infiltrated by the Jews. Thus the Jesuits are seen as a group of Jews who took over the Roman Catholic Church and used it as a front for their Zionist politics![45]

In the autumn of 1939, Ratcliffe went on holiday to Germany and returned to fill the pages of the *Vanguard* with praise for Hitler and calumny for the Jews. He thought that the Protestant churches had nothing to fear from the Nazis: "The Jews have been dealt with, not because of their religion but because Germany found them to be a menace to the German nation. That, surely, is Germany's own affair".[46] In June 1940, he was to be found praising Nazi harassment of Roman Catholics: "We are very kind to Roman Catholics in Scotland, of course, the reason being seemingly that we have no Hitler in our midst to eject Popery".[47] His support for Hitler slotted into his pacifism to produce a rejection of the "Jewish-papist anti-German war which Britain is now involved in".

> Britain's War Minister (Hore-Belisha) is a Jew, hence we can rest assured that the young conscripts, baptised the militia but known in Jewish circles quarters as the Melisha, will probably be drilled and instructed how to get after Hitler, that bad German man who so cruelly trampled upon the Jew's toes! A Great Protestant Nation

this! Jews and Papists in command. The small minorities over-ruling the big majority! God Save the King . . . from Jewry and Popery![48]

He pointed out that Britain had gone to war to defend Poland, a Catholic country, from a predominantly Protestant country. He listed the dominant religion of the countries in the western alliance; France was Catholic. Rumania was Old Catholic. Turkey was pagan. In Ratcliffe's view Britain was entirely unsupported by Protestant countries. The conclusion was obvious:

> The working classes of Britain are stupid. They are so simple that they do not realise that they are being used for an ulterior purpose. They cannot see that this is a war in the interests of the Jews and the Roman Catholics. They cannot appreciate facts when they are submitted to them.[49]

The working classes of Glasgow were so stupid that they began to abandon the League. The unpopularity of his opposition to the war became clear to Ratcliffe and he tried to repair the damage, promising in November of 1939 to drop all further items about the war. But the damage had been done. There is some evidence that Ratcliffe later changed his position on the war. In 1943 his daughter was called up: "I served in the WAAF as a wireless operator for three years. My father told me he was very proud of me and I did wonder then if he had changed his views". This may have represented a change of heart or it may have represented the very common phenomenon of people holding extremely dogmatic views about abstractions and yet being quite willing to moderate such views in the case of actual known individuals.

But either way it hardly mattered. The League had become publicly associated with opposition to the war and it was in decline. Ratcliffe had given up the use of the Forum because of the expense of keeping an auditorium of that size when audiences had dropped. He had given up all the League's full-time staff. In a curious return to his roots, he opened up a bookshop in Edinburgh which was run by his brother, who also edited the last few editions of the *Vanguard* after Ratcliffe's health had broken. In 1946 Ratcliffe was supposed to speak in London. A Member of Parliament raised the possibility of banning him, a reaction that pleased Ratcliffe immensely. The government decided that he was so unimportant as to be best

ignored, which was by then the correct decision. Ratcliffe and the
League were both finished. There was talk of rescheduling the
meetings but Ratcliffe was again seriously ill. In January 1947, he
died of a heart attack. Two of his supporters tried to keep the
remnant together as the Open Bible Fellowship with weekly
meetings but attendence was very poor and soon even these
meetings ceased.

Explaining the Decline

Some of the major changes that help to explain the rapid decline of
the League will be dealt with later in the general review of the
decline of anti-catholicism. Here I want to make a few observations
about the League and its leader. One of the obvious weaknesses of
the League was its leader's inability to create any organisation. The
SPL was rarely anything other than Ratcliffe and his secretary, Nan
Dykes. At times there was an "executive committee" but this had no
authority and it was wound up by Ratcliffe in his embittered
reaction to the defections of 1934. His attempts to find and groom
an assistant and potential successor were feeble and always ended in
failure. Each of the four full-time SPL workers left the movement
or was expelled. Even John Meacher, the Edinburgh railway worker
who had been with Ratcliffe since the formation of the League and
who returned to the League later, defected and joined an anti-
Ratcliffe group for a short time. The English minister only lasted
six months. Walter Allen, a leading anti-catholic author, stopped
writing for Ratcliffe and started to write for Cormack's magazine.
The lack of solid organisation meant that Ratcliffe was free to
follow his own whims both in method and in ideology. It should
have been obvious to anyone that his bitter and strident attacks on
other Protestant leaders did nothing to assist the movement. His
feud with Cormack, culminating in Ratcliffe sending people to
Edinburgh to distribute anti-Cormack literature at the council
elections, was obviously damaging to both parties. The lack of
restraint extended to philosophy. The shift to anti-semitism is not
novel; many anti-catholic organisations are also anti-semitic. But
however respectable a pedigree such a combination had in extreme
Protestant circles, making it a major part of an organisation's
platform when the country was going to war with Nazi Germany

was patently foolish. Previously his supporters had been asked to take a great deal in terms of doctrinal "deviation". Ratcliffe did not believe in eternal damnation. He did not believe in the Trinity. These points would have alienated a lot of Calvinist supporters. The Calvinists might have liked his criticisms of the pagan rituals of Christmas and Easter and his total abstinence, but then those positions would have alienated some less theologically Protestant working-class supporters. Performing plays, even if they were anti-papist plays, would have offended many old fashioned Presbyterians. There were thus already enough problems with the nature of his ideology without the introduction of an element that was pretty well unknown in Scottish Protestantism. Luther may have been anti-semitic but most Scottish Presbyterians were not.

The problem with the adoption of unpopular ideas and declining support is that they feed off each other. While the League was winning elections and looked like it might become a major force, even such an individualistic character as Ratcliffe had his innovatory instincts curbed by the desire to reach the largest possible audience. Once the League's support had started to fall away there was no such block. In fact, the decline almost encouraged Ratcliffe to be outrageous and to pursue his own hobby-horses into the sunset. One common reaction to rejection is the amplification of the characteristics that caused one to be rejected. One needs some reason to compromise one's own beliefs. Political success is a good reason. Playing down one or two beliefs seems like a small price to pay for promoting one main goal. In the absence of success there is no good reason to compromise and a very good reason to exaggerate one's distinctive qualities. Then the fact that the movement is not doing very well can be read as a sign of its doctrinal purity and all competing movements can be rejected as compromisers and apostates who have only done well because they compromised their principles. The Bible provides a variety of texts which can be used to interpret failure as proof of ideological rectitude. Thus failure breeds further failure because it causes the leader to give up hope of success through rational considerations of strategy and tactics, through trying to work out ways to present those ideas which will appeal to potential audiences. "Sensible" politics is abandoned in favour of the politics of the miracle. The leader proclaims his unpopular truths, tending all the time to make them more and more unpopular, and asserts that he will finally succeed because God is on his side. Reliance on the miracle of a "great revival" means that the leader no longer has to try to be popular. This leads inevitably to further unpopularity. Failure breeds irrelevance which breeds failure.

3

Cormack and the Protestant Action Society

WHEN Alexander Ratcliffe moved his Scottish Protestant League to Glasgow a number of people tried to fill the gap left in Edinburgh with their own militant Protestant organisations. The only movement that lasted more than a year or two and which achieved any sort of political power was the Protestant Action Society led by John Cormack.[1]

Although a slightly younger man, Cormack had much in common with Ratcliffe. Both had lay preachers for fathers. While Ratcliffe's father was missioning to the fishermen, Cormack's father was running a Soldier's and Seamen's Home and preaching at the Mound (an open patch of ground just off Edinburgh's main thoroughfare, Princes Street) at weekends. But while Ratcliffe acquired his sense of vocation early on in life and deliberately coached himself for his future career by attending evening classes and learning "the controversy", Cormack was late in discovering his life's work. He joined the army in 1910 — the 2nd Battalion of the Argyll and Sutherland Highlanders — and served until 1922 when he retired with the rank of corporal. The last three years of his service were crucial to his later career: it was spent in Ireland, fighting alongside the Black and Tans. According to the accounts Cormack gave of his own "conversion", it was this period which added a political dimension to the basic evangelical anti-catholicism that he had acquired from his father. He mentioned finding devices that suggested fraud in shrines that were supposed to have miraculous curative powers.

He did not mention, but an objective observer should, the crude racism that armies always develop. As the few candid accounts of the attitudes, language and behaviour of the British Army in Ulster show,[2] soldiers quickly develop justifications for their actions in terms of supposed characteristics of the people they are fighting or policing. It is difficult to be in a position of feeling threatened by, and trying to impose order on, a population and still view members of that population in the same way as one views one's own friends, colleagues and "people". The normal reaction to violent conflict is to develop stereotypes of "my side" and "them" that glorify "my side" and present "them" as the forces of darkness. Cormack's experience in the army in Ireland probably goes a long way to explaining the differences between himself and Ratcliffe that will be explored below.

When he returned to Edinburgh Cormack went to work for the Post Office and at the same time became involved in anti-catholic organisations. He was first drawn to Ratcliffe's Scottish Protestant League and for a short time, the two men worked together. One account mistakenly says that Cormack was the Edinburgh secretary of the League. He was not; John Meacher was, but the error captures the essence of how Cormack saw himself. He had discovered that he had a talent for public speaking and he felt that he deserved to play a major part in the League. Ratcliffe, as he was to do so often, felt threatened by Cormack and assigned him various menial roles. Cormack wanted to be on the platform. Ratcliffe wanted Cormack to work on the door.

Cormack left the League and joined the Edinburgh Protestant Society, a small group that contained a number of defectors from the League, but he found little satisfaction there. In 1933, complaining that the EPS was nothing but a talking shop, Cormack and four others left to form the Protestant Action Society. The name was the key to Cormack's vision. All previous Protestant societies — the League, the Scottish Reformation Society, the EPS — just talked. Protestant Action would *act* and act decisively to repel the tide of Romanism that was sweeping the country. The stated aims of the movement did not differ markedly from the goals of the League, as the following statement from an advertisment shows, but the method was different.

> All "Protestants" are eligible as Members. Members can be of every degree in Society, and of any political party, but having the following objects as their aims:
> (a) The Defence of our Protestant Faith.
> (b) The Repeal of the 1918 (Scotland) Education Act.
> (c) All Institutions founded on superstition — such as those of the Popish belief, Monasteries, and members of Roman Catholic Religious Orders — will have no permanent domicile in this

country, and members be served with Expulsion Orders.

(d) Prohibition of Papist Irish emigration into this country.

(e) The Promotion and Protection of Protestant Rights and Interests.

(f) No Romanists to hold Commission in our Navy, Army or Air Force, or have positions on Judicial Bench.

(g) As Romanists deal with Protestants in countries where they have full power, so will we deal with Romanists in this country.[3]

It is object (g) which suggests the ways in which the SPL and PAS diverged. Although nothing is spelt out, those who heard Cormack knew what was meant by "As Romanists deal with Protestants". He argued that Romanism was intolerant and oppressive where it had the upper hand. Only when Roman Catholics were in a minority did they advocate tolerance and religious *laissez faire*. Thus from the first there was a clear element of aggression in PAS which was largely absent from the League.

Protestant Action rose rapidly. Cormack was fired from his job for allegedly tampering with mail going to officials in the Catholic Church. Whether he actually did or not, his public speaking was bringing him notoriety and his employers preferred not to be associated with sectarian political activity: a position taken by many of the employers of the prominent Protestant Action members. A lot of leading PA people had erratic job histories! In 1934 Cormack stood for the council in the North Leith ward and was elected. In 1935 two more PA men — James Marr and George Horne — were returned. The following year, six more were added to give Protestant Action nine councillors.[4]

Like Ratcliffe, Cormack did not stand simply as an anti-catholic candidate. There was also a populist theme in his oratory. He frequently criticised the conservatives on the council (who were called the Progressives) for their corruption and inefficiency. He borrowed wholesale Roosevelt's New Deal philosophy of public works as a solution to economic stagnation. He wanted new roads, the electrification of the railways, the construction of a large airport, and the building of a new sewage system. Naturally, this reconstruction would be designed to favour Protestants. One election manifesto said: "we will vote that all contractors working for the Corporation employ at least 90 per cent Protestant Labour". Similarly, Protestant Action campaigned for Protestant privilege in housing: "we will vote that

Protestants get first claim for any Corporation houses".[5]

Unlike Ratcliffe, who produced enough words to keep the *Vanguard* — at times a full-size 12-page weekly newspaper — full, and still had some left for his stream of pamphlets, Cormack did not write. He left school at fifteen and had no further formal education. Critics made much of his prose, which was worse than poor, but he was a gifted public speaker. As a result, the public meeting formed an even more important part of the life of Protestant Action than it did in the Protestant League. And by all accounts the Protestant Action meetings in the middle thirties were very large and impressively staged affairs. The following observations of a meeting in the Usher Hall were made by an American:

> The meeting was organised in a manner that would warm the cockles of the heart of Billy Sunday. Perfectly ushered. A truly excellent brass band — Edinburgh Trades Silver Band — playing the highest type of music that obviously was hugely enjoyed by the great audience. Mr Donald Cormack introduced four candidates on the "Protestant Action" ticket . . . The four . . . were forceful, humorous, and tremendously earnest. One I will mention — Rev Wm Trainer, who for 25 years has laboured as a social worker among the very poor of the city, and he gave a word-picture of the degrading poverty he comes in contact with, that kept his audience in wrapt silence. He placed the blame for most of the poverty on the Roman Catholic Church, in its grip it has on the public-houses (saloons) of Edinburgh . . . In a former letter I described to you the reception given Councillor John Cormack as he arose to speak. Again this reception was elemental, overpowering, it went on and on in volley after volley of cheering that died down and started up all over again. I make the statement without fear of contradiction, that there is but one other individual in Great Britain that can move a great mass of people as this little Scotsman can, and that is David Lloyd-George.[6]

The little Scotsman may have been able to move people with his oratory but he could not write and his critics were quick to expose this weakness. Ironically, Cormack fell victim to a device that Ratcliffe commonly used to make fun of his Catholic critics: the unedited letter. Ratcliffe frequently published his hate mail with no attempt to correct spelling, grammar or punctuation. The *Glasgow Weekly Herald* did the same to Cormack in June 1935 when it printed Cormack's reply to a letter that had been critical of the Protestant Action demonstration against the granting of civic honours to Lyons, the Australian Premier who was a Roman Catholic.

"A REPLY TO THE BAILIE"

"Sir, — In this weeks issue of the *Glasgow Weekly Herald*, I read an open letter to myself. The only point that appears to be open is the Abysmal Ignorance of yourself, the writer. Firstly you state that after Mondays disgraceful proceedings, you do not want to know me, well that is where you Mentality and mines differ, I like to come out in the open not to hide under a Nom-de-plume. Who are you anyway? dictating lying and malicious statements and who are you speaking for? An open letter indeed! I did engineer as you term it, the proceedings, I did Protest, and I am not ashamed of it all, let that sink Sir, I protested in the Usher Hall on behalf of the 100 per cent. Protestants in Britain and Australia, I have letters and a cable from Australia advising me what to do with the same; the term Honoured, Guest, Lyons he is hated there, and the Scullin and Lyons, are known as the White Ants, of Australia, You question if many Edinburgh folks knew that Lyons was a papist? Every 100 per cent. Protestants knew, thats our mission in life to know our own business, I wish you knew the angles of your own job, I would not be answering to such vapourings, The High Constables who acted as Chuckers out should have been doing my job as they were brought into existence among other things, to repress Popery, Sneeze Bailie your Brains are dusty, Criminals as a society have a right to existence but where? in Prison to prevent them carrying on with their criminal tactics to the detriment of Good Citizens, likewise R.C.'s, or Papists, The doctrine they must believe prevents them giving an undivided loyalty, to our Protestant Throne. They are not even citizens, as a citizen is loyal, therefore we must not given them all the privlages of Citizenship, got that clear? Scotland does not want the good opinion of Lyons, or any other Papist, thats impossible unless Scotland goes Papist, and when the day comes along that I have to ask the craven unknown, Bailie, for advice, as to what Propoganda, is and how, to Propogate, my Protestant Principles, then I trust that the hole in Mother Earth will be open, waiting on my remains at least. I'll be buried as John Cormack not under a Nom-de-Plume, Go Give Up the Ghost, Bailie, there are too many of your kind busying around. If you feel like it come to the Calton Hill or the Usher Hall on June 23 I will give you the Great Unknown, the chance to repeat your article verbally to that great audience.

JOHN CORMACK
(Councillor).

The letter was reprinted in a pamphlet by Compton Mackenzie, a recent convert to Catholicism, in 1936.[7] It is impossible to know what sort of impact the exposure of Cormack's weakness in writing had. Perhaps Protestant Action had very little support from the literate middle classes who might be offended by such an inadequacy, but one can suppose that the ridicule had some effect in reducing bourgeois fears about the new demagogue and thus in preventing an over-reaction. In that sense, there may have been lasting damage done to the cause but there was no obvious short-term loss of support. Far from it; the November elections in 1936 saw a further increase in PA's popularity.

Elaborate staged meetings with bands and ushers were the great set-pieces of Protestant Action but the staple diet was the open-air meetings at the Mound. Here, every week, Cormack and other leading PAS speakers would declaim on whatever was topical. Opponents heckled them and minor skirmishes were common. But almost as important as its own meetings in the public perception of Protestant Action was the frequency with which its members disrupted other people's meetings. Free speech was not a right that Cormack accorded Roman Catholics, for the reason already mentioned. He did not believe that Romanism would give Protestants that right were it to become the dominant ideology and so felt justified in denying Roman Catholics that right in order to prevent such an outcome. As a slogan at the bottom of one front page of the PA periodical put it: "Toleration overdone is an evil".[8]

In 1935 the Catholic Young Men's Society announced that it planned to have its international meeting in Edinburgh. Ratcliffe tried to organise a united Protestant protest and wrote to the Protestant Action Society, the Scottish Reformation Society, and all the other smaller groups suggesting a common front. None of them replied. But Cormack determined to stage his own demonstration. Ratcliffe instructed his supporters to have nothing to do with it. In the event the demonstration passed off peacefully. A large crowd gathered outside the city chambers to heckle people arriving for the civic reception but there was no riot.

The following year there was. The Catholic Truth Society had booked the Music Hall in George Street for a meeting at which Monsignor Ronald Knox was booked to speak to the subject: "Wanted a World Leader — Why not the Pope?" The Protestant Action Society intended to answer that question. About 3,000 people gathered to barrack the meeting and police moved in with horses. Cormack and two other Protestant Action councillors were charged with causing a breach of the peace and found guilty. Cormack refused to pay his fine and was sentenced to sixty days in Saughton Prison.

The leaders of political movements normally benefit from a short spell in prison. It gives them "martyr" status and deprives their followers of their presence long enough to ensure a rapturous reception on their release. In Ulster Ian Paisley was markedly more popular after his short prison sentence. Cormack's sentence had the same effect. The rest of 1936 was probably the zenith of Protestant Action. The rising part of the curve was the Canaan Lane protest. The Catholic hierarchy had arranged for a Scottish Eucharistic Congress to be held in Edinburgh. About thirty thousand Catholics were expected to collect in Canaan Lane Park, celebrate mass and then march in procession along Princes Street. Protestant Action was determined to make sure they did no such thing. Cormack used his meetings to call for a massive Protestant turn-out. A flyer on "Why the PROTESTANTS of Edinburgh should demonstrate against POPERY in the City of John Knox" was printed. In it Cormack wrote: "The Eucharistic Congress really means the Propogation of a Blasphemous and Idolatrous worship of a Wafer-God . . . The Mass is a dangerous and Pagan institution — was, is, and always will be — offensive to Protestant people". After calling for "every Protestant to turn out on the streets of Edinburgh" Cormack signed off with "No Compromise, No Surrender, and No Popery". On the day, between thirty-five and forty thousand Protestants encircled the park. Again there was violence with the police charging the protesters and Action members retaliating with their newly acquired knowledge of anti-horse drill. The technique they had developed in earlier encounters involved pulling the rider's foot out of one stirrup and then jabbing the horse with a sharp instrument, causing it to bolt and dislodge its rider. The demonstration was a success: the procession was cancelled.

In November the public responded to Protestant Action's militancy by giving the society another six councillors to add to the three members already in place.

At the time, critics were quick to depict Protestant Action as a movement of unprincipled thugs, and even Ratcliffe — who sympathised with PA's aims — condemned the violence that surrounded many of its activities. Cormack was an aggressive man who saw no problem in using force to preserve the Protestant heritage. At one of the meetings leading up to the demonstration against the CYMC civic reception he warned potential hecklers before going on to his vision of the future:

> If there is even one little interruption the police outside will have to phone for an ambulance to take you away (loud applause) because the stewards have my instructions to deal with you any way they like . . . Once we capture the local authorities, we are going to have Parliament also (prolonged applause) and this despite the civil war that will ensue. We are going to take away the vote from every papist in the British Empire.[9]

In his sketching of the Catholic reaction to the rise of Protestant Action, Cormack asked "Are we afraid of bloodshed?" with the clear implication that he certainly was not. He once called the PA policy "applied physical Christianity".[10] The brute force of PA worked not only in the large public demonstration but also in dark corners and alleys. Like Ratcliffe, Cormack had formed a special cadre within PA called Kormack's Kaledonian Klan (KKK). The full range of Klan symbols were borrowed. The fiery cross was burnt, officials were given titles that began with a forced K: Kommissionaire, Kustodian and so on. There was even a Klan song which was sung to the tune of The Old Rugged Cross:

> Over dear old Scotia,
> The Fiery Cross we display,
> The Emblem of Klansmen's domain.
> We will for ever be true,
> To the Red, White and Blue,
> and British will always remain.

In an interview with a journalist Cormack is supposed to have said: "We are a secret body, and have agents in Glasgow along the west coast of Scotland, in Aberdeen and in Edinburgh . . . We meet once a week in cowls and masks and discuss plans of action. We are not out for aggression but if our opponents do anything they can expect retaliation".[11] At the funeral of one Protestant Action member who had been in the Klan, an actual "fiery cross" was burnt. Most sources think that Cormack's use of the Klan symbolism was frivolous. He did not actually intend to identify with the American southern states white supremacist movement and it is likely that Cormack was borrowing not so much from the original Klan as from Ratcliffe's version. Yet there was a basic similarity and the name was appropriate because the Kormack Klan shared with its American forebear the rationale for its use of violence. Part of the justification was that the action was retaliatory. There is no doubt that working-class Catholics often attacked Protestant militants. Meacher's potential assailants in Fauldhouse were not unique. James Russell, for a time President of Protestant Action, was once seriously assaulted by two Catholics. When he came out of hospital he found that his two assailants had been beaten up. The second part of the justification for the Klan's use of violence was that it made up for supposed deficiencies in the legal system. Just as the original post-Civil War Klan had legitimated its operations in terms of re-imposing "law" on a disrupted society, so the Edinburgh Klan argued that the police and the courts were not doing their job properly and so direct action was needed.[12]

For the most part the Klan used the threat of violence rather than actual violence. Typical of its actions was one case where Cormack had been approached by a woman who claimed that she had been sexually abused and harassed by the priest — John Gray — for whom she worked as a house-keeper. The priest had apparently grown tired of her and turned his attentions to her daughter. A leading PA member gave the following account:

> The evening of the following day he, with seven colleagues in two cars arrived at Gray's residence. Admission was denied but there followed a notable altercation with exchange backwards and forwards between Cormack and his supporters on the pavement and Gray and his fellow priests at upper windows . . . Cormack in his blunt style warned and promised Gray — "Touch again as much as one hair of either woman and I'll be back with a razor and I'll cut it off (it — Gray's penis).

A similar message seems to be the import of the following item from the *Protestant Action:*

Ask a certain Roman Catholic priest who has been hanging around
Gullane for months, except when he was having dinner parties in
hotels in Edinburgh. What about the cork of the champagne bottle he
gave to one young lady and told her to tie in her garter? Oh yes, friend
priest, we've been keeping contact with you, so behave yourself or we'll
get you sent to No Woman's Land. Compre?[13]

There is also a hint of menace in an item under the heading "Things
we want to know?": "Who will be the next Italian to shut up shop?
What about the SMT cafe in St Andrew Square? It is run by an Italian.
So, Protestants, will you get busy?"[14]

It would be misleading to suggest that the Klan and the
encouragement of anti-catholic violence were typical of Protestant
Action. Few PA members were in the Klan section and few of them
were directly involved in violent action. Most core members spent
their time in activities such as Jimmy Marr's Speakers Club where they
learnt how to address meetings, or in whist drives and dinner dances.
This is a part of the organisation's life that tends to be forgotten. Like
the Scottish Protestant League, and the Orange Order, Protestant
Action offered its members not only a campaign, but also a social life.
It offered companionship and opportunities to meet potential
spouses.

The Renfrew Case

The increasing notoriety of Cormack and his Protestant Action Society
brought him to the attention of an Alexander Renfrew. Renfrew had
been a successful business man in Glasgow and had married a Catholic
lady. In 1927 he was approached by A.J. Macdonald, then the Lord
Abbott of St Benedict's Abbey in Fort Augustus. Macdonald wanted
Renfrew to send his son to the Abbey school, which Renfrew did.
Macdonald began to ask Renfrew for financial advice and Renfrew
gradually became the Abbey's investor advisor. Renfrew was surprised
to discover that the Abbey had very large sums of money at its disposal.
He claimed that "in a matter of 18 months I had cleared a profit on
their behalf of well over £100,000. This was made on the Stock
Exchange, Rum Running and Greyhound Shares".[15] Renfrew became
personally involved in a number of large and complex deals with the
Abbey and borrowed some of their funds to shore up his own business.

The relationship soured and in June 1929, Renfrew told the Abbott that he wanted no more to do with their business. Renfrew was charged with stealing £5,000 from the Abbey and with uttering a forged share certificate. In his own account of the case he admitted that he made some mistakes and foolish decisions in trying to accommodate Macdonald's plans but denied criminal intent. He was found guilty and imprisoned for five years. He claims that he was approached by the prison chaplain and assured that, provided he keep silent, his family would be taken care of. In fact, the Abbey bought his business and did nothing for his family.

On his release, Renfrew approached the Catholic hierarchy and seems by a combination of threat and entreaty to have convinced them that he had been wronged. There was talk of compensation and the details of the case were sent to the Rota Court at the Vatican. After he had heard nothing for two years, Renfrew decided to make his case public and he contacted Cormack. Cormack was immediately interested; while Renfrew was in prison, Macdonald had been promoted from Abbot in Fort Augustus to Archbishop in Edinburgh. Cormack announced a special meeting in the Usher Hall to hear "Startling disclosures of how the Abbots, Priests and Nuns keep a vow of poverty" and said he would read letters from Macdonald to Renfrew which showed the corruption of the Church. Macdonald immediately filed for interdict preventing any such disclosures.

Macdonald argued that the contents of his letters to Renfrew were copyright and confidential. Lord Robertson chose to ignore the copyright question but accepted the confidentiality argument. Cormack was restrained. The Protestant Action defendents tried to have details of the case made public by the cunning device of inserting them into the detailed legal averments which would have been made public as part of the "Open Record". Macdonald's counsel defeated that move by convincing the judges to remove all the details. After a year the case was finally closed in Macdonald's favour with him dropping all claims for expenses in return for Cormack undertaking not to publish, in any form, any parts of his letters to Renfrew. Cormack agreed.

A number of features of the case are interesting. The first is Cormack's own reticence. It is hard to believe that he would have kept quiet had the letters contained any really damaging material. He frequently accused John Gray of sexually abusing his housekeeper. He had been willing to serve a jail sentence for his beliefs before and would not have been put off publication by the threat of legal action, although the costs of such action were a factor. One can only conclude from the Protestant Action agreement to the legal restraint that the actual letters from Macdonald to Renfrew did not contain any evidence of fraud and that Cormack was clever enough to see that Renfrew was not a very convincing witness. He had after all tried to reach an agreement with the Church that would have meant money in his pocket: his conscience and sense of public duty only asserted themselves after he had waited for two years and been given no compensation.

The other main point to be drawn is the comparative weakness of the militant Protestant cause in face of a legal system designed to serve universal ends. Although this was the city of John Knox, the courts clearly had little or no sympathy for the argument that the public interest would be served by revelations about the finances of an Abbey. Lord Robertson, himself a Protestant, refused to read the case as being anything other than a normal breach of confidence case. The fact that this was militant Protestantism exposing the chicanery of Romanism was ignored. Thus in the same year as the PAS staged its largest counter-demonstrations and trebled its council representation, it failed to dent the "universalism" of the legal establishment. To the Protestant Actionists this was just further evidence of the power of Rome. In one sense it was, in that it was a clear demonstration that the Roman Catholic Church was not going to be penalised as it had been in the past. It was evidence that Catholicism was completely acceptable in the eyes of the state.

Protestant Action at the Polls

Edinburgh was a conservative town. Until the late thirties the council was dominated by independents and various shades of conservatives. In 1935 only 16 of the 71 seats were held by Labour candidates. In November 1934 John Cormack achieved what the headline writer of the *Edinburgh Evening News* called his "Surprising Protestant Win" when he took the seat for North Leith.

One of the problems of explaining the rise of Protestant Action is that it is difficult to make any very clear inferences from election results. All the numbers can tell us is that a certain number of people voted one way one year and that another year a certain number of people voted a certain way and so on. We cannot actually tell *who* voted which way and in the absence of surveys asking people who they voted for and why, we are left having to guess. But some light can be thrown on PA's support by looking at the results of the various elections they fought and I want to spend some space on the minutiae of those campaigns. The reader who finds numbers dull may skip on a few pages and pick up the story later.

November 1934 saw the entry of Protestant candidates into Edinburgh's municipal elections. Three people described themselves as Protestants; two — Cormack and Aitchison — were Protestant Action candidates and James Mitchell stood for the Edinburgh Protestant Society: the organisation that Cormack had left when he formed PA. Between the three of them they collected 6.4% of the poll. The Moderates had 62% of the vote and Labour (and other socialists) had 38.4%. The next year there were 9 Protestants in the elections; 6 Protestant Action candidates and 3 others from the Protestant Progressive Society and the Protestant Defence Society. The Moderate share of the vote slid to 42% and Labour also lost votes. Its share went down from 38.4% to 33.5%. But the system used in the elections was the "first past the post" method, and, as third parties in Britain have always protested, this method exaggerates the position of the dominant party. For all their votes, the Protestants only won one seat to give them a total of 3, a third seat having been taken by James Marr at a by-election.

Protestant Action got its second seat in South Leith by apparently taking votes from both the conservatives and socialists. But the Moderates suffered most. PA recorded its best second places where there was no Moderate candidate, as in Gorgie, but it also performed reasonably in wards with both Moderate and Labour candidates. Although there was no immediate benefit from all the close second places, the result did give PA a major boost that was reflected first of all in the elimination of the other Protestant societies. In the 1936 municipal elections there were 14 Protestant candidates and they were all standing on the Protestant Action ticket. This was the party's best year. It took 31% of the total vote. More than that, PA pushed Labour into third place in terms of percentage of the total vote but again the "first past the post" system served to prevent PA turning this support into a similar proportion of seats. Only 6 new seats were acquired while there were a further 6 second places, some of them very close. An analysis of the 1936 outcome suggests an interesting observation. With fewer total votes, Labour won more seats than PA. Labour's

support was less extensive and better concentrated. This suggests that
PA was drawing votes from a wide variety of social groups and
geographical areas while Labour had a strong base in particular areas
and a clearer identity. The Moderate vote continued to decline. It was
now down to 37% of the total cast. Labour had slipped slightly to 29%.
Nevertheless, the "first past the post" system (and the fact that only
one-third of the seats were contested each year) meant that the
Moderates still had 46 seats in the council; Labour had 15 and
Protestant Action had 9.

As evidence for the varied nature of Protestant Action's support
one can examine some of the ward results. In the Canongate ward the
party percentages for 1935 and 1936 were as follows:

	Canongate Ward	
	1935	1936
PA	22.4	48.3
Labour	34.9	32.4
Moderate	20.0	17.2
Others	11.4	2.1

In this ward PA took votes from everybody. In other wards PA won in
a straight fight with Labour, presumably by taking the Moderate vote
(although some other seats suggest that in the absence of a Moderate
candidate, conservative voters simply stayed home). But in Broughton,
George Ballantine won the ward against a Moderate with no Labour
candidate. It is clear that the Moderate vote was on the decline but it is
not obvious whether it was going to PA or to Labour. It is possible (and
later elections suggest this) that the main trend was from Moderate to
Labour with some people stopping off at PA on the way. As a counter
to the thesis that Protestant Action was simply a new home for
conservative voters, one may examine the voting in the North Leith
ward.

	North Leith Ward		
	1934	1935	1936
PA	2054	1927	2143
Moderate	1819	2384	
Labour	1141	950	2451

When all three parties contested the ward for the first time, PA came out ahead of the Moderates and well ahead of Labour, presumably because the PA candidate was its leader, John Cormack. The second time, the PA vote remained much the same but the Moderate vote increased and the Labour vote declined. At the third election, there was no Moderate and yet there was no major increase in the PA vote. Instead, the Labour party found one and a half thousand new voters. Thus in Leith at least, Protestant Action was not just the home for disgruntled conservatives who had previously voted Moderate. When one adds the case of West Leith, where the Moderate won twice as many votes as the Labour man, and almost three times as many votes as the Protestant Actionist, it seems that the situation in Edinburgh was considerably more fluid than it was in Glasgow, where Ratcliffe's support came predominantly from conservatives.

1937 should have been a good year for Protestant Action. The various public protests and demonstrations were making the party well-known (or notorious, depending on one's view) and it had 9 councillors. 14 candidates took the field but PA's percentage of the total vote was down on 1936.

Percentages of the total vote polled by the major parties

	1935	1936	1937
Moderate	42.5	38.2	37.1
Labour	33.9	29.8	37.4
PA	23.6	32.1	25.6

Far from continuing the success of the previous year, Protestant Action actually lost a seat. This was a function of a combination of a feature of the system and a tactical mistake. The tactical mistake was Cormack's decision to stand in two wards. Quite why he did this is not clear. It was a tactic usually only used by "no hope" candidates (such as the socialist and pacifist Guy Aldred in Glasgow) who wanted to get their name and their cause mentioned as often as possible and who had no realistic chance of winning any seats. Cormack stood in two wards and came second in both. The function of the system was its "three year drag" effect. With only one-third of the seats being vacated each year, a party's standing did not only depend on how well it performed in this year but also on how well it did in the previous two. Thus there was a built-in conservatism that allowed a party whose present popularity was declining rapidly to maintain a presence it no longer deserved. From the position of an up-and-coming party, this inertia

meant that three good years were required before the party's public
standing was reflected in seats in the council. Protestant Action had
had two good years but that was not enough. Had the 1936 pattern
been repeated twice more the party would have been established as a
major force in the council but, instead of a repeat of the previous
success, there was a decline in the PA vote which was further reduced
in impact by the party's main vote attractor — Cormack — wasting his
popularity with two second places instead of the one first he would
have undoubtedly registered had he confined himself to the North
Leith ward. Where the PA support went to is no more obvious than its
source. The following table shows the voting in Canongate over the
three years.

	Canongate Ward		
	1935	1936	1937
Labour	34.9	32.4	64.8
PA	22.4	48.3	34.0
Moderate	20.0	17.2	
Others	11.4	2.1	1.2

With no Moderate, PA should have had a clear run but instead it seems
that a lot of Moderate voters moved over to the Labour candidate.
Alternatively, it may have been that the Moderate vote went to PA and
the PA vote moved to Labour.

Although the evidence is at best ambiguous, it seems from these
results that PA took votes from both Moderate and Labour and that at
least a good part of its support was working-class. This picture is
confirmed by the 1938 election. More than anything 1938 showed the
signs of a party in decline. Only 8 candidates stood on the Protestant
Action ticket and there is some doubt about the relationship of three of
these to the party. Thomas Sprott now described himself as an
independent, although the advertisements for his undertaker's
business still appeared in the Protestant Action paper, which suggests
that he was not totally alienated from the party. The Rev Percival-
Prescott, the minister of Buccleuch Evangelical Church, who had been
a PA candidate before and was at one time treasurer of PA, also called
himself an independent.[16] Leitch, standing for his old seat in the
Canongate, was described as a PA candidate but he had resigned the
whip of the party sometime in 1937 and then been reinstated in early
1938. John Cormack won a seat in South Leith where he joined George

Horne, another PA councillor, but there were no other PA wins and the party's share of the total vote fell to just 12%.

As a political party, Protestant Action was well and truly on the skids. Had there been elections in 1939 it is likely that the party would have been wiped out and it was only the suspension of municipal elections for the duration of the war that allowed the party to claim a presence.

The general pattern that emerges from these figures is that of a steady decline in the Moderates' position. In 1937 and 1938 the Labour Party matched the Moderates and laid the foundation for a major victory after the war. For a few short years, Cormack's Protestant Action looked like a serious contender and gave him some reason to think of his movement as a base for an entry into Westminster politics. But as quickly as it came, Protestant Action's vote disappeared.

Explaining the Decline

The collapse of Protestant Action is to be explained in much the same way as the decline of Ratcliffe's Scottish Protestant League in Glasgow. To take the environmental features first, one of the main elements was the response of the Catholics. Sectarian conflict requires two parties. Had the Catholics of Edinburgh (or Glasgow) formed their own political party as Hugh Murnin suggested then the battle-lines would have been clearly drawn. Instead they chose to work through the Labour Movement and the Labour Party. The absence of an obvious political enemy forced the militant Protestants to argue that a vote for Labour was a Catholic vote; a claim that was patently not the case when a large number of working-class Protestants were active in the Party. It also forced Cormack to become more and more anti-Labour to the point where his manifestos of the late forties and fifties made scant mention of either Protestantism or Roman Catholics and instead concentrated on being "one hundred percent opposed to communism and socialism". Although he retained the Protestant Action title, Cormack's post-war council career (and that of George Horne, once a PA member and later an independent) seems to have been based on individual popularity and basic conservatism.

If the Catholics were not playing ball by making themselves an easy target, other Protestants were not helping much either. Although Cormack and most of his supporters were active in the Orange Order,

the Order as an institution did little to help Protestant Action.
Cormack's relationship with the Order was never as poor as
Ratcliffe's, mainly because he was not as vicious in his attacks on the
Order. In the sixties he was a regular contributor to the Orange paper,
the *Vigilant*. After his death, Cormack was commemorated by the
changing of Lodge 188's name to "Cormack's Protestant Defenders"
and the County Grand Lodge of the East of Scotland is presently
having a new bannerette prepared which carries a portrait of
Cormack. But for all that, the Order did little to boost Protestant
Action when it could have been a political force.

And if the Orange Order was not a great help to Cormack, the
Protestant clergy of Edinburgh were conspicuously absent from the
ranks of his supporters. Only one minister of the Kirk, J. C. Trainer,
was active in PA; PA's other cleric was an independent evangelical,
and many of the Edinburgh ministers were vocally opposed to
Cormack. This was only to be expected given Cormack's anti-
catholicism and the Kirk's conversion to, if not active ecumenism,
then at least a desire for peaceful co-existence with its Roman Catholic
neighbour. But even more damaging was Cormack's problems with
non-Church of Scotland evangelicals. Putting the source of tension at
its simplest; was Cormack a Christian?

The political dimension to militant Protestantism has always
created semantic problems. When someone is called "a Protestant"
does this mean that they hold certain religious beliefs or does it mean
that they are part of an "ethnic" group which identifies itself by its
opposition to Roman Catholics? Ratcliffe usually reserved the term to
describe those with evangelical Protestant religious beliefs but even he
was capable of slipping. He once described someone as "a Christian as
well as a Protestant".[17]

I have no intention of belittling John Cormack's motivation but it
is clear that he was not an evangelical Protestant. One of the bitterest
arguments between him and Ratcliffe concerned his statement "once a
Catholic, always a Catholic". He did not believe in sincere conversion.
He thought that those who were born to Catholic parents or who had
once been practising Catholics were incapable of being "born again".
This is in clear conflict with orthodox Protestant teaching on
conversion. As Ratcliffe put it:

> Any person claiming to be a Protestant protagonist and who declines to
> put the points of Protestantism before Roman Catholics and who says

"No Roman Catholics Admitted" is two things. He is a coward and a humbug . . . Mostly such persons are afraid that Roman Catholics will ask them questions which they cannot answer. The Protestants are warned against such sham Protestants.[18]

Ratcliffe's militancy caused many evangelicals to shy away from the SPL even when they supported the League's principles. Cormack offered the same militancy but did not even have the right basic theological principles.

Of course, Ratcliffe's dislike for Cormack was not just a matter of theology. There was a good deal of plain envy. Ratcliffe's own political hopes had been shattered at just the time that Protestant Action was becoming obviously successful and Ratcliffe was always one to hold a grudge. His dislike for Cormack reached the point where he was actively campaigning against him and this almost certainly played a part in Cormack's 1937 defeat. Ratcliffe had sniped at Cormack from the day he founded Protestant Action and by 1936 the feud had got to the stage where Ratclifffe was writing and circulating pamphlets with titles such as "Is Cormack a Christian?" and "Protestant Action Finances: interesting disclosures for the Protestant Public". Members of PA attacked SPL members at an open-air meeting on the Mound. Ratcliffe hired Leith Town Hall to accuse Cormack of cowardice. Cormack retaliated by claiming that Ratcliffe was a "Romaniser" and a "compromiser". Although Ratcliffe had little organised support in Edinburgh, such public feuding can have done little to advance the cause of Protestant Action.

The movement was further weakened by internal problems. The next chapter will consider the persistent factionalism that is found in militant Protestant movements. Although PA was never as fractured as Ratcliffe's League there were defections and doubts about the loyalties of some councillors. Leitch resigned and later asked to be reinstated. Esta Henry also resigned the whip: according to one PA activist she "was a person who should not in my opinion have been selected as a candidate. She used her position to enhance her business (she was an antique dealer in the High Street and an Orthodox Jew) while in the council". James Marr did not stand again once he had served his first term: "Jimmy Marr was one of the first councillors, and a very able one, but he was also a fine looking young man and one of our lady members trapped him and a scandal ensued. We did not need a scandal so Jimmy left the arena."

The War and After

The serious setback in the 1938 election did not mean the immediate
end of Protestant Action. In fact, the routine activities seemed to have
carried on much as before. The magazine was published every month.
There were open air meetings at the Mound and indoor meetings in
various halls. There were dances in Leith Town Hall and the Marine
Gardens, Portobello. There was the annual picnic and the Covenanter
Commemoration rallies. There was an annual fund raising concert for
Leith Hospital. This period can perhaps best be described by referring
again to a principle of movement development mentioned in the last
chapter: institutionalisation. Social movements are relatively well-
organised attempts to promote some kind of change, or to build
resistance to some perceived change. People get involved in social
movements to achieve some particular aim or goal. But there are also
immediate benefits that come from membership itself: the sense of
friendship, of being with one's own kind, of being part of a great
endeavour, the feeling of doing something worthwhile. It is quite
common for a member's perception of a social movement to change.
At first, it is the striving after the goal (in this case, the establishment
of Protestant Action as the major force in Edinburgh politics) which is
the most important thing. But if this goal is not readily achieved then
the movement tends to settle down for the long haul and the benefits
of just being a member tend to become the main attraction for those
involved. The movement becomes "routinised": the active pursuit of
the original goals becomes displaced by the regular round of routine
activities. This is precisely what happened to the SPL in Glasgow after
1934 and one can see it happening in 1938 and 1939 with Protestant
Action. This is not to say that Cormack or the other activists
welcomed or encouraged this settling down but in the absence of any
signs of hope for political success then the routine activities became
the best the movement could provide.

The war had a paradoxical effect on PA. In the long term, it
removed what relevance it still retained in early 1939 but in the short
term, by delaying council elections for six years, it allowed the party to
pretend to an importance which would not have been reflected in a
popular election. Cormack continued his open-air meetings at the
Mound and even achieved a new notoriety by being charged with

treason for one speech he made. One of the core of PA worked in Leith Docks and he observed that the destination of some arms shipments was clearly marked on the cases. He tore off a piece of board and Cormack displayed this as an illustration in some of his attacks on the gross inefficiency of the government. He was found guilty and given a small fine.

Unlike Ratcliffe, Cormack was an active supporter of the British and Allied war effort. He was not a pacifist nor did he believe that the war was a Roman Catholic plot to destroy Protestant nations. But nonetheless, the war effectively killed Protestant Action. In the first place, it caused massive movements of population. Most men and a lot of women went away for long periods of time. Whole communities were uprooted. All communal activities were disrupted but such dislocation was particularly damaging to activities built around an ethnic identity. Being "Protestant" and "Catholic" was not just (or hardly) a matter of religious beliefs and practices; it was a sense of identity, a sense of shared belonging and it was very much a matter of location. In the thirties one could readily identify the Grassmarket as being a Catholic area and Bridgeton in Glasgow as being Protestant. Any major movement of population would disrupt that part of identity that was linked to place. Of course, the effects of dislocation depend on what caused it. In Belfast between 1968 and 1973 a very large number of people moved but in this case the movement strengthened group identity because it was a movement of people from marginal areas into their own ethnic strongholds. Catholics on the edge of Protestant areas moved into *more* Catholic areas for safety.[20] But the dislocation in Scotland was not related to sectarian conflict and did not lead to people moving because of their religious and ethnic character. Hence the movement just fragmented community identities.

In addition, the requirements of war overrode considerations of religion. In peacetime it was possible for Protestants and Catholics to practice "ritual avoidance". It was quite easy for people on one side to never meet those on the other. That ended with the war. Although the first wave of army recruitment tended to group people together in units that mirrored communities and hence maintained the segregation to some extent, later reorganisation of units to cover for casualties and new operational strategies were carried out with no thought for such niceties. The result was a considerable mixing of Protestant and Catholic. It is a mistake to suppose that simple

proximity always produces amity; it does not. People who hate each
other at a distance may hate each other even more when they are
forced together but this mixing did produce a greater sense of
tolerance. A number of conservative Protestants who fought in the
war have told me of the way their attitudes to Catholics changed as a
result of the experience. One leading Protestant Action member
recalls chiding Protestants in his platoon for ragging a young Catholic
who was doing his rosary; he suggested that they might be well advised
to pray. There is no reason to suppose that this experience was
restricted to those whom I have interviewed. If it was at all common, it
would account for a major change in attitudes.

These two observations about the effects of the war concern social
boundaries and social distance. A third point concerns people's hopes
and aspirations. The war was a watershed in the development of social
attitudes. It marked the end of an era that many people still associated
with the depression and, once it became likely that the Allies would
win, it was a time of considerable optimism and social planning. The
planning that had been necessary for the war effort could be harnessed
to the creation of a new world; a better world the advantages of which
would justify the sacrifice of war. In that sort of climate, the
animosities of the Reformation, the Seige of Londonderry and the
response to "papal agression" seemed obsolete. People were no longer
interested.

This climate of optimism explains the Labour landslide. Churchill
had won the war and no one denied the value of his role but they
wanted something new. In the "khaki" election of 1945 the Labour
Party overturned a Tory majority by taking 179 seats from them, 16
seats from the Liberal-National group, and 17 seats from various
Liberals, Nationals and Independents. The result was a Labour gain of
212 seats creating a parliament with 393 Labour MPs, 198
Conservatives and 36 others.

Edinburgh was not in the forefront of the Labour landslide but the
same trend was reflected there. Of the five seats in the city, three did
not change hands. One of these was already Labour and the candidate's
majority increased from just over a thousand to over six thousand
votes. The Conservatives held on to two seats but with much reduced
majorities and lost two other seats to Labour. John Cormack stood in
the Leith constituency and won just 2,493 votes in a potential total of
46,450. The seat had been held by a Liberal National with a majority of
over 11,000 in 1931 which had been reduced to about 5,000 in 1935. In

1945, the votes were cast as follows:

Westminster Election 1945: Leith

Hoy (Labour)	19,571	(60.8%)
Brown (Lib Nat)	10,116	(31.4%)
Cormack (PA)	2,493	(7.8%)

A decade earlier Cormack had talked about gaining control of the council and then taking over Westminster and depriving Catholics of the vote, with the use of violence if necessary. In 1945, he had his first chance to stand for parliament and in the constituency which contained the ward he had represented in the council for a decade he was wiped out by a Labour landslide. In 1947 he stood for the council in his old ward and gained almost six thousand votes! There were thus at least three thousand people who were prepared to see Cormack as their man in the town council but who would not vote for him in a national election.

This should not have surprised him. It was simply the return for the problem that had haunted Ratcliffe in Stirling in 1929. Any fool knows there is no point in voting for a party that has only one candidate. Cormack's presence would have made no difference to Westminster. This problem is endemic to regional parties; even if all their representatives are elected they will not form a block large enough to have any power and influence unless there is an unusually fine balance between the major parties. Protestantism was worse than a regional issue; it was a minority concern even within the region. Protestantism was not on the political agenda for the post-war world and therefore neither was John Cormack.

The Fifties and After

Protestant Action continued with two council members: Cormack and Horne. The end of PA as a serious political force was underlined by the defection of some of its councillors and candidates to what they hoped would be greener pastures. Esta Henry, who had stood as an independent before her success with Protestant Action, reverted to that label and still only managed a third place in the Canongate ward. Mrs Laughton, a Grand Mistress of the Orange Order, stood for PA in 1945 but changed to independent for the next elections. When that failed she switched to the Progressives (as the conservatives now styled themselves) but the electorate continued to be unimpressed.

Through the fifties Protestant Action shrunk, catching the headlines only sporadically when its members did something that was seen as provocative or outrageous. James Russell was arrested and charged with disturbing the peace when, in 1954, he led the chant of "One, Two ... No Popery" at the annual Covenanter commemoration rally in the Grassmarket. The charge was dropped. There was always some publicity to be had by protesting at various Church of Scotland activities that showed an increasing desire for accommodation with Rome but these were small affairs and they were *reactive*.

For example, in January 1969, members of PA barracked a Roman Catholic priest who had been invited to take part in a service which was being broadcast from the Church of Scotland parish church in Braid, Edinburgh. When Father Walter Glancy began his sermon, the PA people stood up and shouted "No Popery" and "Traitors to John Knox". The protest worked; the broadcast was stopped and replaced with classical music. Gordon Gray, the Roman Catholic Archbishop of St Andrews and Edinburgh, suggested: "It would have been better if the BBC had allowed the listeners to hear the calibre of people who were making these interruptions".[21] Although flamboyant, this sort of protest did not impress the electorate.

In 1971 it was decided to contest John Cormack's old South Leith ward. The candidate was good. Jim Maclean was a local man, Vice-President of PA, District Master of the Edinburgh Orange Lodges and an active Mason. He was supported by a large and efficient organisation which, in the estimate of one person campaigning for the Scottish Nationalist candidate, worked harder than all the other organisations put together, and yet he gained only 217 votes. In 1972 he won only 151 votes. The result might have been better had PA put up a candidate the year Cormack retired and the old loyalties been kept in place, but it is unlikely. By the sixties, Cormack's support had largely ceased to be a Protestant support. It was personal loyalty (and an agreement with the conservatives not to oppose him) that kept Cormack in his seat. Looking back one had to suppose that the effort put into Jim Maclean's first contest mobilised the total "Protestant" support in South Leith and it was only two hundred people strong.

As with other Protestant organisations, Protestant Action was well and truly in the doldrums until the outbreak of the present wave of "troubles" in Northern Ireland once more made sectarianism an issue. Yet, as I will argue, while Ulster gave Protestant Action a renewed reason for existence it also created a general climate in which the majority of people became positively opposed to the mixing of religion and politics.

4

The Protestant Popes and Internal Conflict

RATCLIFFE concluded one review of the League's development by saying: "But division, traiterous work, surrender of principle, envy and jealousy have divided our ranks in recent years".[1] He was not wrong but he could have extended the proposition to militant Protestantism at large. It seems as if the impulse to "protest" is so strong that Protestants feel impelled to turn against each other.

A good deal of the internal fighting can be attributed to the personalities of the leaders. I have already suggested that Ratcliffe was more than difficult. He was an open advocate of authoritarian leadership:

> There is no room in the SPL for any man or woman who questions the leadership of the founder of the Protestant League . . . I have been challenged over and over again, not in the open but in an underhand way; and I want to say this: I am not the man, I never was the man, to tolerate a challenge from any person in so far as my own position in the Protestant League is concerned.[2]

In defence of this attitude he offered the analogy of an army with one commander and (rather grandly) mentions the case of the single person of Jesus Christ! His own arrogance and unwillingness to tolerate initiative and leadership in others caused a constant stream of defections; Lord Scone, John Cormack, almost all of his councillors, all of his full-time workers.[3] Leslie Hope and Frederick Watson, the two Church of Scotland ministers who had been keen supporters before the League was moved from Edinburgh and whose support had played a large part in convincing Ratcliffe that the Glasgow pastures were greener, turned against him. His two attempts to find assistants and possible successors failed, with neither man lasting more than a few months.

Ratcliffe for his part was not slow to turn on those who were disloyal. His attacks on Cormack were vitriolic. He did not hesitate to use Cormack's lack of education against him: "He who would teach the people to shout 'No Popery' should really learn to know popery beforehand. But this is not considered to be necessary by the novice who sets himself up as a Protestant leader".[4] The same page of that issue of the *Vanguard* contains a long attack on H. D. Longbottom of Liverpool. Often two or more pages would be taken up with "open letters" to other Protestant leaders. Once in a while these letters would begin with some faint praise but more usually they consisted entirely of detailed listings of the addressee's faults. Ratcliffe neatly summarised his view of all other Protestants: "other Protestant bodies in Scotland, every one of them in fact, compromise with Rome one way or another".[5] But Ratcliffe was not alone in seeing himself as the sole defender of Protestant rectitude. Cormack had a similar vision and a similar style of leadership. Like Ratcliffe, he was poor at creating and training a supporting cadre. James Marr tried to give the organisation some depth by "bringing young men on" in his Speakers Club but Cormack continued to run Protestant Action as if it were simply an extension of this own will. One President of the Society argued with Cormack over his "once a catholic, always a catholic" at a committee meeting and was shunned by other members for months. After the electoral defeat of 1937 and the publication of Ratcliffe's critical pamphlet on Protestant Action finances, Cormack said: "I am going to re-organise the party from top to bottom, and to allay any suspicion of dictatorship on my part a new executive committee is being formed, who will then consider all my plans for the future and O.K. them if they consider in their judgement they are correct".[6] But this was only dressing. Cormack so closely identified the organisation with his own person that he fully expected it to be dissolved when he retired and for a few years after his retirement was on very poor terms with the other members who insisted that the Society should continue.

But any explanation of the feuding within Protestantism that only mentioned the character of the leaders involved would miss the point. It was not just Ratcliffe, Cormack and Longbottom who could not work well with each other. Many other examples could be produced. Ian Paisley has a similar history of feuding. He was once very close to

Jack Glass (whose career will be examined in detail in a later chapter) and for a short time the two of them, with Brian Green, were united in one organisation. The parting of the ways was ostensibly over a theological argument. The basis of faith of the umbrella organisation was clearly Calvinist. Paisley became very friendly with the American fundamentalist, Bob Jones Snr, who was not a staunch Calvinist. Glass demanded that Paisley denounce Jones and then "separated" from him when he refused to do so. Since then, David Cassells, an Ulsterman who is on very close terms with Paisley, has started his own evangelical church in Glasgow and Glass has been vocal in his criticism of Cassells, even going so far as to take an advert in a local paper to denounce Cassells and assert that his was the only orthodox church in the city.

Twenty years earlier there was considerable ill-feeling between the remaining members of Protestant Action in Edinburgh and the Glasgow Orange Order. This seems to have stemmed from the failure of the Glasgow branch of PA which operated from September 1951 to May 1953 and which, according to the secretary of PA, collapsed because of "local LOL antagonism". The secretary later offended the west coast Orangemen by writing the following description of the Orange Walk for the *Ulster Protestant*.

> Never has the Orange Order been so leaderless and never so much in need of leaders. The shuffling amorphous mass which walked in the Orange demonstration at Shotts, Lanarkshire, on the 12th of July cannot claim to have taken part in a dignified and impressive parade. The ridiculously late start, the proliferation of drunkenness, the jazzing of bands, in fact the crass disregard of the rules as printed in the official programme causes one to wonder and doubt the literacy of many district organisers . . . After the initial parade the marchers retired to Shotts Park. Out of an estimated attendence of 45,000 only some six hundred bothered to gather for the public meeting. A pity, for this included the best thing of the day — a fine speech by the Rev Maurice Brown which took the form of an attack on the Orange Order. Unfortunately, however, the Rev Maurice Brown and the other speakers had to contend with blatant discord caused by the simultaneous efforts of bands in all parts of the field . . . The Loyal Orange Institution of Scotland has its banners upside down, its sashes inside-out and seems to be merrily marching backwards into the River Clyde.[7]

Alice Adam, wife of the Grand Secretary of the Order, wrote a bitter letter to the *Ulster Protestant* and the whole correspondence was reprinted in the columns of the *Vigilant*, where Maurice Brown (despite the nice things that had been said about his contribution to the day in Shotts) added his piece and suggested that all true Orangemen should boycott the *Ulster Protestant.* This suggestion was accepted by the Grand Lodge and the December issue of the *Vigilant* carried on its back page, blocked and in headlines, the following announcement:

> The Most Worthy Grand Master, Bro. Thomas Corry directs that until such time as the allegation contained in the September issue of the *Ulster Protestant* are withdrawn unreservedly, members of the Loyal Orange Institution of Scotland SHOULD REFRAIN FROM PURCHASING THE ULSTER PROTESTANT.[8]

Once more it seemed as if the brothers were more intent on fighting with each other in public than they were on opposing "papal aggession".

An American example of Protestant divisions can be found in the career of Carl McIntire. McIntire was a theology student at Princeton when J. Gresham Machen resigned from the faculty over the increasingly liberal tone of the Presbyterian Church. McIntire went with him to the college he formed — Westminster — and for a time served as a minister in Machen's new Presbyterian Church of America. He fell out with Machen over the Church's position on the nature of the "end times" and split the Church; the smaller part following McIntire and becoming the Bible Presbyterian Church. Eighteen years later, the Bible Presbyterians dumped their leader and withdrew from his two organisations: the American Council of Christian Churches and the International Council of Christian Churches. Once again he started to rebuild. By 1971 he had created a large and popular theological college. That year the president, more than half the students and all but two of the staff left because of McIntire's authoritarian leadership style and his view that the Vietnam War should be won by "nuking" the North.[9]

This degree of fissiparousness is not especially modern. The history of the Scottish Presbyterian Church is a history of continuous division. In the eighteenth century the Seceders left the national church to protest at its loss of evangelical fervour. To justify their withdrawal the seceding ministers drew up detailed memorials listing all the faults of the national church. Within one generation, the Seceders divided over whether they could take a loyalty oath required of all burgesses which made a reference to supporting the "true religion". Did this imply support of the apostate national church or could Seceders take the oath and mentally argue that it was their own church that they were supporting? They split. The two groups then each divided over theology: liberals forming "new light" sections and the conservatives being called "old lights".[10] So one denomination had become five in two generations! These were shortly added to by the Free Presbyterians and the Free Church. Although the trend was reversed at the end of the nineteenth century with most of the Presbyterian organisations uniting, this did not reduce the number of competing organisations. When two organisations merged, each left behind a dissenting rump, and thus each act of union produced three churches.

The conclusion has to be that Protestantism is peculiarly prone to schism. One qualification to that proposition is that distance helps. Paisley and Glass separated but Paisley gets on well with Bob Jones who is in South Carolina. Cormack and Ratcliffe were at each other's throats but Cormack got along well with Longbottom in Liverpool. Recently a very disparate group of evangelicals in Ireland formed themselves into a fraternal organisation. I asked one member, a clear Calvinist, how he could be in fellowship with some people of quite different views. He replied that it was quite easy to overlook such differences when the other fellows were hundreds of miles away. When two groups or individuals are not competing for the same audience, fraternal relations are much more likely than when they are working the same patch. The other qualification is that some people preserve the peace by not competing. Brian Green has remained on good terms with Ian Paisley for twenty years because he is quite content with the subordinate position of being someone who "does everything I can to help Paisley". He has a full-time career in insurance and is opposed to professional ministry.

The Structure of Beliefs

The range of examples given should be enough to show the weakness of a "personality" explanation of Protestant factionalism. It is simply too pervasive a phenomenon to be explained in terms of the individual characteristics of the leader involved. The fact that Ratcliffe was an egomaniac did not help but there is something more general that needs to be considered. I want to suggest that there is something about the nature of Protestantism, and the views of knowledge and authority that the Protestants hold, that accounts for the susceptibility to fission.

Wallis has cast light on this problem by looking at schism as a process in which the people involved have to make calculations about the likelihood of taking the majority of members out with them.[11] And the key consideration in those calculations is the problem of authority. How does one justify some new course of action or some new revelation? Different sorts of movements have different kinds of authority. For the Nazis, the person of Hitler was the sole source of authoritative knowledge. Thus anyone considering leading a schism would be in a very weak position because "the person of Hitler" could not be appropriated for the schismatic group. In contrast, a "tradition" can be claimed by lots of different people. A fixed body of ideas, such as "Marxism", can be claimed by a variety of people and thus it is always possible for someone to lead a split from a Marxist party by claiming to have some greater insight than the dominant leadership into the canon. The crucial question is this: how accessible is the source of authoritative knowledge and who can claim it?

Different types of Christianity have very different answers to that question. With some simplification and generalisation it is possible to divide modern Christianity into four types based on the answers given to the question "how do we know the truth?".[12] All types would say firstly, "because God told us" but when one asks the subsidiary question "how did he tell us?", then the differences become clear. Conservative Protestants believe that the Bible is the only source of salvational knowledge. Liberal Protestants accept that but add that we can only understand the Bible in the terms of our own culture. The values of whatever passes for human reason and knowledge stand as a filter between the actual words of the Bible and our understanding of them. Hence we have to "interpret" what the Bible says. In practice this position leads to embracing contemporary rational culture as the basic source of values and then finding interpretations of scripture that fit modern man's reason. The Catholics and the Orthodox temper their reading of the Bible with the Church's traditions. They also see a problem of "interpreting" the Bible and give a predominant position to the properly appointed officers of the Church as the correct interpreters of the Word. Hence their commitment to the idea of an "apostolic succession". Christ appointed and anointed those who were to perpetuate his teachings and in so doing passed on to them his powers. Only the successors of those people, properly anointed, have the power of interpreting his teachings. Thus for the Catholics and the Orthodox the main source of authority is the Church. Pentecostalists and Charismatics differ from the three traditions already outlined in believing that the gifts of the Holy Spirit are still available today to all believers. Hence they look for the presence of the gifts of the spirit: the ability to "speak in tongues", to heal, to read prophecies and so on. The four main traditions and the corresponding course of authoritative knowledge can be displayed in a table:

1. Liberal Protestantism   Culture/Reason
2. Conservative Protestantism   Bible
3. Orthodox and Catholic   Church
4. Pentecostalism/Charismatic   Spirit

Of course, no actual living group of Christians relies on one source exclusively. Most create some sort of combination. Most Protestants, both liberal and conservative, use some sort of church tradition. Pentecostalists vary in the degree to which the workings of the Spirit are institutionalised in traditional teachings that do not change a great deal. Some Catholics combine their allegiance to the Church with a belief in direct spirit revelation and others become slightly "Protestantised". Nonetheless the model does identify the major differences.

The four traditions have very different tendencies to schism. The Catholic and the Orthodox, with the emphasis on proper church order and tradition, has a structure which prevents leaders emerging to lead factions and breakaway movements. The power and influence belong to the office and not to the person who inhabits that office. There are elaborate procedures for defining "knowledge" and for resolving disputes. Anyone who refuses to accept the outcome of proper procedure can be stripped of his office. Outside of the church there is no salvation and potential leaders and followers of schisms know that. Of course, this does not entirely prevent factionalism and schism — the case of Archbishop Lefebvre in France is a counter example — but it acts as a very strong curb on the tendency.

The other three traditions all have a high potential for schism. None of them has one centralised organisation which claims sole possession of authority. All Protestants and those who believe in the present day activity of the Spirit assert a "priesthood of all believers". Anyone can hear the Word; anyone can read the Bible; anyone, in theory, can receive revelations. This being the case it is easy for inspired individuals to believe that they have the truth, that the Word has spoken to them. It is also conceivable for such leaders to convince others to follow their revelation. There are no institutional obstacles to schism. In practice, most Protestants moderate this democracy by adding ideas about training and proper government. Presbyterians are especially fond of a trained, learned ministry. Being "called" to lead is not enough. One must also study and although Presbyterian organisations maintain the rhetoric of a congregation testing a potential minister to see if he has truly been "called", in practice the profession is only open to those who have been through certain procedures of training and who have thus been socialised into the profession. Thus while they may have no ideological commitment to a notion such as the apostolic succession, in practice most Protestant Churches have restrained the democracy inherent in their ideas about universal availability of the scriptures with a *de facto* church organisation, outside of which there may be salvation but it is a grudging "may be".

So some Protestants continue to believe that the organisation of the Church is important and that revelation is more likely to be found within such an organisation than without it. This reduces the likelihood of the factionalism that concerns us here. The rest of the Protestants reject such notions as "popish" and continue to emphasise the democracy of the believers. But this remainder needs to be divided into conservative and liberal groups. Here the crucial division concerns what sociologists of religion call sectarianism.[13] We can view our beliefs in one of two extreme ways. We can suppose that we have the complete truth and that everyone else is wrong: this is the sectarian position. Or we can suppose that no one has the complete truth, that everyone may have some of the truth, and that hence, we should not reject as "damned" those who may disagree with us. This is the denominational attitude. Conservative Protestants, like conservative Catholics, are sectarian. They believe that they have a unique grasp of the truth. Outside of what they hold, there is no salvation. Liberal Protestants do not hold such views. Once one has allowed that the Bible does not speak directly to us, that it must be interpreted, then one has to recognise that there will be differing interpretations.[14] The liberal Protestant thus tends to be inclusive in his views of who is saved. Even if this is not articulated in overt universalism— the belief that all of God's creatures will be saved — it is the practical attitude that comes from problems in deciding just who is and who is not saved. The liberal Kirk member will probably offer some "good" reason for being in the Kirk rather than anywhere else but he does not insist that only other Kirk members will be saved. This is the tolerant spirit of the ecumenical movement. It is the ethos which holds that all (or most) Christian groups have got a part of the truth. The important thing about this denominational position is its resulting psychology. Liberals do not feel impelled to associate only with those who hold identical beliefs. They do not have detailed tests of orthodoxy.

The democracy of Protestantism has different results depending on whether it is attached to a sectarian or a denominational attitude. The combination that produces the greatest number of splits is the *sectarian democracy*. It combines two propositions which are guaranteed to produce endless divisions. Conservative Protestants have no centralised church organisation to settle arguments about precisely what the correct teaching is on any issue, yet they are vitally concerned to know just what is the correct teaching. As a result, conservative Protestant movements are perpetually dogged by internal disagreements.

It is common for the critics of men like Ratcliffe, Glass and Paisley to denounce them as "greater Popes than the Pope" but there is truth in this observation despite the *animus* that usually motivates it. Because the Pope and the other senior officials of the Catholic Church, Orthodox and Episcopal Churches derive their power from their *office*, their authority is limited and circumscribed. While Bishops have considerable power, that power is defined. Their subordinates know what their superior can command and what he cannot. The irony of the primitive democracy is that it allows individuals to become very powerful. Where the power comes through some nebulous channel, such as "the spirit talking to the preacher", it is possible for the preacher to make claims that a Bishop cannot make.[15] The only recourse for those people who do not want to accept the leader's claims is schism. There are no institutional structures for limiting or testing the authority of the leader. Thus it is common for supposedly democratic conservative Protestant and Pentecostal movements to become movements led by an extremely powerful authoritarian leader. The Exclusive Brethren,[16] the no-name preachers,[17] the churches of Jack Glass, Ian Paisley, Bob Jones are all examples.

These observations offer a better explanation for the high degree of internal conflict found in conservative Protestant movements than the claims about the personality of the individuals involved. Their own personal psychology is clearly important but so long as they hold to certain beliefs, they must work within the social organisations, the structures that are built on those beliefs. If we understand the basic nature of authority in conservative Protestantism, we can see how, irrespective of the personality of any particular Protestant leader, the type of beliefs held creates a structure that is ripe for internal division.

The Baptist Connection

Almost every single modern British militant Protestant leader has been a Baptist. Alexander Ratcliffe was a Deacon in the Madeira Street Baptist Church in Leith. One of the League's Presidents, John Kirk, was a minister in the Evangelical Union who had strong Baptist leanings and who sold his church in Gorgie to a Baptist group. John Cormack was raised a Baptist. His father was a Baptist lay preacher, as was George Horne, one of the PA councillors. Of the ministers who were associated with Protestant Action, one was a Baptist, one an independent evangelical, and the other, though Church of Scotland, had no charge. H.D. Longbottom and his predecessor in Liverpool, Wise, were Baptists. Of the modern leaders, Glass and Green call themselves Calvinistic Baptists. Ian Paisley calls himself a Presbyterian but was a Baptist. His father was a Baptist minister and he shares most of his father's beliefs.[18] The church he heads has many of the symbols and forms of a Presbyterian church but it differs from the elected democracy model of the main Presbyterian Churches in that it does not have a different Moderator each year; except for one year, Paisley has been the Moderator since its formation. There is, however, good rhetorical value in calling it a Presbyterian Church, given that most of its members were dissidents from the main Presbyterian Church of Ireland who were attracted by Paisley's assertion that he offered a return to the pure tradition of Ulster Protestantism. That tradition was predominantly Presbyterian and so he has been keen to present himself in some sort of continuity but his beliefs and practices owe as much to those of the Baptists as to any other type of

Protestant. The last chapter mentioned the Rev Percival Prescott, a
Protestant Action council candidate who was an independent
evangelical. James Brisby was another independent evangelical
minister who was involved in Protestant politics. An Ulsterman who
came to Glasgow around the turn of the century, Brisby founded his
own church, launched the *Scottish Protestant Review* (which was very
similar to Ratcliffe's later publications) in 1910, and was elected to the
Glasgow School Board on an anti-catholic platform. He organised the
signing in Glasgow of the Ulster Covenant and formed his own
Volunteers in readiness to defend Ulster from incorporation in the
Free State.

What makes the coincidence of almost all the militant Protestants
being Baptists (or similar independent evangelicals) even more
noteworthy is the relative numbers of Baptists and Presbyterians in
Scotland (and Ulster). Protestantism in north Britain is Presbyterian.
There are representatives of all the dissenting denominations but
these presences are token. The following table gives the figures for the
various denominations and their congregations in Scotland in 1870:[19]

	Churches
Church of Scotland	1254
Free Church	873
United Presbyterian Church	600
Scottish Episcopalian	157
Roman Catholic	132
Congregationalist	96
Baptist	83
Evangelical Union	77
Reformed Presbyterian	44
Wesleyan Methodist	34
United Original Seceder	25
True and Original Cameronian	11

Thus the Baptist presence in Scotland was about 3% of the total
Protestant representation. Presbyterians of one sort or another made
up over 80% of Protestants. Membership figures are always less
reliable than numbers of buildings but the average Baptist congregation
was always smaller than that of the Presbyterian churches and a
comparison of the most reliable statistics suggests that there were
about 7,000 Baptists and 850,000 Presbyterians in Scotland in 1870.

Expressing Baptists as a proportion of Presbyterians gives a percentage of less than 1. By 1930 the Baptists had improved their position — 23,000 as compared to 1.3 million Presbyterians — which is more than 1.7% but this is still minute.[20] It is a small tick-eating bird on the back of a rhino. And yet it was from that small section of Scottish Protestantism that almost all of the vocal militant Protestants came.

The first part of an explanation of this finding concerns the theme that runs through this book. In common with most developing societies, Britain has become secularised. Religion has been pushed to the edges of the society. Where religious beliefs are still strong it is on the geographical edges of our society — Ulster, the highlands and islands of Scotland, Wales — and in the middle classes. Despite the great efforts made by Thomas Chalmers and the other Free Church leaders, the urban working class was never incorporated into the Presbyterian Churches. By the turn of the last century, the Presbyterian Churches were well on the way to becoming solidly middle-class institutions. The Free Church was especially prone to this development. Unlike the Established Church, the Free Church (and the earlier Seceder groups which united in the United Presbyterian Church) was not supported financially by the state. Its clergy, colleges and schools were supported by the contributions of its members. The "voluntary" churches always tend to be the homes of the better off: the people who could afford to support their religious preferences. The major exception to this was the highland half of the Free Church. The middle-class nature of the Presbyterian Churches has been reinforced by the professionalisation of the ministry. The emphasis on an educated clergy means that entry to the profession was restricted to those who had been through long periods of university education. Thus even those people who were from working-class homes, were they to join the ministry, would be socialised into middle-class values and attitudes. Similarly, the position of "elder" in the local churches was normally held by the most articulate, respectable and wealthy members of the congregation. To some extent, *all* the Protestant churches were gradually becoming the preserves of the middle classes, but the Baptists, the small "tin hut" gospel halls, and the little mission churches retained more contact with the industrial working class.

A further obstacle to the Presbyterians throwing up the militant Protestant leaders has been the contacts between the Churches and the state. Although far less influential than they were, and than they would like to be, the Presbyterian Churches still have the ear of the élites in a way that the small dissenting groups never had. The General Assemblies are attended by the Queen's representatives and by government officials. Church bodies such as the Church and Nation committee did have, and still have, some influence on state policy and legislation. There is thus a career structure for those within the Presbyterian Churches who wish to attain some influence; a career that is denied to the small dissenting bodies.

The general point here is that people tend only to direct action, to "street politics", to social protest and social movements, when they feel themselves excluded from the institutional channels for achieving their goals.[21] The position of the Presbyterian Churches allowed their members and leaders to feel more involved and more incorporated into the state. Hence the militant anti-catholic movements, were they to arise, would tend to come from outside those churches.

The second part of the explanation of the failure of Presbyterianism to produce anti-catholic leaders is the universal part: as I have argued above, the Presbyterian Churches had moderated their claims about the democracy of their religion by supporting a professional bureaucratic style of church government. The formal structures did not allow ambitious, committed leaders to assert themselves, except through the institutional structures of the church. Thus in the Church of Scotland someone like Jacob Primmer could be constantly isolated and repressed. Such a person could be denied a lucrative parish. Primmer never had the security of his own parish; he was a missioner all his life and thus his income could be tampered with by the Presbytery and other means of control could be used to isolate him. The maverick could be kept off the important committees. He could be given no say in major church appointments such as theology chairs. Even if he could get to the General Assembly, he could be outvoted.

Such actions were the "stick". The "carrots" were many and persuasive. Following the lead of the senior figures in the Church led to the best "calls" to the most affluent congregations and appointments to the important positions and committees. The structure of the Presbyterian Church could thus operate to offer potential mavericks good reasons to follow the safe line.

In contrast, the independence of the Baptist congregations is almost an encouragement to personal entrepreneurship. Anyone feeling himself "called" to lead can "have a go". The only test of one's leadership is the ability to acquire a following. There is very little centralised structure to suppress deviants. The independents are the classic conservative Protestants. The Word is open to anyone who has ears to hear. Long periods of university training are not required. There is no incorporation in the state. If anything, the position of being a dissenter produced an instinctive distrust for powers and principalities that proved fertile for anti-catholicism when the state began to remove the restrictions on Catholics. Although some dissenters made common cause with Catholics to protest against their joint exclusion from the state, for others the increased toleration of Catholics was just further proof of the essential corruption of the élites. In the tin halls and small missions in the towns and cities of the Scottish lowlands, the sense of isolation, of frustration and exclusion produced a fertile soil for populist politics and anti-catholicism.

5

Rome, Rum, Rebellion . . . and Rape

RATCLIFFE, Cormack, Begg, Hope and Primmer disliked Roman Catholicism and the nature of their campaigns will have given some idea of just what it was about the beliefs and behaviour of Catholics that offended them. I want now to bring these objections together into a coherent picture of the content of anti-catholicism.

In the first place, the militant Protestants objected to anything which offered either practical or symbolic comfort to Catholics. They wanted to maintain Protestant supremacy and campaigned vigorously against anything that eroded that supremacy; the establishment of Catholic religious houses, a Scottish hierarchy, the Catholic Emancipation Act, the Education Act of 1918, all of these were objected to as giving Roman Catholics rights they did not deserve. But this leaves the central question unanswered. What was it about Catholicism that made its followers unacceptable?

The starting point has to be religious difference. It is easy in these liberal and tolerant times to suppose that it is improper to disagree seriously with other people about religion. It is tempting to see as pathological those who continue to think that religion is important enough to wish to treat differently those who share one's religion from those who do not. Terms like "extremist" are happily banded about in bad studies of militant Protestantism. Such an approach misses one brutal historical fact. Protestantism began life as anti-catholicism. It was the Roman Catholic Church which provided the organisational home for the ideas and actions against which the reformers *protested*. In the view of Protestants, Catholicism is an apostate system because it has added to the basic truths of Christianity, as revealed in the New Testament, a number of later perverse teachings. The institution of the confessional and the resource of penance, the elevation of Mary, the ritual nature of the Mass, idolatry, all of these are regarded by Protestants as impediments to true faith and hence to salvation. In particular, the role of the priesthood and the church is challenged. As Lloyd-Jones puts it:

> the Bible says that there is only one mediator between God and Man, the man Christ Jesus. Not so in Rome — Mary, the Pope, the priests and all the hierarchy and all the underlings are necessary. What is the result of this? Their people are kept in ignorance and in a state of superstition.[1]

The Protestant rejection of the role of the priesthood in salvation is coupled to beliefs about democracy and personal independence. Protestantism teaches self-reliance. Every man is his own monk. Each of us must make our own peace with God and live righteously. We can gain no salvational benefit from the prayers of our friends or of priests. If we sin, we cannot buy our way out of it by confessing and doing penance. Protestantism makes us all independent and simultaneously makes us all equal before God and man. Rome is repressive and authoritarian.

> She claims to govern us in what we believe and in what we do. She claims to be responsible for our soul and its salvation. We must therefore submit utterly and absolutely to what the Church tells us and what the Church teaches us. She has a totalitarian system. There is no question but that she binds the souls of her people absolutely, as much as Communism does, as much as Hitler did under his horrible system. It is a totalitarian system.[2]

Thus Rome is not only in doctrinal error. She also leads people into the wrong politics. Theological mistakes cause social and political evils.

The linking of religious and political error was not difficult in the British context. The Hanoverian defeat of the Jacobites meant that the Protestant party defeated the Catholic and Episcopalian parties. Oppositional movements such as the 1715 and 1745 Risings in Scotland and the nationalist movement in Ireland were predominantly anti-protestant movements. Apart from the odd short-lived liberal Protestant coalition with the nationalists, as happened in the United Irishmen in Ulster,[3] the religious division matched the political conflicts. Protestantism could then be read as the loyal religion, the religion that supported the Crown and the Empire, while Catholicism was seen as the treacherous religion, the faith of those who opposed the state. Protestantism became Unionism and Loyalism.

Although the religious and political divisions did not match so neatly in other contexts such as America, Protestants in, for example, the Know Nothing Party,[4] could still mobilise the same rhetoric of rebellion by pointing to the *international* nature of Catholicism. The fragmentation of Protestantism into hundreds of sects and denominations allows it to develop in harmony with local interests. A good case in point is that of the Dutch Reformed Churches in South Africa, which are in theory "sister churches" of the Reformed Churches in Holland and elsewhere and yet which developed a quite distinct ideology supportive of Afrikaner supremacy.[5] The gulf between the South African Churches and those in America and Europe has grown to the point where they are on the point of being expelled from the World Alliance of Reformed Churches. Although the Roman Catholic Church has regional divisions and conflicts (for example, the radicalism of some of the Latin American priests as compared to the conservatism of the Italian Church), it still has one formal institutional framework whose headquarters is Rome. Add to that the Roman Church's inflated rhetoric of papal titles (such as "ruler of the world") and one has an excellent opportunity for arguing that Roman Catholics owe their allegiance to Rome rather than to the sovereign state in which they are resident. The fact that it is very difficult to find an example in the last two hundred years of Roman Catholics betraying their country for Roman interests (whatever they might be) makes little difference to the plausibility of the rhetoric.

The solution to the lack of obvious evidence is simple: suppose a secret conspiracy. It took very little imagination to translate the reality of a religious order, with "branches" in lots of different countries and with its senior officials, often foreigners, appointed by Rome, into the myth of a worldwide secret organisation bent on taking over the world. The history of the Roman Catholic Church's political intriguing could then be culled by evidence. The retort that such evidence was anachronistic could be dismissed by repeating Rome's own claim to be always the same, never changing. All it then needed was one or two ex-Jesuits willing to claim that they had been privy to such conspiracies, and there were plenty of those about. Books such as *The Jesuit Conspiracy: the secret plan of the Order detected and revealed by the*

Abbate Leone[6] provided detailed grist for the conspiracy thinker's mill.

Roman Catholics were not only rebellious; they were also wretched. First in Ireland and then in Scotland, they were poorer than Protestants. In Scotland, Protestants were distributed across the whole social spectrum but the conservatives of the lowlands in the Seceder Churches and the Free Church tended to be located in the rising bourgeoisie and the skilled working class. Catholicism was the religion of the poor Irish immigrants. This allowed the Protestants to make a ready equation. They were better off because they deserved to be. The truth of their religion was evidenced by their greater wealth. Few writers would have expressed it as bluntly as that, but that was the conclusion arrived at (even if not often voiced) by Protestants.

If asked to detail the causal chain that connected false religion and poverty, most nineteenth-century anti-catholics would without hesitation have pointed to the demon rum. It is common for poor, hopeless people to seek solace in narcotics. Bolivian miners forget their tiredness and pain by chewing coca leaves. The Irish in Glasgow, like the residents of most early British cities, drank a lot. At the same time, the temperance movement was having a major impact on the evangelical Protestants, who could then explain their own increasing prosperity as a result of sobriety. While it is likely that the Irish drank because they were poor, the Protestants argued that they were poor because they drank. A second causal link was gambling. Again, it is common to find people who have no great hope of achieving high wealth and status through diligent labour and saving turning to fortune and chance. Lotteries provide the possibility of miraculous release from drudgery. For this reason they offend against the rationality of Protestantism with its emphasis on pain-staking work with each man responsible for his own fate.[7] Although orthodox Protestant doctrine always argued that salvation could not be earned — it is a sovereign grace offering from God — in practice Protestant ethics implied that it could be acquired provided one went about it in a diligent and worthy manner, glorifying God by honest striving in an honest vocation. Drinking what little money one had and then hoping to get rich by gambling was seen by Protestants as just the social equivalent of the Catholic's belief that one could sin a lot and then get free of the consequences by some simple (and relatively painless) acts of penance and contrition.[8]

It is not easy to separate the religious, political and social themes in anti-catholicism. They are so closely interwoven that one thread leads readily into another. There is, however, some value in distinguishing intellectual anti-catholicism from its popular counterpart. In the absence of social surveys and opinion polls it is unwise to be too specific about which elements in anti-catholicism appealed to which markets but it seems safe to suppose that the theological arguments were not the pressing concerns of most people who opposed Catholicism. What was more arresting and immediate was the empirical *evidence* — the disloyalty, the poverty, the vice — that these people had the wrong religion.

Nuns in Bondage

One of the main planks of popular anti-catholicism was sexual licentiousness. The supposed sexual depravity of the priesthood, the priest's use of nuns, the dark areas of sexuality probed in the confessional, these were themes that were returned to over and over again. The 1845 meeting organised by the Scottish Protestant Alliance was arguably one of the last great anti-popery occasions for the main Scottish Churches. 746 churchmen attended the three days of meetings; half of them sent as appointed representatives of their various churches. Among the convenors one finds John Hope, a couple of baronets, a member of parliament, and the leaders of the Free Church: Candlish, Guthrie and Begg. Very few major figures in Victorian Protestantism were not present at the meetings. The introduction to the published report states the need for "action for the overthrow of Popery in every form". Romanism apparently "teaches the destruction of innocent life as a duty". It is also guilty of a "conspiracy against the liberty, lives and property of British Protestants". And tagged on to these accusations is the demand that priests should not be allowed to immure Protestant wives and daughters in their "monkish prisons".[9]

The meetings resolved to petition the government for a ban on priests in state institutions such as prisons, an end to all grants to Catholic organisations such as Maynooth College, and called for government inspection of convents. The purpose of the first two points seem obvious enough. They were ways in which the state could continue to deny Roman Catholics the rights granted to other citizens. But the inspection of convents seems a curious aim for such an august body of Scottish churchmen — even given their anti-catholicism — to desire.

Thirty-eight years later, Jacob Primmer was campaigning on the same issue. On a visit to Carlisle he was informed of a convent that was supposed to possess a dungeon for refractory nuns. With some deceit about his identity, Primmer and a companion toured the convent and "discovered" two cellars which he claimed were designed as prison cells. While in Carlisle, Primmer met Helen Golding, a woman who claimed to have been a prisoner for 25 years in 18 different convents. She had finally been rescued from a French convent by a Scottish lawyer. With Primmer as her promoter, Golding toured Dumfries, Dundee, Dunfermline and other towns recounting her life story.[10]

The tradition of campaigning against convents continued with Ratcliffe. He promoted the lectures given by Edith O' Gorman Auffray, an ex-Carmelite nun who had previously spoken for the English Protestant Alliance. She gave Ratcliffe copyright to her life story and he published that, and other anti-convent material in pamphlets with titles such as *The Horrors of Convent Life*, *The Life of the Carmelite Nun*, and *Convent Life Unveiled*. Ratcliffe's criticism of convents, like those of Primmer and others, had two main strands. The first was imprisonment:

> The Nunnery system at all times, ancient and modern, has had for one of its fundamentals, the seclusion or imprisonment of its devotees. To say that Rome's nuns are prisoners is to understate the case. Because most prisoners are set free at one time or another. But Rome's nuns are *prisoners for life*. They are jailed women who are never set free except by death.[11]

Ratcliffe referred often to the age of girls going into convents. They were too young to have made decisions and once inside, they were kept imprisoned. Poignant references were made to the slamming of the door behind the neophyte and the heavy bars across the window through which parents and daughters could talk.

But alongside this concern for individual liberty is a second objection. Ratcliffe and others before him believed convents to be hotbeds of sin and vice. In his lecture on a Carmelite convent, illustrated with apparently authenticated slides, he dwelt at length on the various rituals of humiliation which were part of the social process of becoming a nun. In common with most institutions that are concerned to change people's characters (prisons and army induction camps are obvious examples), convents employed what Garfinkel calls "degradation ceremonies",[12] in which the old identity of the new nun was symbolically stripped away and a new identity conferred. The fact that some of the rituals had an element of physical contact — one of them involved the recruit prostrating herself on the floor while others walked on her — was used by Ratcliffe to imply some sort of masochistic sexual gratification. Just as the term "bondage" now has the meaning of a certain kind of masochistic sexual practice, so Ratcliffe's exposure of the bondage in which nuns lived always had that subtle implication of sexuality.

But Ratcliffe went beyond innuendo. In the *Vanguard* and in his pamphlets he frequently reprinted ex-nun's claims to having been sexually abused by priests. One ex-nun claimed that illegitimate children were frequently born in convents, baptised and instantly strangled, in this way being assured of a place in heaven.[13] His illustrated talk on the life of a Carmelite nun reached its climax with a story of Barbara Ubryk, who entered a Carmelite convent in Austria in the 1830s. She was drugged, sexually assaulted by the priest and then imprisoned for resisting further assaults. She was kept there for 21 years and was only found during a government inspection.[14] Ratcliffe gave the local Bishop his due and reported that he sacked the priest. Ubryk died in 1869. The case thus dates from at least 80 years before Ratcliffe delivered the lecture, a point that will be taken up later.

The accusations of sexual depravity were not limited to the convent. Other Ratcliffe pamphlets are *Why Priests Don't Wed, The Priests' Immoral Questions to Women,* and *The Abominable Confession.* The first of these was reprinted over ten years and sold about forty thousand copies. It is basically a reprint of an American book, supposedly written by an ex-Catholic priest, B.L. Quinn. Quinn tells the reader that a number of "blessed confraternities", established by Pious IX in 1866, were organisations of women whose task it was to serve the priests:

> The female, to be a suitable candidate, must be perfectly pliant, docile and obedient. She must be sound and healthy in mind and body, free from scrofula and all impurity, as nothing diseased can touch the sacred bodies (?) of these "holy fathers". She must be considered good looking.[15]

The priests recruit and then dominate their women:

> How carefully, and with what specious arguments, these smooth-tongued villains ingratiate themselves into the favour of their flock, the initiated alone can tell; suffice to say, they rule, they sway, the bodies and souls of their dupes, touching as with a magic wand the secret springs of passion and lust, till, like a mighty chorus, the spirits of evil seem to congregate about them and revel in a villainy such as never before was perpetrated under the sanction of any religion claiming to be Christian, thus rivalling in enormity the worst and most licentious institutions of paganism.[16]

The basic elements of Ratcliffe's obsession are all here: women are seen as weak creatures, barely in control of their own sexuality; priests are sexual deviants who use their influence to lead women into evil. "The priest will visit the home when the husband is at work . . .the priest is the Lord and Master of the Roman Catholic wife these days, not her husband."[17]

The institution of the confessional is attacked on similar grounds. In *The Abominable Confessional* the case that it is unscriptual is dealt with in four pages; the case that it is also immoral takes the following ten. "Thousands of women have been sent on to the street and kept there because of the confessional. Ninety percent of the women walking the streets of our cities and large towns are Roman Catholics and victims of the priest's confessional."[18] Such women are turned to prostitution by the priest:

> The idle and luxurious habitués of sexual vice of almost inconceivable filthiness — they, as confessors, could by their questions, prompt and initiate into the comparatively pure and innocent mind of their penitent, refinements and subtleties of vice and crime that could have their origins only in the heart and brain of a lazy, luxurious and licentious priesthood.[19]

Even if those Catholic men who join the priesthood were not corrupt before, their part in the confessional would *make* them corrupt:

> and what must be the state of mind, the Confessor's, into which is daily poured the accumulated filth and vice of a neighbourhood. He cannot decline the dreadful office. He must be the depository of all the

imagined and all the acted wickedness around him. To him it gravitates,
as to its centre. Every purpose of lust, every deed of vengeance, every
piece of villainy, forming a fresh contribution to the already fearful and
fathomless mass of known wickedness within him. This black and
loathsome mass, he carries about with him, within him.[20]

It is often glibly asserted that those who advocate puritanical controls
of sexuality are themselves the victims of sexual obsession. The
puritans are the ones who are continually thinking about sex. One
critic of the American evangelist Billy Graham noted with relish a
Freudian slip in which Graham said "fertility" when he clearly meant
"fatality".[21] I do not want to pursue that argument but it should be
noted that Ratcliffe and others premised their attacks on the sexual
morals of priests on the belief that no one could actually remain
celibate. He once said: "Rome's priests cannot live without their
mistresses, being denied wives".[22] Ratcliffe does not believe the ascetic
claims of the celibate. Everybody needs sexual release. Those who are
not married thus need to find it outside marriage. Hence all priests
have mistresses.

The climax of Ratcliffe's attack on the morals of the Roman
Catholic Church comes in his pamphlet *Liguori the Filthy*. Liguori was
an early eighteenth-century moral theologian and founder of the
Redemptionist Order who was canonised as St Alphonsus Liguori in
1839. He wrote a number of texts which have often been used by
Protestants as proof of the immorality of the priesthood. Liguori was
concerned with sin. He discusses certain sorts of acts in great detail in
order to make fine distinctions between those that are sins and those
that are not. For example, he poses the question: "if a husband
withdraws after spending but before his wife has spent, can she
immediately, by touches, excite herself in order to spend?"[23] and then
goes on to consider the pro's and con's of the case. An interesting
aside: it is obvious that Liguori thought that orgasm was essential to
conception. Were it not, then he would have had no hesitation in
describing that case as sinful. What is more striking about the writings
of Liguori to the modern eye is the hair-splitting involved in these
treatises. There is no discussion of general moral themes but rather a
legalistic picking of nits. Thus, for example, when Liguori is
considering the cases in which the confidence of confessions may be
called into question, he does not offer the general principle that the
priest should remain silent on anything he has learnt through the

confessional. Rather he asserts that anything learnt in the confessional *is not known*. The priest is thus told he may swear on oath that he does not know something which he has been told in the confessional. This doctrine of *reservation* allows Ratcliffe to assert that priests are told by Liguori to lie.

Accusing People of Deviance

Why were Ratcliffe and other militant Protestants so keen to accuse Roman Catholics of sexual perversion? The simplest answer would be that they were confronted with overwhelming evidence that such perversion was common in the Roman Catholic Church; they made the claims because the claims were true. It is hard to know just what would count as the evidence that overwhelms. A critical perspective suggests that the sources were not very good. The main evidence came from ex-priests and ex-nuns. B.L. Quinn, Pastor Chiniquy, Edith O' Gorman Auffray, P.J. Maurin, Helen Golding, and the almost certainly fictitious Maria Monk, these were the sources of most of Ratcliffe's material. If one were naive about it, one might suppose that these people were the best possible sources; they claimed to be either perpetrators of the things they condemned, or victims of the vices that they delineated in loving detail.

But one ought to be extremely cautious about defectors. In the first place defectors have a large axe to grind. Very often they have turned their backs on a belief-system and a pattern of activity in which they have invested an enormous amount of emotional energy and commitment. In some cases, the Catholic Church had spurned them; in other cases, they withdrew, but either way one might expect a considerable amount of grudge in their reactions to the previous life which once meant so much to them. The second reason for caution is well known to students of conversions. A common element in the accounts of converts is an exaggeration of just how bad they were before they got saved. Sinners who get religion; alcoholics who dry out; slobs who become health fanatics; in all of these dramatic alterations, there is a perfectly understandable tendency to mentally rewrite the previous biography, to heighten its awfulness in order to make more clear the benefits of the new life. Young evangelicals giving their "testimony" are especially prone to stressing their previous sinfulness.

Another neglected consideration is the converts' need to explain their previous mistakes. Young adults who have devoted years to ceaseless fund-raising for the Moonies and who cease to believe in Sun Myung Moon have the serious problem of explaining to themselves and to others how they could have been so wrong and so foolish. And a ready explanation is offered to them by the critics of the Moonies. They are invited to claim that it was not *really* them that did these terrible things; they were not in control. It was not their (now seen as mistaken) choice to become a Moonie; they were brainwashed. They were externally controlled. Although Ratcliffe did not use the language of brainwashing, he offered a similar account of how people could be so mistaken as to be committed Catholics. They were controlled by the priests who seduced their minds at an early impressionable age. Hence young girls did not choose to become nuns; they were conned and then kept imprisoned in convents.

The third reason for being cautious of taking defector stories at face value is an extension of the first. There was not only good reason for amplifying one's previous sinfulness in order to please the audience and boost one's new belief system. There were also good financial reasons. Patrick McMenemy, the charlatan who so successfully conned James Begg, was an extreme case, but there was money to be made. There was an audience of evangelical Protestants who would not only make welcome any ex-priest or ex-nun but who would also pay large sums of money for the entertainment provided by the public confessions and denunciations.

Quite how lucrative the exposure business was is not clear but we can get some sense of it from a number of biographical details. Primmer managed to support himself through theological college working as an agent for the Scottish Reformation Society: he sold membership and magazine subscriptions on a percentage basis. In the late twenties, Ratcliffe sponsored Edith Auffray on her "Life of a Carmelite Nun" tour. He paid all her expenses for six weeks and gave her a cheque for one hundred pounds at the end of the tour. He offered a Maltese ex-priest, P.J. Maurin, all expenses and 40% of the entrance fees. In the Caird Hall in Dundee, at prices between 6d and 1 shilling per ticket this cut would be thirty pounds per night. Then there was the income from pamphlets and books. The sums involved were by no means enormous but the defectors were singing for their suppers and the better they sang, the bigger the supper.

I am not impugning the motives of most of the defectors. At this distance it would be improper to make unsupported guesses about why these people earned their livings from denouncing the Catholic Church, or to guess how the fact that they were earning their livings might have biased their perceptions and presentations. All that needs to be said is that such people would have had to have great strength of character not to exaggerate the atrocity stories, given the great public pressure to do so. Thus one has to take their accounts with a great deal of salt.

Another weak feature of Ratcliffe's sources was their age and datedness. Edith Auffray was an old lady when she toured for him. The experiences she related in the twenties, and which Ratcliffe continued to publish until the end of the second world war, dated from the middle of the nineteenth century. His other source of material — the writings of Catholic theologians — was even older. Liguori wrote in the early eighteenth century. He can only be taken as a contemporary source if one supposes that the occasional later endorsements of his work by Catholic institutions were a full-bodied commitment to them in their entirety, and that is an almost certainly inappropriate supposition. In full flow, Ratcliffe was prone to cite the immoral state of Scotland before the Reformation as proof of the essential evils of the Roman Catholic Church and one of his most popular pamphlets — *The Horrible Lives of the Popes* — lists the vices of Pontiffs from the fourteenth and fifteenth centuries. It concludes with the life of Rodrigo Borgia! Another ancient source was Cardinal Sermoneta's letter of *1556* describing the lewdness of Scottish nuns: "they even admit all sorts of worthless and wicked men within their convents and hold with them unchaste intercourse. They defile the sacred precincts with the birth of children, and bring up their progeny about them".[24] Ratcliffe constantly used this letter as evidence of the sinfulness of the convent. The idea that the lives of most people, irrespective of their religion, might have been pretty lewd in the sixteenth century does not occur to Ratcliffe, nor does he notice one crucial feature of his source. The complaint was being made by a Roman Catholic Cardinal; the behavour of the nuns in question was thus obviously frowned upon by a senior representative of the religion that Ratcliffe claimed produced the lewd behaviour.

Ratcliffe's use of crime statistics displays a similar lack of causal charity. The following are the statistics for the religious identity of the inmates of the central Scotland prisons in 1933.[25]

Prison	Total	Protestant, etc	Catholics
Barlinnie, Glasgow	7276	4340	2936
Duke Street, Glasgow	1775	955	820
Greenock	672	368	340
Edinburgh	2259	1546	713
Dumfries	254	174	80

Given that only some 12.3% of the adult population was Catholic, these figures, as Ratcliffe correctly points out, show that Roman Catholics were considerably over-represented in the prison population. Ratcliffe then claims that such statistics prove that Roman Catholicism causes crime.

The fallacy here is in supposing that because a particular social group shares two characteristics (Catholicism and "being in prison") that the former cause the latter. It is often the case that there are other characteristics shared by the group that can be used to tell a much more plausible causal story. What most Catholics also shared was a social and economic position lower than the Protestants of the same area. They were poorer and less powerful. Their poverty offers a better explanation than their religion for their committing more crime (if indeed they were). And their lack of power offers a good explanation for their being more often apprehended and sent to prison, even if they only committed crimes at the same rate as their Protestant counterparts. Many recent studies of the operations of police forces and courts demonstrate that there are a series of complex social variables that intervene between the commission of any crime and being imprisoned.[26] The most important one is visibility. Poorer social groups lead more public lives. A basic lack of private property means that most activities are played out on the public stage; in public houses, on the streets. Because more of all their activity is public, more of their *criminal* activity is public. The more private property one has, the more of one's life, decent or indecent, legal or illegal, that is conducted in the sort of privacy that makes it less open to police scrutiny. There is also a simple "hassle" factor. The richer and more powerful one is, the more trouble one can cause the people and agencies who want to sanction parts of one's behaviour. A police force does not have to be consciously reactionary or bourgeois to concentrate its policing on powerless minorities; it simply has to be aware of the different "costs" of policing this or that group. The richer can cause more trouble and thus are less readily available for policing.

While the detailed sociological research to support such arguments is new, the basic line of reasoning is not, and it was used by both Catholics and liberal Protestants to criticise Ratcliffe's simplistic causal models, but such arguments made no impact on Ratcliffe. His obsession with self-evident "facts" allowed him to pass over such alternative explanations.

The thrust of my presentation thus far is that it is hard to suppose that Ratcliffe and others were driven against their wishes by a great weight of evidence to conclude that Roman Catholicism had an especial propensity to encourage sexual licentiousness, and deviance in general. The final point to make is that Ratcliffe operated a double standard of causality. He was aware that Protestants committed crimes but he explained those as the natural triumph of evil over good. A Protestant committed crimes by *falling away from his religion;* by not being Protestant enough. In contrast, the honourable Catholic was the exception. Catholics committed crimes *because they were Catholics.* One can only conclude the obvious; that Ratcliffe wanted to believe that Catholics were especially evil. And in particular, he wanted to believe that Catholic priests were active encouragers of sexual promiscuity.

The Sins of the Fathers

Militant Protestants were not the first nor the last to accuse their spiritual enemies of sexual misdemeanour. What is apparent from the history of any new religious movement and from public reaction to religious innovators is the ubiquity of such claims. The Edinburgh bourgeoisie of the 1850s were generally "moderate" in their religion. They liked moral behaviour and intellectual pursuits but they were not at all keen on enthusiastic religion. When the highlanders became converted to evangelical Calvinism, the Moderates attacked not only the highlander's stupidity and superstition; for good measure they also threw in immorality. One critic of the large open-air prayer meetings claimed:

> It is too well known that much immorality is the consequence of such stimulants. Not a few young people of both sexes, of light and thoughtless character, frequent these meetings for no good purpose;

and the scenes exhibited are frequently exceedingly derogatory to religion.[27]

It may have been "too well known" to the author but there is scant evidence for it in any worthwhile sources. But being the victim of such ill-founded attacks did not prevent the highland evangelicals using the same device. The highland revival was largely a lay movement, led by "the Men" and, as shown in the first chapter, most of "the Men" were not separatists. Although they did not like most of the actual ministers of the Kirk they remained committed to the idea of an established national church. But some were separatist. John Grant of Sutherland was one, as were Alexander Campbell and Norman Macleod. This extreme party had come to conclude that the Church of Scotland was so rotten that even the popular evangelical ministers must be tainted. They were a very small minority. Of the 200 parishes that made up the highlands only about 10 had any significant number of separatists. But the evangelical Thomas Brown, after extolling the virtues of "the Men" and the evangelicals of the north, condemns the separatists on the grounds of their holding "Antinomian views, which at times they carry into practice".[28] The Edinburgh bourgeoisie accuse the highland evangelicals of being perverts and the highland evangelicals accuse their own extremists of being perverts!

Numerous examples could be added. The targets for the accusations seem to fall into two distinct groups: public displays of enthusiasm and charismatic leaders. The open-air meetings in the highlands were an example of the former type. The great frontier revival meetings in North America were often attended by scenes of great emotion. People who came under "conviction of sin" were given to rolling around the ground in fits. There was much wailing and gnashing of teeth and comas were not uncommon. The respectable dwellers of the eastern towns and cities were appalled by such behaviour and the usual claims about immorality were trotted out.[29] The reasoning here seems to have been that, if these people can so forget their sense of decency as to roll around having fits, then they are probably engaging in all sorts of other indecencies. In the Canadian revivals, the preachers took such accusations to heart and segregated the sexes at their meetings.[30]

The other type of accusation concerns the individual religious leader who is held to have great power and influence over his following (or in the case of Aimee Semple Macpherson, *her* following). William Irvine, one of the founders of a small evangelical Protestant sect called the Cooneyites or the Nameless sect, was removed from his position of leadership by his lieutenants who felt that he had become unreliable. One of the critics compared Irvine to David who: "when he didn't go forth into battle himself, but sent his armies out, fell into temptation of adultery . . . There is no question that William had a weakness along that line and . . . that he had fallen. I know positively that there were women who have confessed to me of trouble with him along those particular lines."[31] Henry Ward Beecher, the nineteenth-century "new light" theologian, was cited in a court case by a husband for seducing his wife. John Taylor, the leader of the Exclusive Brethren, was accused of committing adultery and the arguments about whether he had or not played a part in splitting the movement. When John C. Bennett defected from the Mormons and began to campaign against them in 1842 he accused the sect of encouraging sexual immorality.[32]

I have come across these examples without any great searching. Doubtless serious investigation would generate hundreds more, but the above cases are enough to make my basic point that accusations of sexual impropriety are the common currency of attempts to blacken the character of individuals or groups that one wishes to oppose or denigrate. Why is this?

An explanation is possible, although it is complicated by the layers that must be peeled off. The first layer concerns the existence of the conflict. Why do people attack religious innovators, or those with different religious views? That is simply answered. The innovator is offering a serious challenge by claiming either that one's religion is wrong or that one has become lax in observance. But this raises the question of why the counter-attacks do not focus on the religious beliefs of the protagonists. The answer is that most of the traditionalists are not excessively religious themselves. James Begg, Jacob Primmer and Alexander Ratcliffe were committed Christians and often argued against Catholicism on theological grounds. But much of their audience would have had only a formal attachment to a church. John Cormack was not himself an evangelical Protestant (although his father was). He was anti-catholic on a variety of grounds but few of these were directly related to religious doctrine. Strictly theological arguments would not have been close to the hearts and minds of the audience for anti-catholicism, just as today the readers of the popular press who feel great indignation at the Reverend Sun

Myung Moon and the Unification Church are not generally committed Christians. So the fight has to be taken at another level, and one easy method of changing the level of discourse is to move attention away from the beliefs of the new religious movement to the *motivation* of the advocates of those beliefs. So the issue becomes not "Are the Moonies correct in their theology?", but "Are they honourable in their motives?".

The topics chosen for denigrating the motives of religious innovators then seem to reflect two things: the claims of the innovators and the concerns of the public. Most western religions are ascetic in their drives. They are connected with the *control* of bodily impulses, temptations, and especially sexuality. Religious innovators are often claiming not only that they have the better theology, but also that they are more *moral*. The counter-attack then takes the form of not only denying that claim but actually reversing it. Those people who claim to be puritans are really no better than the rest of us: and, in fact, they are a great deal worse! Ratcliffe just did not believe that people could remain celibate. His criticisms of one particularly trivial piece of Catholic teaching for the priesthood — what a priest should do at a difficult childbirth to baptise an infant that might die shortly after birth — displays this lack of faith in sexual control: "Rome's priests are all unmarried men, many of them young unmarried men, and is it right, is it decent, that these carnally-minded victims of an enforced celibacy should be permitted to witness the birth of infants, under any circumstances whatsoever? What sink of iniquity is this horrible system, the Papacy!"[33] Celibacy is "enforced" and its victims remain "carnally-minded". Rome claims that celibacy is some sort of higher moral state, some more spiritual calling, so Ratcliffe counter-claims that, far from it, celibacy produces corruption and sin and vice on a grand scale.

A Jimmy Crowley song extolling the virtues of "boozing" uses a similar device:

> What does the Salvation Army put down?
> Boozing, bloody well boozing!
> But what are they doing in every town?
> Boozing, bloody well boozing!
> What they preach they don't practice,
> Of that there's no doubt.
> For at the street corner

They stand and they shout.
What are they doing when the lights have gone out?
Boozing, bloody well boozing!

An even more unlikely form of the same reversal was used in 1964 by Ned Sherrin, whose television programme, *That Was The Week That Was,* was criticised by the morality campaigner, Mary Whitehouse. Sherrin countered by claiming that Mary Whitehouse was a prostitute![34]

So sexual activity is a suitable topic for accusatory claims about people one wishes to denigrate because it avoids strictly theological arguments which have only limited interest value, and because the control of sexuality is often at the heart of the claims that the various groups are making about their superiority. By simple reversal one can accuse those claiming to be new puritans of actually being dangerous perverts. But there is another set of reasons for using sexual misdemeanour in such public contests.

The first is so obvious it is easy to overlook. Some kinds of sin and vice, or to use a more neutral term, deviance, require special skills, apparatus or opportunity. Only those in a position of financial trust can embezzle or commit fraud. Only those in positions of leadership can be accused of manipulating their followers. But the equipment for sexual activity (and hence for illicit or illegal activity) is universally distributed. The number of people who are genuinely incapable of sexual action is so small as to be discounted. Thus everybody *could* engage in sexual deviance. If accused, one may claim that one did not do it, or that one had no desire to do it, but one cannot claim that one *could not have done it.* Thus the accusation has a basic universal application and plausibility.

The second observation leads on from the first. Sex is universal. All human beings engage in it. Hence all societies have rules about who may do what with whom under what circumstances. So in all societies there is the possibility of the rules being broken. Other kinds of deviance are limited to certain cultures and certain times. It made sense to accuse old women in Puritan New England of being witches because that culture believed in witches. We do not believe in witches and so the accusation of witchcraft has no great import in our culture. However, we believe in private property and we have tax advantages for religions, so it makes sense for us to accuse religious innovators of being only in it for the money, and it is precisely this accusation that is frequently made against American evangelists, faith-healers and new movements such as the Unification Church. But sexual deviation is possible in *all* cultures and so the claim of immorality can be tagged on to more specific accusations. The Puritans accused the witches of sexual intercourse with the Devil and Billy Graham was so sensitive to the threat of being accused of taking advantage of a woman in need of counselling that he always kept a male witness with him when he toured and stayed in hotels.

The third great advantage of sexual impropriety as a claim in denunciation is that sexual activity normally involves only two or a very small number of people acting in private. One does not expect it to be visible and hence the lack of witnesses is not something that undermines the claims. The appearance of illegitimate children might be evidence but then according to Ratcliffe's nun, these were strangled at birth! Anyway, illegitimacy is not an immediate visible character- istic. The problem of evidence is clear in the difficulty of judging rape cases. It is very hard to prove that something untoward happened. For the same reason, it is very hard to prove that *nothing* happened. It is one person's word against another. The lack of witnesses or documentary evidence does not undermine an accusation of sexual deviance in the way it might well with other forms of deviance. We do not expect witnesses.

These observations show the general value of making claims about someone's sexual misdemeanours. The nature of the activity makes such claims hard to refute. If one is predisposed to believe them, the lack of good evidence for doing so is not a problem. Hence the popularity of such accusations.

The obsession of militant Protestants with Catholic sexuality does throw light on another part of Protestant culture. While one can understand Ratcliffe's revulsion at the supposed sexual deviance, it is a little harder to understand why he was so revolted by Liguori's writing on moral theology. After all, Liguori was not advertising or promoting sin. He was documenting it and examining its forms in order to prepare priests for their role as the *controllers* of sin. There is a similar incongruity in the nineteen-thirties opposition to Frank Buchman and the Oxford Group (later known as Moral Re-Armament).[35] Evangelical Protestants were appalled at Buchman's technique of getting young people to confess their sins (which were usually masturbation and homosexual encounters or thoughts) to either their "soul surgeon" or to a small group. Yet the whole purpose of

Buchman's method was thus to embarrass the sinner out of repeating the sin. Liguori would have said that he was on the same side as Ratcliffe, the side of strict control and the repression of sexuality. His treatises were written on the "know your enemy" principle. Yet Ratcliffe and others were disgusted by them. The answer to this conundrum lies in the different models of control being used by Liguori and Ratcliffe. Liguori had the *externalist* model of control common to most Catholics. He accepted that people sin and educated the priesthood to use the confessional to ferret out the sin and then pass the appropriate penance. The Catholic sinner is thus purified by a limited externalisation of the sin. The sin is made "public" and the solution is returned by the public agent, the priest. The sin is thus recognised as existing and a ritual is provided for what Weber called "a periodical discharge of the emotional sense of sin".[36]

For Ratcliffe and other evangelicals, control is an internal matter. the conscience of the saved Protestant is the agent which prevents the sin. It is not recognised and punished; it is forced into non-existence. The saved Protestant does not need to make public his potentially sinful thoughts and actions and then be told whether or not they are sins, and if so, how bad they are. The internalised conscience of the Protestant will prevent such sins even arising as a possibility. Hence for Ratcliffe, writing about such things, even if the purpose in so doing is to prevent them, is a further commission of the same sin, and even worse, can be seen as an *encouragement* to more of the same.

Hardly surprisingly, Ratcliffe was sexist in his views on sexuality. Like other evangelicals, he held most of the traditional Christian views about male superiority which were legitimated by reference to Paul's teachings. The fact that the Catholic clergy were all male suited well his general philosophy. Thus he deals almost exclusively with the dangers to women from the male priests. In his writing on the moral perils of the confessional, he never mentions young men being led astray. Either young Catholic men were of no interest to him, or he thought they were less vulnerable to the corruptions of the clergy. This is an important point not only because it locates Ratcliffe in a particular culture but also because it is an unconsidered part of conflict with the new religious movements. The documentary evidence is not yet available because no one has chosen to study the phenomenon but I am intuitively sure that most recent western cultures have been willing to let young men experiment with deviant religious positions and yet have been horrified when young women do the same.

Ironically the best recent example was provided by the Roman Catholic Church in Ireland. Every year, numbers of young men leave the Catholic Church and become members of evangelical Protestant churches. Some even become ministers. This has provoked no public response yet the conversion of one rural Catholic young woman of 19 provoked a hostile reaction bordering on a moral panic. The West of Ireland Catholic Bishops used their Lenten pastoral letter to warn the people about "new religious movements" (in which they seemed to include the almost century-old Elim Pentecostal Church) and much press coverage was given to the case. The girl's parents and her brother claimed on radio and television that she had been "brainwashed" by the Elim Church. Forty or fifty friends of the family picketed the Elim bookshop. In listening to those broadcasts, reading the press coverage, and interviewing some of the protagonists, I was left with the clear impression that a similar reaction would not have been offered had the young person defecting from the faith been male.[37] Although no one openly articulated this sentiment, it seemed that women were expected to provide the continuity, the backbone for the tradition. This fits well with the evidence on church membership. In all religions, it is the women who form the bulk of the membership. There is almost a spiritual division of labour, especially in societies that are well on their way to becoming thoroughly secular. Men are "too tired" or "too busy" to go to church, but they encourage their wives and daughters in their support of the dominant religion. Hence, when women fall away from the faith or deliberately reject it in favour of some alternative, this is an especially deep cut.

Ratcliffe and Cormack seem possessed of the classic Victorian ambiguity towards women. Women were seen as *both* the precious and pure bearers of the tradition *and* as potentially wild sexual beasts who would be expecially vulnerable to the blandishments of the priest. Neither of them was prepared to accept women as equals in the struggle. Ratcliffe refused to have women on his executive. Cormack, as late as the nineteen-sixties, was asserting that women should not be allowed to speak to the Council chamber.[38]

Yet both men were pioneering in the opportunities they gave to women. The Orange Order denied office to women and only reluctantly allowed them to form separate women's lodges (which were, and still are, regarded as inferior to the male lodges). The Protestant churches allowed women to do little other than arrange the flowers and make the tea. In contrast, Ratcliffe depended on women.

His life-long secretary, assistant editor, and during his illnesses, *de facto* leader of the SPL, was a woman. Most of the movement's supporters and fund-raisers were women. About one-third of the SPL candidates, and two of the seven councillors, were female. Ratcliffe argued that women should be allowed to preach and rejected the traditional conservative interpretation of Paul's statments about the role of women in the church.[39] His appreciation of the importance of women led him to make special appeals for their votes at elections with pamphlets that contrasted the independence of Protestant women with the subjugation of women in the Catholic Church. Cormack's own behaviour was at odds with his later statements. In 1936 Protestant Action fielded three women in a slate of thirteen — a much higher proportion than either the socialists or the Moderates. The following year there were again three women and only nine men.

There is a very large element of irony in all of this. Ratcliffe and Cormack frequently agitated against convents. Yet women's religious orders in the nineteenth century offered one of the rare opportunities for women to achieve some sort of status and recognition. The SPL and PA offered a rare opportunity for Protestant women to achieve some sort of status in active political campaigning against the very system which did something similar for Catholic women!

Changing Fashions in Accusations

The most striking thing about pamphlets like *The Priests' Immoral Questions to Women* is how dated they now seem. Modern Protestant leaders no longer use such accusations (at least, not frequently and not often in public). A campaign for government inspection of convents would not be a great cause even in militant Protestant circles. The obvious reason for this is that the Catholic Church has changed. There has been a gradual liberalisation in the orders and the convents. One now finds nuns having almost normal working lives outside their convents. For this reason the old claims would now sound strange. But they would also be unexciting because the standards of the rest of the world have changed. Sexual impropriety is not a strong accusation anymore. The *News of the World* still prints "vicars-and-choirboys" stories but the claim of sexual deviance seems to have been almost completely displaced by the accusation of greed and peculation. The most common claim against the various perfectionist "messiahs" who were popular in Victorian America was that they were sexually corrupt.[40] The most common claim against L. Ron Hubbard and Sun Myung Moon is that they are consciously selling a hokum religion for financial gain. The general increase in sexual promiscuity has moved the definition of what is normal sexual behaviour so far to the left that the typical Protestant will no longer be the figure of moral rectitude that he or she was fifty years ago. If one is engaged in premarital or extramarital sex one can hardly deploy accusations of impropriety against Catholic priests or be much moved if such accusations are deployed by others.

Changes in the Roman Church also reduced the plausibility of the other objection to convents: authoritarianism. Even before the liberalising pronouncements of Vatican II, the convents had become more open. In the late fifties, Pius XII emphasised the need for sisters, especially those involved in teaching and nursing Orders, to be competent professionals. The aim was for nuns to be as well trained as their secular counterparts. Given that the Church did not have the universities and the advanced facilities required to achieve that aim, nuns had to use secular educational facilities. The result was a quite radical change in the climate of the convents. Where before the sisters had been trained in obedience, now they were being challenged to scepticism and to open intellectual inquiry. The consequence of this was the great wave of liberation that swept the convents, and the monasteries, in the sixties.[41] Many nuns ceased to wear distinctive clothes, a large amount of democracy was introduced into the organisation of the Orders, and the convents became so open that the pleas for government inspection became entirely redundant.

And while the Catholic Church was changing, the rest of the culture was in revolution. The sexual climate became so permissive that the Roman Church soon seemed, even to the conservative Protestants, to be the last defender of sexual rectitude. The failure of the Vatican to go along with this movement, its rejection of contraception and abortion, allows atheists and liberals to continue to accuse it of authoritarianism, and the man who succeeded Cormack as the main PAS speaker at the Mound frequently used that line of attack, but such a position causes problems for militant Protestants. They cannot make too much fuss about Rome's position without themselves appearing to countenance sexual laxity. They can claim that while Rome's heart is in the right place, its autocratic methods are wrong, but the fact that some of the most conservative Protestants share

Rome's position on abortion makes this issue poor grounds for a controversy. The result is that anti-catholicism can no longer with conviction or with success accuse Roman Catholics of sexual depravity.

Conclusion

In this chapter I have tried to explain why Protestants' opposition to Romanism rarely focused on detailed theological arguments. A large part of the audience for anti-catholic sentiments were not themselves committed and devout Protestants: their interest in matters religious was never great. So the fight was taken at a more general level. Protestants claimed to be the possessors of all virtues and all worthwhile social characteristics. Catholics were depraved and disloyal. Because of general changes in the wider social climate, accusations of sexual depravity came to have less conviction. Convent inspection became *passé*. In the Scottish context accusation of disloyalty were also hard to sustain. The Irish who settled in Scotland maintained some links with their old country and culture but they never rebelled against the state. They saw themselves as people who lived in Scotland and had little ambition to drag Scotland into another political formation. In the absence of any good grounds for claiming that Roman Catholics were disloyal, the militant Protestants in Scotland and England had to resort to the less powerful claim that the Roman Catholic Church wanted first to dominate the British state and then subvert individual liberty and freedom of worship. The collapse of the Scottish Protestant League and Protestant Action demonstrates the lack of interest in such claims. Few believed them and even fewer cared about such abstractions as "the British constitution". Even the possibly more immediate claim that the Roman Church was authoritarian and prevented its members making their own decisions about schooling, choice of ritual in the case of "mixed" marriages, the use of contraception and so on, was undermined by the relaxation in the Church that produced, and was amplified by, the meetings of Vatican II.

The absence of any strong local issues made the sectarian conflict in Scotland almost entirely parasitic on the conflicts of Ulster. Scottish militant Protestantism languished in the doldrums in the fifties and sixties precisely because the relative peacefulness of Ulster in that period removed Ireland from the agenda of British politics. The

Catholics in the west of Scotland settled to making their way in their
new country and continued their active involvement in the Labour
movement.

This is not to say that anti-catholic sentiment vanished. The
generation born in the twenties and entering adulthood in the forties
was strongly influenced by a nebulous suspicion and vague dislike for
Catholicism.[42] But the attitudes were changing enough for that
generation to weaken in its support of the organisational expressions
of anti-catholicism. The sentiments may still have been there but they
were not strong enough to produce the issues.

6

The Orange Order

ON a clear day, one can stand on the deck of the Larne-Stranraer ferry, mid-way on the crossing, and see both Ireland and Scotland. It is geographical proximity that has entwined the histories of the two countries. Scotland got its early Christianity from Ireland. When the north and east of Ireland was settled by Scots, Scotland returned the compliment by exporting its Presbyterianism and, for almost half a century, the Presbyterian churches in Ireland were under the General Assembly of the Scottish Church. In the next turn of the screw, Ireland gave Orangeism to Scotland.

Ireland in the eighteenth century was littered with secret societies and informal militias. These were largely agrarian movements. Protestant and Catholic small farmers and peasants banded together in defence against each other in movements such as the Defenders and the Peep O'Day Boys. The Orange Order was founded after a skirmish at the Diamond in 1795 by Protestants who saw that battle as just the first in a likely series.[1] The movement was organised, like so many others of this period, along the lines of the Freemasons. The name was chosen to demonstrate support for the religion and politics of King William of Orange, the man who had saved loyal Protestants from the dark machinations of the Catholic Stewarts. At first the gentry were ambivalent about the Orangemen. They were of the right religion but there was always the danger that they might develop their activities from destroying and expropriating Catholic property to stealing from their aristocracy. It was only when the United Irishmen, with their French Revolution rhetoric, seemed to be an even greater threat that the gentry entered the Order. In the relatively peaceful period of the first two decades of the nineteenth century, the movement declined

and there was considerable internal dissension, with rival factions
claiming to represent the "true spirit of Orangeism".

It was a pair of actions, one to outlaw the movement, and the other
to celebrate its demise, that revived the Order. In 1825, Sir Robert Peel
banned the Order; he and other representatives of the British
government in Dublin Castle did not like the idea of an armed and
organised power-base that was not within their direct and immediate
control. Daniel O'Connell organised a march in favour of Catholic
emancipation to Belfast. Led by John Lawless, the march soon ran into
organised Protestant opposition.

> As O'Connell's forces approached Ulster the Orangemen turned out in
> thousands, carrying their arms. Yeomen out of uniform, well-trained
> and well-disciplined. Despite rumours that he had tens of thousands of
> men, Lawless did not get very far. At Ballybay, two of his supporters
> were killed and a party of Orange yeomen under an innkeeper called
> Sam Gray prevented them from entering the town. A few days later,
> when he attempted to enter Armagh, the Orangemen again turned out
> with their muskets . . . O'Connell now called off the march and ordered
> Lawless to return but the damage had been done. All the old fears of
> mass attacks by Catholic peasants were revived in Ulster and the
> nobility and the gentry, who had been fighting shy of the Orange
> movement because of the legality question, now come out in support of
> it again. And when, as we have seen, O'Connell secured first a seat in
> Westminster, then full Catholic Emancipation, and finally started to
> work for the repeal of the Act of Union, the Orangemen started to
> march again.[2]

The Order had little significance in the period from 1860 to 1886
but in that year fear of the Home Rule Bill brought professional and
business people in Ulster into the movement. Henry Cooke, the
leading conservative voice in the Presbyterian Church, had succeeded
in resolving the intra-Protestant conflict between the Presbyterians,
largely urban and middle-class, and the Church of Ireland, with its
support from the agrarian peasants and gentry. The temporary
alliance (the importance of which is usually exaggerated) between
some liberal Presbyterians and Catholics in the United Irishmen
movement and the abortive 1798 rebellion was buried. The Presbyterians joined the Orange Order and it became the popular voice of
Irish Protestantism.

Orangeism was exported to all corners of the Empire. It was taken to Scotland by soldiers of the Scottish Fencibles who had been posted to Ireland to help quash the 1798 rebellion. As was the case with its Irish progenitor, Scottish Orangeism saw its fortunes fluctuate with the prominence of the Irish question and Catholic Emancipation.

Being an Orangeman

The development of the modern state, with its monopoly over the means of organised violence in its standing armies and regular police forces, removed the militia role of the Order. For the last century, the Order has largely been an "ethnic identity" organisation which offers its members social, cultural and charitable activities. It has usually also been a vote-delivering machine for the Unionist candidate.

Membership is defined by some version of a theological statement such as: "having sincere love and veneration of his heavenly Father, and a humble and steadfast faith in Jesus Christ, the Saviour of Mankind, believing in Him as the only mediator between God and man".[3] Admission to the Order involves a ceremony performed with an open Bible and the Bible is carried at the head of Orange processions. For all this, it is obvious that the majority of Orangemen are not committed evangelical Protestants. While meetings are opened and closed with prayer, religious beliefs and rituals do not occupy much of the average Lodge's time. Even in Ireland, which was considerably less secularised than Scotland, only 6% of the resolutions passed by the Grand Lodge between 1886 and 1920 dealt with religious beliefs. In the Scottish Order, the overtly theological element was even smaller.

For reasons that need not concern us here, Scottish Presbyterians were generally supporters of the Liberal Party. There was no Henry Cooke (nor the conditions that would have produced a Cooke) in the Scottish Presbyterian Churches. There was no imminent threat to the power and prestige of the Scottish middle classes, as there was in Ireland, which could have persuaded them to throw their lot in with the urban working class in opposition to Roman Catholics. The Scottish working class was not unusual in being unchurched. Even with the impact of the Methodist movement on the cities, the English urban working class existed largely outside the ministry of the Church. Taking the general pattern of the decline in religion, it is the case of the Ulster working class that is unusual and in need of explanation. Thus the people in Scotland who had the religious basis for anti-catholicism, because they were not in competition with Catholics, had little reason to engage in anti-catholic politics and those who felt themselves threatened by the Irish immigrants did not have the religious background. Hence Orangeism in Scotland was always less seriously religious than its counterpart in Ireland.

Furthermore, the Scottish Presbyterian middle classes' tradition of support for the Liberals meant that they had little sympathy for the party alignment of Orangeism. Although the Order in Scotland was never as closely tied to the Unionists as it was in Ulster (where the Order has of right a large number of seats on the Unionist Council, the governing body of the Unionist party[4]), it was still the case that leading Orangemen were also leading Unionist (and later, Conservative) politicians. The Order tried once, in the twenties, to break this relationship with the establishment of its own Orange and Protestant party but it only ever won one seat and was quickly re-absorbed by the Unionists.

Nonetheless, however peripheral evangelical Protestantism might be in the biography of any particular modern Orangeman in Scotland, it still provides the logic and rhetoric for Orangeism. Evangelical Protestantism provides the first set of reasons for being anti-catholic: Romanism is not the true faith. In the rhetoric the focus is on the *system of Romanism* and Orangemen are careful to argue that they have nothing against individual Catholics (who after all are simply the victims of an evil institution). Such claims are enshrined in the constitutions of most Orders which require a member to abstain from "all uncharitable words, actions and sentiments towards his Roman Catholic brethren".[5]

However, anyone who has ever spent any time in the company of working-class Orangemen, especially if they have been drinking, will be aware that "uncharitable" does not begin to describe the practical attitude that many of them have towards Catholics who are regularly talked about in the basest and most vulgar stereotypes. Anti-catholic violence is often boasted about and there is a rich and extremely vulgar tradition of popular song which displays almost everything except tolerance. I would not want to deny that there are Orangemen who do exemplify the best Christian virtues. Some — including one Master of a Lodge — marry Catholics. But the Order also contains a lot of people who simply hate Catholics. The following, which needs no comment, comes from a broadsheet produced by young Orangemen associated with the Scottish Loyalists (who will be discussed further in chapter nine):

> Coatbridge youth Sean O'Brien (16) died recently whilst doing a YOP course at a factory. Sean (a good British name) went to dry himself at a heater unaware that his boilersuit was soaked in paraffin. He immediately turned into a human torch and died in agony in hospital five days later. Everybody say Aah. Sean's father Dennis said it was a pity this had happened as Sean was just warming to the job. The company involved was fined £800 for the incident which is outrageous as Sean was only an RC and no friend of the Protestant Community. Sean disproved the old theory that Shite does not burn and it is thought that his parents are keeping his ashes for Ash Wednesday. We can safely assume that Sean is still feeling the heat where he is now but cannot confirm that his favourite record was "Great Balls of Fire".[6]

Beyond a basic anti-catholicism, the Order has little shared religion. Ironically one good reason for this is the presence of clergymen as chaplains. The religious rhetoric requires the legitimation conferred by the presence and support of those people who are public spokesmen for that religion. But unless the Order is to accept only clergymen of one particular denomination its religion has to be that of the lowest common denominator. Every addition of a particular belief (for example, in "predestination" or in the need for adult rather than infant baptism) will alienate the professionals and, if they are interested enough, the laity, of denominations that do not hold those beliefs. Thus the only other "religious" elements usually found in Orangeism are sabbatarianism and temperance. These are two supposed consequences of having the true religion: one keeps the Lord's Day and refuses strong drink because "it is a mocker", and they are two consequences to which most turn-of-the-century Protestants would have at least paid lip-service. As we shall see when I come to discuss the career of Pastor Jack Glass, it is the Order's abandonment of these two characteristics that has eroded what little support it had from committed evangelical Protestants.

The political ideology of Orangeism is similarly thin on details. Its main elements are loyalty to the crown and a strident imperialism. The loyalty to the monarch has a variety of sources in different historical periods. Conservative Presbyterians have generally been royaltists, even when the royalty in question was of the house of Stewart. The original Scots Covenant of 1641 (the model for the twentieth-century Ulster version) recognised the reciprocal obligations of the true Church and the "civil magistrate", at that time represented by the monarchy.[7] Many of those who accepted the covenant felt bound by it even though they knew that Charles Stewart had no intention of keeping his side of the bargain. The arrival of William of Orange resolved that tension. Thereafter, loyalty to the abstraction of the monarchy was made easy by the actual monarch being a Protestant. The presence in the coronation oath of the proposition that all future monarchs must be Protestants because freedom could not be trusted to a Catholic gave the Protestants ground for seeing the throne as a "Protestant" institution. The arrival on the throne of the pious and "low church" Victoria further reinforced the ties and the "loyal Protestant" could contrast his own virtues with the vice of the "rebellious papist". The Victorian period was also the heyday of the Empire and imperialism seems to have given Protestants an alternative to the nationalism of the Catholic Irish.

The Rise and Fall of Alan Hasson.

The present Grand Master of the Orange Order in Ireland is Martin Smyth, a Westminster MP and a minister in the Irish Presbyterian Church. The last clergyman to hold such a senior position in the Scottish Order was Alan Hasson and his career took him in five years from a Church of Scotland parish in the Vale of Leven to being Grand Master of the Order, a spell in a mental hospital, exile in Canada and finally to trial for fraud in a Glasgow court.

   Hasson was born in Glasgow but taken away from his mother by the local authorities and raised by pious Free Church foster parents in Inverness:

> It was there that I got my basic grounding in Free Church theology, biblical theology, very soundly bible-based. The books that I got to read, the books that I got as Sunday School prizes, and even in school, were all pro-Protestant type of thing. There was also the old chestnut: Fox's *Book of Martyrs*. And quite honestly when you are a kid and you get that sort of propaganda and you don't get the alternative and you've never

met Roman Catholics because there were none at school: I never met
them in my early days as a kid.

He was later moved to Tiree and then to Portree where he stayed with
a Church of Scotland couple for two years. After leaving school he joined
the Army. He considered staying in after his basic service but felt called
to the ministry. He applied to the Church of Scotland and was accepted.

It was while he was at Glasgow University that Hasson joined the
Orange Order. Looking back from his present disillusionment with
the Order, he sees himself as someone who then too naively accepted
its rhetoric of being a religious organisation motivated by only the
highest values.

> I more or less got conned into the Orange Order because all I saw was
> the good side. I never saw the background. It didn't bother me. I thought
> I was doing the right thing when I joined the lodge in Partick.

After graduation Hasson went to Union Theological Seminary in New
York and while in the States he applied for the vacant charge of
Bonhill in the Vale of Leven. He was accepted and soon became a
popular parish minister. In Bonhill, his background in the
conservative theology of the Free Church, his membership of the
Orange Order and his new environment came together to encourage a
career in militant Protestantism. The Vale of Leven is thoroughly
representative of those parts of Scotland that have strong sectarian
traditions. Between 1850 and 1900 its population doubled, almost
entirely as a result of Irish immigration. The Irish came into the labour
market at the bottom, with the skilled jobs and the working-class
organisations such as the local Trades Council continuing to be
dominated by Protestants.[8] Although the two wars and the
intervening depression had eroded some of the ethnic divisions and
part of the Protestants' commitment to their churches, the Vale was
still a place where "Protestant" and "Catholic" played a large part in
identifying people and channelling them into different social, cultural
and political divisions. Here Hasson found a keen audience for his
Protestantism and he saw his congregation grow from having less
than 300 members to almost 1000. At the same time he came to the
attention of the Order as a good speaker and was gradually drawn into
both local and national Orange activities.

In 1955, Hasson began to build his own base in the movement. He helped to form "The Vigilance Committee" of the Grand Lodge and to launch a new magazine called the *Vigilant*. Although Hasson was aggressive in his anti-catholicism, there were early signs of tension between Hasson and the Order. Before one annual walk the *Vigilant* carried an article signed by the three Grand Chaplains — Hutchison, Hasson and Kelly — calling for Orangemen to be on their best behaviour at the Walk: "we will all be 'on view' to multitudes of people. Among these will be many of our enemies eager to pounce on any deviation from good conduct, and exploit it in Roman Catholic propaganda".[9] Already one has the appearance of that conflict that dogged Ratcliffe's relationship with the Order. For the religious *virtuosi*, participation in the Order was an *extension* of religious beliefs and was thus always conditional on the Order living up to standards set by those beliefs. Although the Grand Chaplains were extremely circumspect in their warning, it is clear that it was the temperance issue that was the problem.

Hasson took over the editorship of the *Vigilant* in late 1955 and in his first editorials made clear his militant anti-catholicism:

> I am now absolutely convinced that the Roman Catholics will resort to every lie, every trick and every crime in the annals of society to defeat the Protestant freedom we enjoy. They hate us.[10]

The bogeyman of "papal aggression" loomed large:

> As Protestants let us remain vigilant to recognise the underground threat of Roman Catholic infiltration today, which will become the Roman Catholic persecution of tomorrow. Only a strong Protestant faith can keep us safe. The recent increase in open activity by Roman Catholics is a sign of their increasing confidence that they now have a controlling power in the country. If you ignore them, you're their ally. Watch them.[11]

But there is a noticeable change in the content of the *Vigilant* under Hasson's editorship. While there are still the shock revelation stories with titles like "From Convent to Christ", and reprints of crime stories involving priests, there is an increase in the material which expounds the key elements of the Protestant faith. Hasson was beginning to appreciate and trying to counter the lack of religiosity at the heart of the ordinary Orangeman's participation in the movement.

Hasson had the advantage over previous and later Orange leaders of being able to pursue his issues in the courts of the Church of Scotland. In the Dumbarton Presbytery, the Synod of Clydesdale and in the General Assembly, he frequently tabled motions to either present his own principles or to oppose what he and other conservatives saw as the "Romeward trend" in the Kirk. He raised Ratcliffe's old issue of the unfairness of the 1918 Education Act and tried to embarrass the Kirk by pointing out that the Assembly had in 1935 accepted a committee report which argued for changes in the Act and had then done nothing about it. When the Moderator sent a telegram of sympathy to Rome on the death of Pope John XXII, Hasson persuaded the Synod of Clydesdale to pass a motion of censure on that part of the message which seemed effusive in praise of the deceased Pontiff, describing him as "a constant influence for good". These actions brought him a great deal of publicity in a time when the secular press still had enough interest in the affairs of the Kirk to give such motions publicity. The Synod's motion was considered important enough to merit a reply from the *Scottish Daily Express* leader writer!

The high point of Hasson's career was his part in the opposition to the "Bishop in Presbytery scheme". In the middle-fifties, the Free Churches had a number of discussions with the Anglicans about the grounds for church unity. The discussions were long and complex but in Scotland the public reaction to the report focused on the organisational question of Episcopacy. One of the report's tentative proposals was that the Presbyterian system of elected elders should be combined with the Episcopal system to produce Bishops as "managing directors" of a basically democratic system. The report produced a great amount of heat at the 1957 Assembly and, in the Synod and Presbytery discussions that preceded it, it was obvious that there was general opposition to the report. As an active member of the church courts and as an Orange speaker, Hasson could play two hands. In the church courts he could argue, with the certainty of a lot of clerical support, both that the discussions on church unity had been predicated on the notion that there was something wrong with the existing system and that the proposals were anti-Presbyterian.[12] He could also play off the widespread resentment that there has always been in the Kirk about the reality of its democracy. Like all large bureaucracies, the Kirk is nearer to oligarchy than democracy. A small group of well-placed and influential ministers had considerably more power than their number should have produced and any claim that the majority of the Kirk were being railroaded by a small liberal élite always went down well with the lower church courts. At Orange rallies and demonstrations, the proposals could be attacked as further evidence of a "Romeward trend" and a Roman Catholic plot to subvert democracy, first in the Kirk and then in the country at large.

Not surprisingly, given his oratorical talents, his energy and his status as a minister, Hasson rose rapidly in the Order and within five years of his return to Scotland he was Grand Master. He had become sufficiently well-known in Glasgow and in the Church to persuade George MacLeod, then at the height of his influence in the Kirk, to debate with him in Springburn's public hall. Newspapers regularly carried reports of his protests. Within the Order he tried to do two things: to get Orangemen more actively involved in local politics and to introduce serious evangelicalism into the Order. He sought to enforce the evangelical faith part of the membership criteria by having new members present signed letters from their ministers. He introduced Sunday afternoon services at the headquarters of the Order in Cathedral Street. Under his editorship and that of his successor Maurice Brown (the minister of an independent evangelical congregation linked to the Bible Pattern Fellowship), the *Vigilant* carried a number of scathing articles on the lack of genuine evangelicalism in the Lodges. These innovations did not pass without comment. Many members were offended by the tone of criticisms such as the following from the pen of Brown: "there is need for the Grand Lodge enforcing those laws that keep our Order morally clean . . . the private lodges need to school their members in the faith and the cause, that each lodge may become a spiritual and patriotic assembly instead of a glorified club for business (internal) squabble".[13] From the first some senior Orangeman had been unhappy about Hasson's rapid rise and resentful of his popularity with the rank and file. At the June meeting of the Grand Lodge in 1956 there was some criticism of the policy of the *Vigilant* and Hasson offered to resign. The bluff worked and he managed to have the independence of the Vigilance Committee recognised. A year later, again as a response to the criticism from some long-serving Order officials, Hasson resigned the editorship to his friend Maurice Brown and bounced back from what might have been seen as a loss to be elected Junior Deputy Grand Master. The conflicts and tensions continued. In September 1958, Maurice Brown was complaining in the *Vigilant* that "the editor, a Grand Chaplain, was not invited to the Stevenson walk as indeed the Most Worthy Past Grand Master was not either. I would like to record in the minds of all my readers this peculiar, to say the least, behaviour of Grand Lodge".

The interesting irony is that while Hasson now presents the conflict as being between the religious element (represented by himself) and the "tribal" element (represented by his enemies), the true picture of support for Hasson can be seen as almost the reverse. Hasson was viewed with some suspicion by those officials who had been in the Order some time. And these people were most often those who still had some formal religious adherence. Hasson was most popular with the rank and file; those people who had very little commitment to any Protestant theology, yet who appreciated and admired a man who "stood up for Protestants" by organising marches to support the right of Protestant flute bands to march past Catholic chapels. It was precisely because he was good at representing himself as an extremist, a "red hot bigot", to use his own words, that he was popular. On one occasion, the council refused to give permission for an Orange march to Balloch Park. Hasson went with other Lodge officials to meet council representatives and when one Catholic councillor entered the room, Hasson is reported to have said "What the fuck is that!" and stormed out shouting that the march would go ahead. The story is probably not true. The important point is that it was told to me by three different admirers of Hasson as an illustration of his soundness for the Protestant cause. The Hasson supporters triumphed over the doubters and at the December 1958 meeting of Grand Lodge, Alan G. Hasson was elected Grand Master.

The conflicts within the Order come into the open in 1959. Hasson had been invited to attend the annual walk in Belfast. While he was there he was involved in a display of Protestant disunity at the Finaghy field when he interrupted Colonel W.W.B. Topping, the Minister of Home Affairs at Stormont, during his speech. The Central Committee of the Grand Lodge of Ireland demanded "separate apologies to the County Grand Orange Lodge of Belfast and Col. Topping for your unwarranted intrusion into the proceedings".[14] McGregor's presentation (which is basically Hasson's account of events) says:

> At this point he paid an official visit to Northern Ireland where he saw what he calls "the depravity and discrimination against Roman Catholics which dominated every aspect of Ulster's life". He was shocked and made some feeble protests about Christian concern for Catholics. The protests were feeble enough to go unremarked at the time and so he returned to Glasgow and unanimous re-election for another year as Grand Master.[15]

According to many, this account badly misrepresents events. Hasson did not offend the Ulster Brethren by being too moderate or by preaching tolerance for Catholics but by being associated with an extremist protest against the policies of the Stormont government. Topping was the official in charge of policing and he had supported a decision by the police to prevent the Boveva Flute band marching through the centre of Dungiven. Ulster Protestant Action, a militant organisation led by the then less well-known Ian Paisley, had made an issue of the Dungiven ban, presenting it as preventing Protestants from exercising the right to be Protestants in their own country. When Topping rose to speak he was heckled by a section of the crowd. Thomas Corry, a past Grand Master of the Scottish Order, appealed for silence and was severely critical of the hecklers for departing from the standards of appropriate Orange behaviour. Some of the rowdies called for Hasson to address them and Hasson interrupted Topping to say, "I will speak afterwards but in the meantime listen to Mr Topping". Topping responded: "I intend to go on speaking. With the greatest appreciation of my Scottish friend for his intervention, I do not need any assistance."[16]

After the speeches were over the crowd sang the National Anthem (the hecklers sang "The Sash") and the guests left. But Hasson remained behind to speak to the Protestant Action supporters. He said that Topping had a rotten job "and I think he has made a rotten job of it". There were many who thought that Topping's conciliatory policies were the best but Hasson didn't: "Because he is a good brother I appreciate the fact that he acted as he did — damn him!" After those comments on Topping, Hasson adopted a faint note of reconciliation and told the crowd that while he supported them: "For goodness sake, think of some other way than putting Topping up against the wall".

Thus, far from Hasson's offence being that he criticised the Ulster Order for its intolerance towards Catholics, it was that he offered some support for the Paisleyite faction which thought the Unionist government was being too soft. Clearly what one has in McGregor's record of Hasson's view of this period is the transfer of what he *now* feels about militant Protestantism into an earlier period. Now Hasson rejects anti-catholicism and so wants to see his conflict with the Order as the moderate versus the bigots. This is certainly not true of the Finaghy demonstration. In that incident the Ulster officials and Thomas Corry were the moderates. Hasson was criticised for giving some support to the "bigots".

But it was not only the Ulster Order that Hasson offended. The same year he addressed an Orange service in the High Church Bathgate and, in a long critique of the Orange Order, he described Grand Masters as "commissars". The District "Commissar", George Watson, charged Hasson with bringing the Order into disrepute. Hasson replied by suspending Watson and lifting the warrant of the whole Armadale district, effectively suspending all the members of one of the largest districts.

In February 1960 a special commission of enquiry was held to resolve the problem. The main part of the meeting was taken up with a long speech from Hasson in which he argued that "an organisation in which discipline ceases to function is doomed", and by a long reply from George Watson insisting that Hasson was acting unprocedurally.

Before the next full meeting of Grand Lodge could judge the issue, senior officials took out an interim interdict to prevent Hasson soliciting or receiving loans in the name of the Grand Lodge, borrowing on the security of Grand Lodge property, or suspending any member of said Grand Lodge without regular complaint or trial.[17] Hasson had a nervous breakdown and went into a mental hospital in Dumfries where he remained for three months.

Accusations of Fraud

The first "pursuer" on the interim interdict was John Adam, the Grand Secretary, Although he had been a friend of Alan Hasson (some members say that he was sponsored for the office by Hasson), he had become increasingly disturbed about what he believed to be the cavalier fashion in which Hasson dealt with the Grand Lodge finances. From the time of his election, there had been a constant stream of minor dealings which were not obviously legitimate. Whether or not Adam suspected Hasson of fraud at this point is not clear but it was certainly the case that the Grand Treasurer gave Hasson signed blank cheques and that loans were being arranged which Adam knew little or nothing about. In August 1959, Adam proposed at a meeting of the trustees of Grand Lodge that all the accounts be frozen pending a professional audit and a full enquiry about the movement's finances. There was no seconder for the proposal. At the end of April 1960, Hasson suspended John Adam and another critic, George

Rossborough. They and twenty other senior Orangemen applied for, and were awarded, the interdict which prevented Hasson doing anything with the Order's funds and which removed their suspensions.

Only gradually did the true extent of the chaos of the Order's finances become clear as various people and organisations began to claim payment from Grand Lodge for loans made to Alan Hasson. In one case, Hasson had asked the Scottish Reformation Society in Edinburgh to lend the Order money to buy premises for a new Ladies Lodge Hall. He impressed on everyone involved the urgency of the case; a Roman Catholic was bidding on the same property! In what one of the senior partners admitted to me was an unusual step, Balfour and Manson, the Reformation Society's solicitors, handed over a cheque for £1,500 to the Dumbarton solicitors acting for Hasson *before* they received the deeds of the Baillieston Orange Hall which were security for the loan. Similarly, the Dumbarton firm handed the money in cash to Hasson without waiting for the deeds. Where the money went is not clear. As the accountant's report said: "there is no lodgement of £1,500 in Grand Lodge bank account but the bank account shows that on April 9th 1960 there is an unexplained lodgement of £400 . . . and a withdrawal on the same day of £400, the returned cheque for the withdrawal being in favour of Rev Alan Hasson and endorsed by Mr Hasson".[18]

In another incident Hasson persuaded Bernard Brogan, an ex-Provost of Motherwell and a keen Orangeman, to act as guarantor for a loan of £5,000 from the Bank of Scotland. When he was arranging the loan, Hasson showed the bank an extract from the minutes of a meeting of the Lodge trustees which said that "after full discussion" it was agreed to raise the loan and that the Grand Master and Grand Treasurer should be authorised to sign cheques on the loan account. In court John Adam, whose signature appeared on those minutes claimed "it was not my signature. I have never signed a document like that. At that time I had no knowledge of a loan of £5,000 being made to the Lodge".[19] And indeed it does seem unlikely that Adam would have agreed to give Hasson that degree of latitude when he had five months earlier asked for all Lodge accounts to be frozen pending a review of the finances. It seems that only about £700 of the loan was spent on Lodge business. The rest was not traced.

It may well be that some of the money was used by Hasson to help the Barrhead Lodge finance a new hall. Certainly he lent them £2,000, more than his Kirk salary would have permitted. The Lodge repaid £900 to Hasson.

In total, something like £15,000 seemed to be missing. Hasson's account of his actions is that he was simply acting on behalf of the Order. He admits that he may have been a little precipitous in some cases but insists that the finances were being badly managed when he became Grand Master and that, while he may not have always followed the proper procedures, he was always acting with the interests of the Order at heart. Nevertheless, one example which many thought open to question was that of three cheques paying a total of £750 (approximately £5,250 at today's value) to one Alex Wotherspoon, whose only connection with the Order was that he was Hasson's half-brother. Certainly the evidence convinced the jury in the 1971 trial. When the verdict was reversed on appeal it was because the judge at the first trial had not offered the jury the possibility of a verdict of "not proven". It is true that Hasson had other substantive grounds for an appeal and that these were not considered because the technical appeal was taken first but it is also the case that one of the appeal judges said that it was "unfortunate that the conviction had to be quashed".[20]

Hasson leaves the Order

The accusations of embezzlement were first made formally at a special meeting of Grand Lodge on the 7th May 1960 called to discuss what Bro. D.M. McGregor, a Hasson supporter, called the action of "22 undesirables" in applying for the interdict against Hasson. The meeting was dominated by a long speech in which John Adam catalogued Hasson's financial speculations. After a short break, the members returned to question and to argue. If it is true that Hasson's enemies were doing all they could to blacken his character, it is also the case that his friends were not helping much. Rev J.D. Maclean, such a close ally of Hasson that he had served the suspension order on John Adam and was given power of attorney by Hasson during his spell in hospital, can have done little for him if the following notes from the Grand Secretary's minutes are an accurate record of the speech:

> We should ask why this man, A.G. Hasson, whom we trusted and elevated to the high position of WGM. Many years ago in a police court, a mother was deprived of her two children, owing to her immoral way

of life, the youngest of these was A.G. Hasson. He was brought up by foster parents. During the war he became a Captain in the Cameronians and influenced by a Chaplain turned his steps to the ministry. Three degrees taken brilliantly. This man, with no social standing found it difficult to live his own life. He has been blackmailed by his half-brother. A letter read, regards the trial of A. Wotherspoon at Old Bailey, robbery with violence against his mother and was sentenced to four years. A year ago he turned up at the manse and proceeded to blackmail A. G.[21]

In conclusion Maclean tendered his resignation and apologised for the "mess he had got Grand Lodge into".

A special meeting of Grand Lodge completed what the interim interdict had started: the removal of Alan Hasson and his supporters from the Grand Lodge. When Hasson left the hospital in the autumn of 1960 he returned to his parish work. For a year, rumours and accusations continued to circulate while the police collected evidence for a case. In February 1961, Hasson emigrated to Canada; on his account, because he could get no peace in Scotland; on the Lodge's account, because the police were about to press charges for fraud and forgery. In Canada, Hasson was given temporary charge of a Presbyterian Church in Norwood. Within two years he was again in dispute with an organisation and in the law courts. Acting on discontent in the Norwood congregation, the Winnipeg Presbytery sacked Hasson.[22] Hasson took half of the congregation and formed the St Boniface Covenanter Church and affiliated to the Bible Presbyterians. Writs and counter writs followed. The Winnipeg Presbytery claimed that Hasson removed equipment that belonged to them and defrauded the Church; Hasson claimed that he had been wrongfully dismissed. Back in Scotland the *Vigilant* took delight in reproducing the stories from the Winnipeg press. Over the next seven years Hasson earned a living as a radio journalist and in a variety of selling jobs. His dynamism and his own sense of self-importance led him into a number of strange schemes; at one point he went to the Middle East to try and convince the Palestinian leadership to engage in non-violent politics!

Then, ten years after he had left, Hasson returned to face his critics. He arranged to have himself arrested at Heathrow and was returned to Glasgow to face charges of 51 incidents of fraud totalling £17,500 (about £122,500 at today's value). Eleven years after the last offence was supposed to have occurred, the trial was hardly likely to establish beyond reasonable doubt the truth of the charges. Hasson felt poorly served by his legal aid lawyer whom he dismissed when the trial started. He was found guilty and sentenced to three years but won the appeal.

In September 1977 Hasson applied for a job with the Church of Scotland's Social Work Committee as the warden of one of its hostels for boys. He found himself in charge of a run-down hostel in the middle of a notorious Edinburgh housing scheme. The hostel was paid for by the local authority's Social Work Department. The Church of Scotland took the money and passed on part of it to the hostel. Hasson soon became frustrated with the Church's lack of interest in the hostel and began to initiate his own schemes for the care and rehabilitation of the boys; and from the evidence of the boys who testified on his behalf at his subsequent trial, it seems that he was well-liked and moderately successful in finding them jobs and keeping them out of trouble. The problem was that Hasson ran the hostel his own way, even going so far (so he claims) as to put some of his own money into the enterprise. Eventually the frustration became too much for him and a year after taking the job he resigned. Three years later he was charged by the Church of Scotland with embezzling £844.00. The initial charge was given a great deal of publicity; the fact that the sheriff dismissed the case and openly questioned the wisdom of bringing it in the first place was given far less publicity.[23]

On the 7th October 1982, Hasson was charged with stealing a deposit cheque from a Glasgow woman who thought she was buying double-glazing. He was convicted on the evidence of the man he worked for: Paddy Mehan, who was himself something of a *cause célebère* in Scottish legal circles following his pardon from a life sentence for murder. Once again that trial was given a great deal of publicity but the subsequent successful appeal was barely mentioned, thus leaving the impression that Hasson was a persistent fraud. It is important to note that Hasson has never been convicted of fraud and he has never been imprisoned, except in that he had spent long periods on remand awaiting trial.

Hasson himself sees his legal problems as the result of a conspiracy by officials of the Orange Order (especially those with strong Ulster connections) to discredit him for his criticism of the discriminatory nature of the Northern Ireland state. It is reportedly the case that a lot of senior Orangemen disliked him and resented both his rapid rise in

the Order and his popularity with the rank and file. And such men may
have been keen to topple him. He was useful so long as he remained in
the role of a militant Protestant bigot. If he was going to abandon that
role and begin to attack the Orange Order then he had no value at all.
But such a conspiracy theory has trouble explaining why they
proceeded against him *before* he gave much evidence of ceasing to be a
bigot and it does not explain the widespread conviction among
accountants and solicitors involved in untangling the Lodge's books
that there had been fraud; the professionals were not all keen
supporters of Orangeism. Although Hasson's enemies within the
Lodge might have wanted him to be guilty, there is no reason to
suppose that any desire for that conclusion had a greatly distorting
effect on the various professional people who examined various
elements of the tangle.

A number of general points can be made from the story of
Hasson's career in the Order. The first is that the Order was badly
organised. While the Order is theoretically centralised, being run by
the two annual meetings of the elected representatives at Grand
Lodge, and by the "executive committee" of the Grand Lodge, in
practice Orangemen owe their loyalty to their local "private" lodges
and the centre tends to be symbolic rather than managerial. This
might account for the obvious lack of management skills in Grand
Lodge in the late fifties. Whatever Hasson's motivation, it remains a
fact that Grand Lodge's financial and accounting procedures were
weak and hence open to either abuse, or to claims that abuse had
occurred.

The second general point is that the Order was stagnant and hence
open to any dynamic leader who could galvanise the membership and
create publicity. Hasson was promoted so rapidly because he was
intensely ambitious *and* because the Order needed strong leadership.
That Hasson was a Church of Scotland minister only made him more
attractive as a leader. Hasson rose because there was no serious
competition for leadership positions from other good speakers with
suitable religious credentials.

It is very difficult to evaluate the effects of the Hasson scandal on
the Order. It certainly created divisions within the Order with many of
the rank and file members being at least sympathetic to Hasson's side
of the story. One still finds people who speak warmly of Hasson as a
great militant who gave firmer direction to the movement than those
who replaced him. One has the irony that Hasson sees his downfall as

the result of a plot against him for his criticisms of the bigotry in the Order and yet the "plotters" who defeated him were more in tune with his present position than were those remaining members who supported him.

The Church and the Order

It is difficult to compress something as complex as the reaction of members of one national organisation to another into a few pages but what is clear is that the Church of Scotland, and the other Protestant churches, had little love for the Orange Order. Alan Hasson was the last minister of the Kirk to be prominent in the Order and he was a peripheral member of the Church of Scotland. In the late fifties, in the few years when Hasson was at his most influential he carried little or no weight in the Church and his counsels only prevailed when they coincided with other better established interests. The spokesmen for the ecumenical movement in the Kirk may have been soundly defeated over the report on relations with the Anglicans but they remained more influential than their conservative opponents. The leading light of the "liberals" in this period was George McLeod, later Lord McLeod of Funeiry. McLeod had served in the first world war and had been decorated, but he became a convinced pacifist. In his search for some sense of community in the Christian witness of the Church, he founded the Iona Community. Young men who had finished their divinity courses would spend a few months on Iona, doing manual work and hearing lectures on social and economic problems and the need for the church's involvement in their solution. This would be followed by a short spell working in a factory and a two-year assistantship in a selected parish, interspersed with refresher visits to Iona. The idea was to end the isolation of ministers, especially of those who chose to work in poor depressed working-class areas. The membership of the Community was never high; in 1968 it was only 143 but the Community did include some of the brightest and most committed of the Kirk's ministers.[24] Although McLeod and some of those associated with him held some almost archaic notions of the nature of the Church, seeking to find a model in a mythical Celtic christianity that would allow them to get away from the old alignments of either Rome or Geneva, they were modern in their social attitudes, seeking to get church members involved in trade unions and community organisations, and they were ecumenical. They made no bones about their desires for more amicable relations with the representatives of other churches, including the Church of Rome. While many of McLeod's wilder enthusiasms fell on deaf ears, his basic radicalism and his ecumenism became shared in the ministry.

There were those who opposed the radicalism and the ecumenism but they did so for reasons that prevented them associating with the Orange Order. Those who remained conservative either from their geographical locations (as was the case with the highlanders) or from conscious conviction, did not align themselves with Orangeism: the former because they had no acquaintance with the tradition and the latter because they could see only too well that the average Orangeman was no more "born again" than the average Catholic. One can point to the example of William Still in Aberdeen. Still had been one of the leading conservative voices in the Church since the forties. Even today, many young evangelical ministers go to Aberdeen to serve under Still. He holds an annual conference in Crieff which now draws more than a hundred ministers. But Aberdeen until recently had no Orange Lodge. It was only in 1981 that the Order planned its first Orange march in the city and the council turned down the application. Once again one is back to the basic division of Scotland. That part of the country that had Catholics — the central and western lowlands — was heavily secularised. That part which remained conservative in its religion — the highlands — had no Catholics and no history of Orangeism.

This barrenness of the environment for Orangeism has shown itself most clearly in the lack of clerical support for the Order. When Hasson was Grand Master there were only five or six clergymen in the Order and of those only two were Church of Scotland. In the sixties and seventies this number decreased and I can only think of three ministers who are either members or open supporters of the Order. And one of these, Arthur Jones, has been the subject of much controversy. After many complaints to his Presbytery about Jones' general competence a formal complaint and petition for his removal was rejected by the General Assembly in 1984.[25] Jones believes that he was being punished for his Orangeism. The Presbytery denies this. In view of the fact that the Jones' case might appear to undermine my claim that the north of Scotland has no active Orange tradition, it is worth pointing out that Jones is a Welshman. His claim to have been victimised because of his Orangeism is given some plausibility by the recorded opposition to the Order of a number of Presbyteries. In 1979 the Jedburgh Presbytery reacted to the formation of a new Lodge in the Borders by asking its members to "earnestly consider whether the mainly 'anti' emphasis which appears in Orange activities is the best way of upholding New Testament Christianity".[26]

The Order's Loss of Power

In the nineteen-thirties, when Alexander Ratcliffe was trying to establish his Scottish Protestant League, he was opposed by an Orange Order which still had some élite support. The Grand Master was Colonel McInnes Shaw, a Unionist MP. One or two member of the lesser aristocracy could be relied upon to support the Order; partly out of shared convictions and partly because the Order could deliver the votes of working-class Protestants. Both of those things changed in the fifties. Fewer members of the Unionist party élite shared the principles of Orangeism and in the early sixties the party was willing to field Roman Catholic candidates. The process has now gone so far that the chairman of the Conservative Party in Scotland is a Roman Catholic. But the working-class has also changed its allegiance. The decline of the Conservative vote in Scotland has been largely due to urban working-class Protestants voting Labour, even if that meant voting for a Roman Catholic. The Order no longer produces the vote and no longer has the ear of the Conservative Party.

It still retains some influence in local politics but this influence is small and is considerably smaller than that attributed to it by radical journalists looking for conspiracy stories.[27] Like the Masons, the Order has some power in that it creates and perpetuates ties of obligation which, like ties of kinship (and they are often based on kinship), require members to look after other members. But a series of complex social and structural changes has reduced the opportunity for turning those obligations into actual clout. Scotland, more than any other part of the United Kingdom, fell prey to "planning" in the late fifties and sixties.[28] New towns were built; old communities were destroyed. To some limited extent the old social relationships were transported to the new towns. Lodges were created in Easterhouse, Livingston and East Kilbride and council housing was allocated along lines that, either deliberately or accidentally, reproduced some of the old ethnic divisions, but the new housing schemes were never ethnically divided to the extent of the old towns of central Scotland. Furthermore, the

changing structure and character of local government in Scotland
seriously undermined local control over such matters as housing
allocation and distribution of educational and health resources. The
creation of large units of local administration such as "Strathclyde"
undermined the ability of Orangemen to discriminate in favour of
their own. At the same time much of local government passed out of
the hands of elected officials and into the control of full-time
professional administrators who followed careers that could take them
from, say, Grampian Region to Lothian and then to Strathclyde.
Coupled to the other dominant feature of local government which has
been the reduction of the authority of local units and the increase in the
power of central government, this has meant that even at the local
level the particularistic values of the Orange Order have been largely
replaced by the cosmopolitan values of the Scottish Office in
Edinburgh and the government of Westminster.

So what does the present day Order do? In the main it is a social
club. Members join so that they can enjoy a range of social amenities. It
also has an important philanthropic role. It raises a considerable
amount of money for charities; in particular it is one of the main
sponsors of the Erskine Home for disabled servicemen. It still claims
to campaign against papist aggression and on behalf of the British
crown and constitution but this aspect of its work is hardly attended to,
even by its members. Its protests against various proofs of a
"Romeward trend" in the Kirk are very poorly supported. For
example, a protest at the 1973 General Assembly could draw a crowd
of only 1,500 when 3,000 had been hoped for, and that out of an
organisation that musters about 40,000 for its annual walks on the
Twelfth.[29]

What has given the Order something of a new lease of life in the
last fifteen years is the conflict in Ulster. Here was something that
actually looked like "papist aggression". Just as the home rule
movement of the last century caused an increase in interest in
Protestant organisations, so this present period of crises in Ulster has
fueled anti-catholicism. Yet even this obvious opportunity for the
revitalisation of the movement has only served to further divide it and
to make public its irrelevence. The main problem is that while the
committed believer in the evil of Roman Catholicism has had no
problem in blaming the present Ulster crisis on that branch of the
Christian Church, the majority of the population have preferred the
more general interpretation of the problem: they have seen it as "what

happens if you mix religion with politics". Leading politicians and other public figures have been careful to avoid doing anything that might lead to Scotland becoming another Ulster. As was the case in the last major crisis in the twenties, the Catholics in Scotland have been careful to avoid taking sides and the leading churchmen, Catholic and Protestant, have responded by making joint condemnations of the violence in Ulster. Far from increasing the sectarian conflict, certainly at the level of the élites, the Ulster crisis has brought Protestant and Catholic Scots together in their desire to remain out of the argument.

The impotence of the Order has been ably demonstrated by their lack of influence on the British government policy in Ulster. There have been demonstrations and petitions but it is fair to say that these have made no impact. The only obvious result has been the widening of the major division within the Orange Order. Those working-class Protestants who retain strong links with Ulster have had to choose between doing nothing and engaging in anti-catholic activity outside the Order. This later reaction is the subject of the next chapter.

7

Protestant Paramilitaries in Scotland

WITHOUT a paramilitary force — the original Carson Ulster Volunteers — there would have been no Ulster and no Stormont parliament. It was only the threat of organised resistance from the Protestants in the north-east of Ireland that persuaded the British government to exempt them from an independent Ireland. One of the elements of the Stormont state's success in securing the support of working-class Protestants was the incorporation of the Protestant militias into the state's police force as the Special Constabulary.[1] From 1921 until 1966 Protestants seemed content to leave "policing" to "their" government and it was only with the tentative reforms of the O'Neill period and the civil rights movement that some Protestants felt the need for a paramilitary force. The UVF was revived.[2] As the next three years saw the escalation of local violence, most working-class areas of Belfast and Londonderry produced their own vigilante groups. In 1971 a number of these combined in the umbrella Ulster Defence Association.

Three years later, the UDA and the veritable "alphabet spaghetti" of smaller groupings had their biggest success in the strike which defeated the government's plans for a power-sharing executive.[3] Then and subsequently, the UDA and similar groups proved that they had sufficient working-class support to defeat any government initiative that seemed to threaten the position of the Protestants in Ulster but they generally failed to produce any popular alternatives of their own. In a very real sense, the Protestant paramilitaries were reactive. Even the military side to their activities was reactive, often taking the form of tit-for-tat killings and attacks on prominent Republicans.

Since the 1974 strike, the UDA has concentrated mainly on

providing relief for the relatives of Loyalist prisoners and on "community" politics. The simmering working-class resentment at the failure of successive Unionist governments to improve the conditions of "poor prods" has produced a variety of community self-help groups giving advice on housing and welfare matters. For most of the last decade, the UDA has been careful to avoid direct confrontations with the police and the army; a reflection of the bind in which loyalists are caught. On the one hand they want to be "loyal"; on the other hand they have to resist attempts to sell them out by the government to which they want to be loyal. The result has been the maintenance of a large organisation which holds itself in readiness for armed rebellion and for a civil war while trying to prevent its members drifting into open confrontation with the state.[4]

Working-class Protestants in Scotland are both intimately involved in the Ulster paramilitaries and important as external allies. There has always been considerable traffic across the short stretch of sea between Ulster and Scotland. Many working-class Protestants feel equally at home on either side and have lived in both countries. The problems of Protestants in Belfast are thus also the problems of their friends and relatives in lowland Scotland. In addition, the Ulster loyalists have few other allies. The Irish republicans have a cause which is popular in large parts of the world. For the American audience, they can tell an old-fashioned nationalism story. For the many nations which have recently won their independence from imperialist powers, they can tell anti-imperialism stories and they can claim various sorts of left-wing credentials. The loyalists appear on the world stage as reactionaries; associated in the minds of many with the repressive white régimes in Rhodesia and South Africa. It is no exaggeration to say that Scotland offers one of the very few places where the loyalist cause commands any sympathy.

It thus made sense for the Ulster paramilitaries to court Scottish support. The initial response from the Scots was good. The IRA atrocities of the early seventies persuaded many Orangemen that "something needed to be done" and the Orange Order did not seem to be doing anything. The UDA quickly gained about one thousand members; the UVF perhaps half of that number. But while the initial support may have been there, it was not channelled into an efficient military organisation.

One of the earliest incidents of Protestant violence was an "own goal". In March 1973 the Apprentice Boys of Derry Hall in Bridgeton,

Glasgow, was wrecked by an explosion. At first it was thought that this might be an IRA action aimed at the many Orange groups who used the hall but shortly after the explosion an anonymous letter was sent to the *Daily Record*. Its author said:

> I am writing to you because I feel that the troubles which have taken place in Northern Ireland over the last few years could be inflicted on us in Glasgow . . . My main reasons for doing this is that I have young children and have fears for their safety should the outrages which are happening in Belfast happen in Glasgow. I phoned 999 about one o'clock this morning and told them that Big Bill Campbell and another man, George — I don't know his second name — had taken explosives into the hall in Landressy Street. I know for a fact that the same two men had collected about twenty sticks of gelly from a butcher's shop in Bridgeton . . . From what I hear, Campbell had stolen or hired a car and he intended making a bomb which he was going to leave in the car and park it outside St Andrew's Chapel in Clyde Street . . . Please sir, these are desperate men and while I'm a good Protestant and have no love for the Pope or his followers, I am very much afraid of the violence and terror that these men and their followers could start here.[5]

"Big Bill" Campbell was a member of the UVF who was living in West Belfast at the time. He had what the judge described as "an enormous list" of previous offences and was sentenced to a total of eight years. George Martin, a first offender, was jailed for five years. The letter writer was correct in identifying the popular Catholic chapel in Clyde Street as the target but in describing them as "desperate men", the author omitted to say that they were either very unlucky or incompetent. The plastic bags containing the explosive had been placed next to an oven in the kitchen and had exploded when someone had innocently switched on the oven to heat pies!

In December of the same year two men, whose house was found to contain quantities of militant Protestant literature, were sentenced to five years each in Ayr High Court for the possession of fifty sticks of explosives.[6]

The following year Colin Campbell, "second in command of the 6th Scottish Battalion Rangers of the UDA" and brother of "Big Bill", was sent to prison for six years after pleading guilty to assault and robbery on a sub-post office in Mount Vernon, Lanarkshire. On trial with Campbell were Sammy Tyrie (brother of Andy Tyrie, the present leader of the UDA in Ulster) and three others. Tyrie and two of them were given seven years for possessing explosives and the fifth man on trial, Malcolm Nicol, was given ten years for possession. The press reports all emphasised the men's previous convictions. Nicol had been convicted of breach of the peace, dishonesty and a National Assistance offence. Colin Campbell had three previous convictions: for assault, for a firearms offence and for breach of the peace.[7]

By 1977, ten years had become the basic possession of explosives sentence. Three men were found guilty at Ayr of having 104 sticks of mining explosives. One of the three was a miner. An interesting feature of this case was the ease of the arrest. The three men were caught moving the explosives in a van and they were apparently under surveillance, which suggests what became patently clear in later trials: the police were perfectly well aware of who was involved in paramilitary activity.[8]

Some of the incidents bordered on farce. In 1973 a sixteen-year-old boy was stopped by the police in a car park and was found to be carrying a home-made bomb. The boy's brother had been an intelligence sergeant in Ulster. He had developed an interest in the crisis and he wanted to "stop the government pussy footing" over Ulster. He used fertiliser to which he had access in his job as a golf course green keeper to make the bomb and then went to a chapel in Milton to plant it. When he got there, he found there were people at the chapel so he decided to go instead to the Town Hall. There were also people there so he set off to take his bomb to a Catholic chapel in Townhead and was stopped on the way. In his statement to the police the boy said he was thinking of starting his own Protestant army.[9]

Roddy MacDonald and the Orange Order

It is difficult to know just how successful the paramilitaries were in the first few years in Scotland. Naturally only their failures, those actions which were discovered, came to the public attention. It is certain that a number of unsolved robberies in Glasgow and the Lanarkshire area were intended to provide funds for the UDA and UVF. It is also clear that the police were not single-mindedly pursuing the paramilitaries. Some senior police officers did not regard them as a serious threat.

Known sympathisers were looked at occasionally but as long as the Protestants kept quiet the police did not go after them. A change to that approach was forced by the high profile adopted by Roddy MacDonald and by the murder of a gun shop owner.

MacDonald, a highlander working in Edinburgh, was the third commander of the UDA in Scotland. In September 1976 he and three others gave an interview to the BBC Scotland television *Current Account* programme which is worth quoting at length. MacDonald began by asserting that the violence in Ulster had been initiated by the republicans. The Protestants were doing no more than defending themselves: "because you can't let a guy keep slapping you all the time without doing something about it, you know what I mean?"[10] MacDonald expressed the basic conservatism of the Protestant position: I've got nothing against a person for being a Roman Catholic but as far as the IRA and communist factions or anarchist factions are concerned . . . There is no doubt that the IRA . . . have amongst their numbers, a number of communists, anarchists and other extreme left-wing factions who would wish to destroy not only the position of Ulster . . . but also . . . the constitution of the country at the present time".[11] Thus far MacDonald was only stating the beliefs of most Orangemen. At this point the interviewer asked: "We have some evidence that members of the UDA and other loyalist organisations in Scotland help their comrades in Northern Ireland by supplying guns, explosives and so on; would you ever do this kind of thing?" One of the four UDA men (it might have been MacDonald but this is not clear from the transcript) replied: "I've done it and I'll do it again gladly". When further asked "Why is that?", the same person said: "Well, the way they're fighting over there it's no use supplying them with snowballs or something harmless. Snowballs never killed anybody!" In a discussion of where arms might come from, MacDonald made clear his willingness to purchase arms: "We'll buy arms from anybody so if there's any good priest who's got explosives in his chapel we will definitely buy them . . . nae danger. We will buy anything from anybody if it will help our cause".

The interviewer pursued his point about the IRA being better supplied than the Protestants, something which the UDA spokesmen accepted but they argued that this would be rectified if there was a great need for weapons. In the discussion one of the four said he had recently been offered a 12-bore shotgun with enough cartridges "to blow everyone here away". The interview ended with MacDonald being asked how many members the UDA had in Scotland, claiming six thousand, and defending the claim by saying:

> Well, lets face it. How many people do you get in Ibrox on a Saturday afternoon? In a good game on a Saturday afternoon, how many Rangers supporters do you get? Well, half of them are members of the UDA. I'm just saying six thousand; that could be generous or there could be more.[12]

Predictably the interview provoked demands for the UDA to be banned but more importantly, it led to demands for the Orange Order to expel MacDonald and all other members of the UDA. Perhaps sensing the amount of grass roots support that the UDA enjoyed, the Grand Lodge executive by-passed the normal disciplinary procedures. Instead of asking MacDonald's private lodge to remove him from membership, they suspended him and tried to have him removed at Grand Lodge level. The three hundred odd delegates at Grand Lodge refused to support this and re-instated MacDonald. Faced with such a challenge to their leadership the executive raised the stakes and threatened to resign *en masse* unless the second part of the Grand Lodge meeting, held a week after the first, endorsed a motion forcefully condemning paramilitary activity. Grand Lodge unanimously accepted the motion. In rather dramatic terms, David Bryce, the Grand Secretary, presented the decision as momentous: "The Loyal Orange Institution was on the brink of a precipice. We could have either gone backwards or continued to go forward. The decision of the membership, an overwhelming decision, was to go forward."[13]

MacDonald tried to appease the Order's leadership by issuing a clarification of the UDA's position:

> The Ulster Defence Association has never at any time been either illegal or unlawful, while we admit that a few of our more over-zealous members have from time to time been convicted of arms and explosives offences. I deny having at any time ordered or asked them to involve themselves illegally. We do however sympathise with them to some extent and care for their families through our welfare section, Loyalist Prisoners Aid. The Ulster Defence Association therefore exists as a paramilitary organisation that fully upholds the forces of the Crown, but however, in the event of British withdrawal from Ulster and a civil war situation arising, the Ulster Defence Association in Scotland would

be prepared to fight and assist in any way the Loyalist cause in Ulster.[14]

Such a statement was no doubt politic but many people in Orange circles knew that UDA supporters were more actively involved, as a matter of policy, in illegal activities than MacDonald's press release implied. One member in Edinburgh was seriously planning to purchase arms in Europe and had approached a pilot to fly them "into Drem or one of the airfields in Fife. I had a couple of furniture vans ready to keep the tools moving around until they were needed over (in Ulster)". UDA supporters in the Orange Order had on a number of occasions pressed Thomas Orr and the Orange leadership to be more active in the supply of weapons.

In its attempts to expel MacDonald, the Order had distanced itself from the UDA but its critics felt that it had evaded the issue. It had confined itself to pious statements and it had held back from implementing the logical consequences of the law and order motion it had passed at Grand Lodge; MacDonald and others had not been expelled. The hierarchy could, with some justification, claim that those involved in the UDA were almost all peripheral members of the Order. Thomas Thompson of Liverpool, who was convicted as part of the Toronto-Scotland-Ulster arms chain, had been expelled from both the Order and the Apprentice Boys of Derry for failing to attend meetings. Others were similarly "lapsed" members. But there were still many Orangemen who were UDA members and supporters and the Orange Order had failed to purge its ranks. As we will see, the same issue came up six years later when the Order was again presented with a challenge from younger rank-and-file members who felt that not enough was being done for the brethren in Ulster.

Having failed to do the "honourable thing" and resign, MacDonald again embarrassed the Order by leading a party of UDA members to Ulster in early 1977 to assist in the second Ulster Workers Council strike. Unlike the 1974 strike, this one was opposed by two of the main Unionist parties and it quickly petered out. But failure or not MacDonald had led a party of about a hundred Scottish loyalists, almost all of them Orangemen, to engage in activities which, if they were not actually illegal, were aimed at forcing the British government to change its policies and were thus hardly designed to support the forces of law and order.

In the end two police actions saved the Order from further embarrassment. MacDonald was arrested for cheque forgery in

London and that was enough for his private Lodge to remove him from the Order. His conviction in connection with a murder case removed him from circulation. In July 1977 Ross Sutherland, an assistant in a gun shop, murdered the manager and stole a number of guns and a large amount of ammunition. Five or six weeks before, he had contacted MacDonald and told him he had guns for sale. He showed MacDonald a number of weapons to convince him that he had a supply and asked for £2,000. By MacDonald's own account, the affair was botched from the start.

> I gave him my car to go and get the guns. He told me he was going to take my car and park it in the car park and he had a van there and my car was not supposed to go near the scene, right, when he was going to get the guns. He never even told me he was stealing the guns. This is the sad thing about it . . . he went away with my car, all lies about the thing to me. I'm working doing my bouncer in a west end disco and he comes to me and says "Right, Roddy, I've got the guns" and I said "Hang on, I cannae get you the money right away. By the way I've gave you about six hundred pounds already". I had a brand new car at the time. I said "Right there's the book and the MOT for the car. You want £2,000. The car is worth more than that. You'll get the money as soon as I get it". He took my car right to the place, went in and shot the guy in the back of the head, right, and then loaded the stuff in my car and two women up the stairs are watching him load the stuff in my car. He took the guns through to Broxburn to Lawrie . . . I told Lawrie to take the guns off him and get him on his way. But he didnae so Sutherland knew where the guns was. I never seen the guns. I am one man who didn't know where the guns was. And that's what happens when people do not do what they are told.

Untangling the elements that led to the conviction of MacDonald is difficult. There are discrepancies between the accounts given by the different people involved but it appears that MacDonald and the UDA were forced to partly co-operate with the police because the murder had raised the costs to the organisation. The gun that had been used in the killing was anonymously returned. MacDonald was in a very difficult position. He made unfortunate legal history by being the first person in Scotland whose trial involved the playing of a video tape as evidence. Once the court had been shown the tape of the BBC interview, MacDonald could not claim that he had a principled objection to arms purchase. Having publicly said that he wanted to buy guns, he could only claim that he did not buy this particular consignment. Although the main witness against him, Sutherland, had a history of mental instability and was known to have committed a brutal and unnecessary murder — two characteristics that should have devalued his evidence — it was clear that MacDonald's high profile required that he be found guilty. The Supreme Commander of the UDA in Scotland was sentenced to eight years. William Lawrie, the Broxburn contact who was supposed to see the guns on their way to Belfast, got five years.[16]

The guns never reached Ulster. They moved around central Scotland until they came to rest in a basement in Dumfries and there they rested for a year. The arms were discovered by the Dumfries police after they had arrested Michael Forteath, a known UDA member. Forteath showed them to the cache. This willingness to co-operate with the police was shared by almost all of the accused. Unlike the "supergrass" trials in Belfast in 1983, this was not a case of one individual being persuaded by a mixture of threat and bribery to give evidence against former colleagues. With little persuasion, almost every member of the Dumfries cell talked long and loud. Most, even those who had been leaders of the various groups — with titles such as "west coast Commander" and "Kilmarnock Commander" — insisted that they had joined the UDA when it had been a fraternal organisation which raised funds for loyalist prisoners' families and that they had been unwilling participants in the move to use the organisation for the purchase and shipment of arms. Almost everyone claimed that they had only gone along with the change in role because they were afraid for themselves or their families. Henry Haggan, who was commander of the Dumfries cell, said that he had taken some boxes which he supposed contained guns because "I was frightened that if I didn't take the boxes something might happen to my wife and family".[17] Even James Hamilton, who took over as Supreme Commander after the arrest of Roddy MacDonald, told the police that he had been reluctant to take the position, had "wanted out of the UDA", and had not been keen to get involved with shipping the guns; he had left that to Haggan. Walker, one of the first people to handle the guns, claimed that he had been "going to throw them on to the rubbish tip at Seafield but I was told by Jimmy Hyndman, no way. I took that as a threat against myself and my family so just did what I was told".[18]

To some extent one would expect that, once arrested and charged, the defendants would try and shift the blame for their actions on to others, especially if those others were already in prison, but these statements seem to be more than rhetoric. When added to our knowledge of how quickly the defendants co-operated with the police, they suggest a genuine lack of commitment to the cause.

The other feature to emerge from the statements in the Dumfries cell trial was the use of threats of violence in internal control. It seems that most of the people involved did "what they were told" because they were genuinely afraid of doing otherwise, and the later trials of members of groups in Paisley and Glasgow produced considerable evidence of brutality against wayward members of the cells. This rarely reached the level of knee-cappings and killings that was almost common in Ulster in this period but "battering" members who got out of line certainly reduced their commitment to the organisation and their loyalty to their leaders. That reduced commitment gave the police a good foundation on which to work. The threat they held over those who had been arrested was a long prison sentence; the reward they offered them was a chance to get even, to get their revenge on those leaders who had threatened them. The result was a great deal of "co-operation with the police in their enquiries".

A further point that emerged in these trials concerns the size of the UDA. MacDonald had claimed six thousand members but Karl Knutsen, who was the Dumfries leader until he was replaced by Haggan (apparently for not doing enough to procure guns) insisted that he never had more than forty people involved in arms handling in this period and most of them were only reluctantly involved. This observation alone probably explains the incompetence of the organisation. It was simply not sufficiently popular to be able to recruit a large pool of potential activists and then promote only the most able. Anyone who volunteered was accepted; anyone who could be cajoled or coerced into taking part was used. MacDonald himself recognises the lack of commitment from many people who called themselves UDA: "Anyone can wear a collarette, drink a few beers and remember 1690. But when it came to doing something, and risking getting the jail, then they was useless". MacDonald sees the problem as one of a general weakness in the membership. Others were more specific and pointed to the failures of the leaders: "We've always had trouble with the guys at the top. The guys in charge have always been bad yins".

Suspicion is endemic in any organisation that pursues some of its

aims outside the law. When money is being raised to purchase and
shift arms, it is not possible to use the services of respectable and well-
qualified accountants and accusations of holding on to the money are
to be expected. Many people on both sides of the water are certain that
MacDonald did get the money for the guns but failed to pass it on. In
different ways this was used to explain his conviction. One person said
of Sutherland: "The lad didn't grass until MacDonald bumped him for
his money". Another suggested that even if Sutherland did not
implicate MacDonald "it was MacDonald's fault he got caught.
Sutherland couldnae get away because he didnae get the money".
Stories about misappropriating funds were also told about other UDA
leaders. Many members think that MacDonald's successor James
Hamilton was also on the fiddle and Thomas Mackie, in charge of the
west coast area from 1976 to 1978, was suspected of collecting UDA
money for his own use. Certainly it is the case that very large sums of
money were raised in Scotland for Loyalist Prisoners' Aid and only
very small sums ever reached LPA in Belfast.

One has to be slightly sceptical of such stories. It was so clearly in
the interest of the police to sow the seeds of internal dissension and
suspicion that they would have promoted such rumours even if there
had been no good grounds for them, but highly placed UDA sources in
Belfast accept that there was considerable speculation. In part they see
it as the result of poor organisation. The UDA and UVF in Scotland
were run "by rascals and amateurs who didn't know what they were
about". A more interesting observation was offered by a senior UDA
man in Ulster who had considerable experience of this problem:

> It costs me a fortune for a night out at some function. I don't drink but
> I'm expected to go to all these dances and I'm expected to buy drinks. It
> costs me £20 or £30 to go to one of these. It's cheaper to buy the tickets
> and not go. If you're prominent, you're expected to be generous and I
> just haven't got that sort of money.

People like Hamilton and MacDonald were expected to maintain a
certain show of status in the community and were thus almost invited
then to live beyond their means. Even if they had no personal desire
for self-aggrandisement, the expectations of their followers would
have tempted them into enhancing their own position with the
organisation's money.

Bombing Catholic Pubs

Except for the wandering boy with his fertiliser bomb, all of the cases that had come to the courts so far had concerned the collection of weapons or money for the paramilitaries in Ulster. It was not until February of 1979 that the west coast of Scotland was faced with an actual terrorist incident. On the evening of Saturday 18 February, explosions wrecked two Glasgow pubs used mostly by Catholics: the Old Barn in Calton and the Clelland Bar in the Gorbals. Less than forty-eight hours later the police had arrested fifteen suspects; again, evidence of the ease with which the Glasgow Special Branch had penetrated the paramilitaries.

The suspects were all members of the Ulster Volunteer Force. One, Edward McLay, admitted acting as a store-keeper for a cache that included fuses, detonators, a rifle, a revolver, two sawn-off shotguns, and ammunition. Although the police work was made easier by the wilingness of McLay and two others to testify against the rest, the case was not entirely dependent on "grasses". Much as "the vegetables" (so called because "UVF" was jokingly taken to stand for United Vegetable Farmers) may have disparaged "the Wombles" of the UDA, their own operation was hardly more sophisticated. The bomb in the Clelland Bar was planted by a young man who made himself memorable to the bar staff by ordering the unusual combination of pints of "heavy" and, instead of the whisky that would be normal, glasses of sherry. The barman recalled the order without any difficulty because he had to go to the lounge bar to get the sherry and then had to serve it in a whisky tumbler because the bar had no sherry glasses. A customer in the bar also remembered the man and his unusual order.[19]

Two of the UVF men arrested had already been in court for explosive charges: Bill Campbell and George Martin. Campbell's brother Colin, who had served time for robbing a post-office, was also picked up. During the trial a detective said that he had over the last year kept surveillance on all of the accused and once seen them all in the same house. This degree of police knowledge of the cell made their precaution of telling the store-keeper McLay to become a "sleeper" and to keep away from the meetings a bit pointless. Even the most rudimentary surveillance of the Campbells and Martin would have led the police to the others involved — McKenna, Thomson, Kane, Von, Menzies and Ross — and although McLay was to keep away from the meetings he met Thomson, McKenna and Kane in pubs to hand over weapons.

As in some of the early cases, the gelignite came from miners. Two miners, one from Lanarkshire and one from Kirkcaldy, had been approached by pairs of UVF men who had asked for explosives. There was apparently no problem in supplying small amounts because of the miners' habit of saving themselves work by leaving any left-over gelignite down the mine for the next day's blasting. Over a few days, quite a number of sticks could be stored without anyone noticing.

The evidence of the two miners against four of the UVF men was added to by those members of the Glasgow UVF group who co-operated with the police. Anderson followed the now well-established pattern of claiming that he had joined the organisation when its main aim was collecting money for loyalist prisoners. The Bridgeton brigade had been altered in its purpose by the return from prison of Bill Campbell. Anderson said that he had been warned by George Martin to get an alibi for the night because there was going to be a "bang". Although he had, on his own evidence, been involved in moving explosives Anderson was not charged. Another UVF man, this time the top money handler, also co-operated with the police and was crucial in identifying the cars used by William Campbell and in testifying that he had passed on considerable sums of UVF money to Campbell.

As in other trials, the police case was assisted by the willingness of the defendants to try and lessen their own responsibility by fingering the others. George Martin had little reason to protect William Campbell who had "punished" him for insubordination by hammering holes in his legs and he claimed that the change in policy from fund-raising to criminal activity had been instigated by Campbell and only carried through because the rest of the members were frightened. John Thomson claimed that he had deliberately tried to subvert Campbell's plans by destroying weapons that came into his hands.

The sentencing in this case seems to have been deliberately designed to be a warning to anyone else who might be contemplating similar activity. All of the accused were found guilty of plotting to further the aims of the UVF by criminal means and four — Ross, Thomson, McKenna and Von — were found guilty of bombing the two bars. Thomson and McKenna were given eighteen years. William

Campbell and Stewart Ross were sentenced to sixteen years. Colin Campbell, George Martin and Peter Duffy got eighteen years. One of the accused, John Pears, was found not guilty but he was later convicted of possession of large quantities of a weed killer that was commonly used to make explosives.

The Paisley UDA

The police success in removing the Dumfries cell of the UDA was immediately followed by the successful prosecution of the core of the Paisley UDA.[20] Four men were convicted on conspiracy, firearms and terrorist charges and a fifth was convicted of possessing a firearm. Two of them — the Paisley commander William Currie and his right-hand man James Currie — were also convicted of assaults on their own members. The evidence in the trial produced a picture very similar to that painted by earlier trials. People had joined the organisation in the early seventies because they wanted to show solidarity with the Protestants in Ulster. Their activities had been mostly confined to paying a weekly subscription and raising money with discos and raffles. They saw themselves as being involved in welfare work by supporting the families of loyalist prisoners in Ulster. The arrival of one or two "hard men" then led to a change in the nature of the organisation with a move to collecting arms and explosives for Ulster. For the most part the violence of the group was internal, with the leader regularly threatening and disciplining the members. Just as William Campbell's assault on George Martin had been enough to make him turn on Campbell in court, so in the Paisley case, Richard McAvoy, a long-standing member who had been beaten up by William Currie, was only too keen to testify against his leader. Three other members who had either been assaulted or threatened with assault were also keen to testify. One of these had actually contacted the police himself: "I wanted to lead my own life. I wanted the UDA to break up in Paisley. It was my way out".[21]

With that sort of resentment in the organisation, the two Curries did not have to be particularly careless to be caught. They were under police surveillance for some time before their arrest and by the time they were taken in, the police knew enough about the UDA in the west coast to be able to destroy the organisation.

The Canada Link

Another case in what was proving to be a very successful police operation was the trial of eleven men for offences related to the shipment of arms from Toronto in Canada through Glasgow to Belfast. Parcels from Canada purporting to contain car parts were intercepted, found to contain arms, re-sealed and delivered under police supervision. Once again the police had no difficulty in rounding-up the members of an active UVF cell responsible for the Glasgow end of the system. The leader, Andrew Gibson, gave evidence but insisted that he did not tell the police anything they did not already know:

> I should have been in the dock with my men. But I did nothing to put them in it. Some of them were put there by their own mistakes. They broke direct orders by keeping stuff in their own homes rather than hiding it somewhere. But I deny doing any deals with the police. In fact when I went into court I thought I could be charged with gun running. At first I told the police a pack of lies. But as the hours and days went past I began to realise that someone else was talking. The police knew more about what was going on than I did.[22]

This UVF cell, based around the Maryhill area of Glasgow, had been re-organised after the 1979 arrests and convictions and one of its members was John Pears who had been charged in that set of arrests. Canada had always been the main source of arms for Protestant paramilitaries. In December 1974, two men had been convicted in Winchester Crown Court of smuggling arms from Canada. The 1981 operation was simple and neat. The guns were put in boxes lined with lead foil to excape detection in the normal X-ray machine checks but once one parcel had been detected and one member of the cell exposed, the rest of the organisation collapsed. It seems that Gibson fell for the classic trick of supposing that someone else was talking anyway so he might as well co-operate and win the benefit of assisting the police in their inquiries. Whether anyone else was passing information at that stage is not known but, to return to the common feature of all the cases, the police had a very good idea of who was involved in paramilitary organisations. This is not that surprising given that being in the UDA was usually an extension of being an Orangeman, being in a flute band, being a Rangers supporter, and drinking in certain pubs and clubs. The network of UDA membership was built on these other social networks. The police knew who had earlier been convicted, who visited them in jail, who their friends were and hence they knew which people to watch. The police also pressed minor villains into "touting" for them: "They done young boys for this and that and then told them to keep an eye out and let them know what was happening and they wouldnae be charged". When the police decided they wanted somebody, they could always charge them under the conspiracy laws which allow any group of known paramilitary sympathisers who meet together to be charged with "conspiring" to further the ends of an organisation by illegal means. Interestingly, the conspiracy charges have not been very successful. When a cell has been charged with conspiracy and with some actual offences, they have often had the conspiracy charge dropped and been proceeded against only on the specific charges but the presence of the conspiracy laws allows the police to begin with a charge that earns a long sentence and use that as a threat to produce co-operation.

Another police tactic in the Glasgow trials was to suggest the guilt of those charged by showing their friendship with others who had already been convicted for arms offences. In the trial in July 1982 of Charles Hamilton and William McLeish, the Crown called as witnesses a number of previous associates of Hamilton and McLeish even though it was known that they would not implicate them in any crimes. They were called to make the point to the jury that, even if there was no good evidence linking Hamilton and McLeish to any particular crime, they were the sort of people who *would* commit such crimes. In Hamilton's case the tactic was successful. He was jailed for seven years for possession of a revolver (which he insists was planted). The Crown failed to link McLeish with arms but managed to have him imprisoned for a year for reckless driving.[23]

"The Union of Dumb Amateurs"

What most strongly characterises all the incidents of Scottish Protestant paramilitary activity is incompetence. The title of this section is the description given by one detective to the Scottish UDA. In part this aura of almost vaudeville cack-handedness was produced by the reports in the press. The reporting of each of these cases had two quite different tones which were usually employed sequentially. The first reports were couched in the terms of shock, horror and

outrage and the offences are described in a sensational fashion which
magnified their importance. So every cache of arms was an
"enormous" or "huge" stockpile. The two pub bombs did not
"damage" the buildings; they "destroyed" them, and so on. Then in the
detailed descriptions of the charges humour was introduced and the
actions were described in such a way as to highlight their ineffectual
nature. The story was told of one man who sent arms to Ulster and
made the police case very easy by putting his own name and address on
the back of the parcel. The purpose of such a tone in reporting seems
to have been to reassure the public. The sensational reports were
designed to catch the attention by suggesting that the outrages of
Ulster were about to become common in Scotland and then the
reporters tried to reassure their readers by implying that there was no
real threat because these particular terrorists were incompetent.

But it is possible to separate at least some "facts" about the cases
from the style in which they are reported. And the essential facts do
testify to a very poor level of operational skill.

Explaining the incompetence of the Scottish UDA highlights the
basic differences between the Ulster and Scottish settings. The
Scottish paramilitaries were far less popular than their Ulster
counterparts and hence they had a smaller pool of talent and money to
draw on. It is hard to run a tight, partly illicit operation when there are
so few resources that rapid promotion, as in the case of Thomas
Mackie who was in charge of first Kilmarnock and then the west coast
are, came about because: "I was the only one with a car".[24]

The lack of popularity left the paramilitaries extremely vulnerable.
Few non-members in their communities supported what they were
doing, or, more precisely, once the long prison sentences made clear
the *cost* of supporting arms collection and shipping, enthusiasm for
those activities decreased rapidly. Some individuals in the UDA and
UVF who showed they had "the right stuff" by not implicating others
when they were convicted are highly regarded in their communities,
but those communities are small.

It is difficult to generalise about organisations as large and
complex as "the police" but there is no evidence that the Scottish
paramilitaries have ever benefited from support within the police
forces in Scotland. This is in contrast to the Ulster situation where in
any large station or division there will be one or two policemen with
enough sympathy for the paramilitaries to occasionally offer them low
level assistance. The Scottish paramilitaries are convinced that the

police are riddled with IRA sympathisers and frequently point to apparent discrepancies between the sentences they receive and those given to "the other side". Also missing from the Scottish situation is any even tacit élite support for paramilitary activity. In Ulster one has the model of the old Carson UVF, fighting to save Ulster from a united Ireland. In the present day one has Ian Paisley and his Free Presbyterian ministers counselling their members to establish defence militias.[25]

Here one comes back to the basic question of threat. The UDA, the UVF, and more recently Paisley's "third force" are responses to a very real sense of physical danger. There is genuine republican and nationalist violence against which to react. There was no actual threat to Protestants in Scotland. Scottish Catholics are not engaged in a war against the Protestants. The Provisional IRA has limited its attacks on the mainland to English targets. In part this is the result of an ideological association: the Scots and the Welsh are brother Celts and they too are dominated by the English. There is also a good practical reason for laying off Scotland. Scotland provides resources for the Provisional IRA. Money is raised and people who are too "hot" to remain in Ireland can be housed in parts of the west coast of Scotland.

The absence of any actual violence against Protestants in Scotland means that retaliatory violence and the preparation for violence only make sense for those who have a strong sympathy for their friends and relatives in Ulster. Scottish paramilitary activity is very much a matter of personal associations with what is happening in Ulster. At first there was a great deal of sympathy for the plight of Ulster's Protestants but, precisely because it was a matter of feeling for the plight of others rather than a personal fear for oneself, this sympathy was rapidly eroded by a knowledge of the costs of being caught, and by the increasing distrust for the character and motives of those most active in paramilitary organisations in Scotland. The knowledge that one of the UVF leaders, and three of the UDA activists had served sentences for murder and manslaughter *before* their paramilitary involvement, coupled to the widely circulated stories about large sums of money going missing and leaders feathering their own nests (one UDA man used his authority to run all his electrical appliances from the meter of a lower ranking member!), undermined a lot of the UDA's credibility. The paramilitaries came to be regarded, even by many of those who shared their loyalist principles, as unprincipled thugs.

War Heroes or Villains?

The press coverage and the public reaction to the Protestant paramilitaries made much of the criminal records of many of the accused. The common perception was that these people were villains first and foremost who used the UDA as a pretext for continuing their criminal activities. Their loyalism was commonly dismissed as a legitimation for a pattern of violence and villainy they would have pursued had there been no Ulster crisis. How valid is this perception?

Two UDA activists had served sentences for murder before they became involved in the UDA. Removed from its context, this information seems powerful evidence that the men in question were primarily villains whose politics were secondary. What is missing from that information is the background. As Patrick's study *A Glasgow Gang Observed* amply demonstrated, the working-class youth culture of urban Scotland in the late fifties and early sixties was extremely violent.[26] Many young people were routinely engaged in gang fights with razors, knives, machettes and axes. Simply coming from another area was ground enough for being brutally attacked and assaults with deadly weapons were so common that it is surprising that more of those fights did not end with deaths. In a very real sense, it was almost accidental that some such fights ended in deaths and others did not. I make the point about the prevalence of violence not to justify or excuse the actions of those involved but simply to establish that such violence was just part of the everyday lives of very many young people growing up in the depressed urban areas of lowland Scotland.

Gangs tended to be organised around locales. This gave most of them a sectarian identity. They were predominantly Protestant or Catholic but in the early sixties this tended to be more a matter of coincidence than design. Patrick's gang — the Young Team — was mostly Catholic but it contained Protestant members and it seemed equally at home attacking other Catholics as fighting Protestants. It was only when the present Ulster crisis raised the profile of sectarian loyalties, that the local "routine" violence became channelled into paramilitary activity. But even now one finds that a common distrust of the police unites some Protestants and Catholics. One UDA activist, talking about his arrest, said:

> I lived across the road and I was the only Protestant in the close. The
> rest were all Catholics and when the Special Branch came to my close

and interviewed everybody, not one of them said a word against me. Not one of them said a word.

The issue has been confused by those mainly middle-class Protestants who have supposed that being a "Protestant" and being prepared to use violence are mutually exclusive. Hence anyone who uses violence cannot be a real Protestant. Such a dichotomy may make sense if one takes "Protestant" in the strictly religious sense and opts for a pacifist view of the Christian message but in the sense of political, local and family loyalties — which is the sense in which the term is used among working-class Protestants and which the Ulster crisis has reinforced — it is invalid. The actual relationship, as it appears in the lives of UDA activists, can best be seen in terms of common ways of doing things. A willingness to use violence was simply part of the cultural background of "means" to achieve certain ends, be they status, the preservation of "face", wealth or whatever. Loyalism — the desire to preserve and protect Ulster Protestants — can be seen as a set of political ends. Those people who have been willing to use the means of violence for "less worthy" ends simply carried that willingness into a new arena when a new set of problems and issues came to the fore.

The other important point is that it is natural for those with criminal records to come to the fore in paramilitary activity, not because only psychopaths would join the UDA or UVF but because those people who are accustomed to violence are less afraid of its consequences and hence more willing to take such risks for what they believe in. One of the strongest impressions left from reading Patrick's study is the almost stoical way in which his kids expected to serve time in a variety of penal institutions. They talked about "doing their borstal" as if borstal was an inevitable stage on a pre-ordained career structure.[27] Young people from a culture in which prison sentences are common can more easily engage in activity that may well land them in prison. What I am suggesting is that being a villain was not an initial source of motives for loyalist activity but it did help in that it reduced the sense of fear that, for others on the fringes of paramilitary activity, acted as an obstacle to serious involvement.

Whatever the validity of the public perception of the Scottish paramilitaries as just criminals, it did have the consequence of undermining their legitimacy. It removed the possibility of even tacit support from the Protestant population of the lowlands of Scotland and it isolated the most militant activists from the religious Protestant

militants. Someone like Jack Glass, the focus of the next chapter, was
forced by both his own conscience and the demands of others to
denounce the "tribalism" of those loyalists who were willing to break
the law to support their brethren in Ulster when the major Protestant
institutions such as the Orange Order seemed to be doing nothing.

8

"Scotland's Ian Paisley":
Pastor Jack Glass

IN February 1972 the Official IRA shot down John Taylor in Armagh
City. Taylor was a rising star on the right of the Unionist Party at
Stormont and he was Minister of State for Home Affairs. The
following month the Westminster government suspended the
Northern Ireland parliament and introduced direct rule. A BBC *World
At One* programme interviewed a number of leading Ulster politicians for their reactions. It also sought Scottish opinion by
interviewing Pastor Jack Glass. Glass was asked how the Scots
responded to this new crisis.

A: There is a general feeling that if the people in Northern Ireland
   needed the people of Scotland, certainly there would be people
   prepared to leave here and go to Ulster and defend their Ulster
   brethren.
Q: To fight?
A: Yes, this is the general feeling. There could be a period of civil
   disobedience in Glasgow or the west of Scotland if there was any
   political initiative which was a capitulation to the IRA or there could
   be street demonstrations or thirdly there could be sending of
   volunteers to Ireland. Now I know it's easy to say these things. The
   real test will be when the crisis comes.
Q: What is your estimate of the number of people who would be ready
   to do this?
A: I called a demonstration within a week and got five thousand people
   out on the streets. I believe a good cross-section of that crowd would

be willing to go to Ulster, perhaps a few thousand anyway.

Q: Are these people with military experience?

A: As far as I know there are no arms caches in Glasgow, in the west of Scotland, but some of these people would have had experience in the armed forces during their national service.

Q: Are you prepared to lead, organise and participate in such a force yourself?

A: This decision would have to be made at the crucial moment. I'm certainly wrestling with it. I realise the tremendous responsibility that rests upon my shoulders. I'm not dealing with my own life here; I'm dealing with other people's lives and I just feel the crisis will precipitate the decision that I have to make.

Q: Are you willing to fight?

A: I would be willing to participate in this sort of thing and defend my country against terrorism whether it be from the IRA or whether it be from the Roman Catholic militancy.[1]

For those listeners who lived in England, Wales or the north of Scotland, this interview must have seemed extremely strange. Who was this man? Why was the BBC asking the pastor of a very small independent evangelical church in Glasgow whether or not he was willing to lead an army to Ulster? Who was Jack Glass?

Glass was born into a working-class family in Dalmarnock, an area of Glasgow bordering on the once strongly Protestant area of Bridgeton. His parents were both committed Christians (although his father was not, as some reports say, a minister) and at the age of eleven he was converted in a Salvation Army Sunday School.[2] As was the case with Ratcliffe, Cormack, Longbottom, Wise and Paisley, Glass lived his religious life outside the main Presbyterian churches. He was a regular attender at Baptist churches and at the variety of small hall meetings that make up the independent evangelical milieu. During his period of national service, he became friendly with two brothers who had "sat under" Dr Martyn Lloyd-Jones, the Welsh Calvinist who pastored the prestigious Westminster Chapel in London. Through them Glass was introduced to the publications of the Banner of Truth Trust: a small publishing house in Edinburgh which specialised in reprinting the works of the great Puritan divines and of the legendary Scots Calvinists such as the Bonars. These influences laid the basis for Jack Glass's theology. He returned to Glasgow looking for a church that combined a belief in the need for adult (rather than child) baptism with the Calvinist belief in predestination and "sovereign grace". He did not find such a church: most Baptist congregations are not Calvinist and the conservative Presbyterian congregations (such as those of the Free Church, Free Presbyterian Church and Reformed Presbyterian Church) do not practise adult baptism.

He intended to train for the Baptist ministry and spent a year at Glasgow University but found himself increasingly at odds with the policy of the Baptist Union on inter-church relations. Although there are many Baptist congregations which are deeply conservative, the Union as an organisation has been involved in ecumenical gatherings and is a member of those bogeymen of the conservative Protestant — the British Council of Churches and the World Council of Churches. The largest Baptist congregation in the Union, Charlotte Square in Edinburgh, withdrew because it wanted no part of the ecumenical movement and Jack Glass did likewise. By now he had decided to pursue an independent ministry and he persuaded the Free Church of Scotland to accept him at their theological hall as a private student. He was a good student and in 1965 acquired his diploma in theology.

An excursion on ordination

A small diversion is called for here. There is a common tendency to suppose that ministers must be ministers in some large organisation such as the Kirk or the Methodist Church. This makes reporters ready to repeat the accusation that ministers of such organisations make against people like Glass and Paisley: that they have not been "properly" ordained and that they are not "real" ministers. Cynics are fond of pointing out that Ian Paisley bought two of his degrees from one of those American degree mills that will send a parchment to anyone who pays enough. He did, but what is not usually mentioned is that before Paisley's pride or insecurity led him to purchase some dubious initials to put after his name, he trained at a Bible college in Wales and at the Reformed Presbyterian theology hall in Belfast. What is involved here are two conflicting notions of how a person is "called" by God to minister. The major churches have developed strategies which are supposed to "test" the validity of a "call". There are examinations and rituals which "certify" to the audience that this person is now a "real" minister. In churches such as the Roman Catholic, the Orthodox and the Episcopalian, the authority comes downwards. The candidate is admitted and "blessed" by his superiors in the organisation. In the Free Churches, the certification takes the form of the members of the congregation, through their representatives in the Kirk sessions, presbyteries and synods, accepting the candidate. In either case it is the organisation which gives its *imprimatur* to the prospective minister. But there is a strong tradition which opposes this organisational initiative and insists that the "call" is a more mysterious phenomenon which cannot be judged or certificated by a church organisation. There are many independents who insist that only the person called knows if he has been truly called and that the test of the "call" is to be found in its fruits. Independency is the church equivalent of the free market system in economics. If a man feels called then he offers himself as a pastor, preaches what he feels to be the Word of God, and if people follow him then he is a "real" man of God. There is no need for an organisation to accept a candidate. That is irrelevant, and some independents go so far as to imply that anyone who could be accepted by such apostate and sin-ridden bodies as the Church of Scotland is almost certainly *not* a man of God. Thus the question of "proper ordination" is seen by independents as an irrelevance.

To return to the biography, having a solid grounding in conservative Scottish theology from the Free Church, Glass started his own church in Glasgow. His first members were one or two survivors from the Tent Hall (a mission hall founded after the D.L. Moody crusades in the 1870s) who had, interestingly, been members of the Scottish Protestant League in the thirties. The rest of the congregation were gathered piecemeal. From the first, Glass was in conflict with the Church of Scotland, whose Glasgow Presbytery refused to sell him one of its many disused church buildings. A group of Americans acted as a "front" and bought a church.

The theological position of Glass's congregation was encapsulated in its rather unwieldy title: the Zion Sovereign Grace Evangelical Baptist Church. The combative nature of the new group's position is made clear from the beginning in the foreword to the *Articles of Faith and Constitution:*

> You are now a member of a church which has declared war on all Modernism, Romanism, Ecumenism and Arminianism, and every member is expected to unfurl the banner God has given him and to display on it the doctrines of Sovereign Grace.[3]

Beliefs and Style

Two of the main elements of Glass's theology — Calvinism and adult baptism — have already been mentioned. It is perhaps worth spending a little time elaborating the features of Calvinism so that Glass's disagreements with most other churches can be understood. Although this presentation will gloss over a deal of detail, it can be said that the main point of argument concerns "free will". There are many who believe that God created us with the power of independent thought and action and that how we behave will have an influence on our fate at the Day of Judgement. Many churches offer routine activities which we can choose to engage in (such as lighting candles, giving money to support the church, saying Hail Mary's and so on) and which will win us "merit" with God. While the Protestant tradition outlaws such routines, it still supposes that those of us who act in a godly manner throughout our lives and avoid sin will impress God favourably. Calvin argued that a God who could be impressed by the actions of puny men was no God. If God is really all-powerful then nothing we do will sway his judgement. This is coupled with the proposition that if God is all-knowing, then he knows the future as well as the past and present. If that is the case, he must know whether we are saved or damned even *before* we are born. These two beliefs lead to the notion of *predestination*: whether we are saved or damned has been decided already and we cannot change that decision. This leads Calvinists to a narrow interpretation of the idea that Christ died for our sins. They argue that Christ died only for the sins of the *elect*: that group of people who are already destined for salvation. This explains the Calvinists' revulsion for American styles of mass evangelism where men like Billy Graham ask people to make a "decision for Christ" and thus imply that men can choose whether to be saved or damned. Crusade evangelism implies something approaching "free will" and hence makes God's grace conditional on something we do. Calvinists use the phrase "sovereign grace" to suggest that God's grace is far from being conditional on our behaviour; it is *independent* of our action.

The Scottish Presbyterians were once thoroughly Calvinist and the Westminster Confession of Faith, which is still the Presbyterian Churches' "subordinate standard" (subordinate to the Bible as the statement of true salvational knowledge), is a clearly Calvinist document. But in reality almost all the major Protestant churches have moved a very long way from eighteenth-century Calvinism and it is a feature mainly of the small highland churches. Thus Jack Glass's

Calvinism separates him from the main stream of Scottish Protestant church belief.

The belief in the necessity of adult baptism causes a further separation; this time from the remaining Calvinists. Adult baptism is very much a reaction to the conformity that affects any religious organisation in its second and subsequent generations. When a new religious movement is created, it is voluntarily participated in by only those who enthusiastically hold its beliefs. But the first generation of believers have children and those children are *socialised* into the church rather than converted. This creates the danger that this second generation does not actually share the beliefs of the church but simply goes along with them, goes through the motions, because that is "just what everyone does". In order to have some evidence of actual personal belief most churches develop a two-stage process. The children of believers are accepted into the church, by baptism, but this membership is conditional. When they reach an age of mature decision making, they are further "tested" and are then admitted into full membership. Most churches have some sort of "confirmation" ritual for young adults. The most conservative and "serious" churches suspect (quite rightly) that these confirmations are little more than empty rituals which do little to test the potential member's faith. Hence they tend to shift the ceremony to a later point in the individual's biography, to "adult baptism", and try to make the tests significant rather than ritual. This, in lay terms, is the argument between child and adult baptism: validly testing the faith of members.

Thus Glass offered a theology that isolated him from the main Scottish churches. He further compounded his isolation by his style of worship. "I'm an active preacher. I put a lot of fire into my preaching. I also try to get a bit of fire and zeal into the singing." Although Glass's services are not the up-tempo, all-singing, all-dancing events common in the black American churches and in some British pentecostal churches, they do use music and hymns. The old Scottish Presbyterian churches reject instrumental music and hymns because these are "human" inventions. The Free Church members sing only the Psalms of David metrical chant; that is God's Word and not human invention. Thus Glass, by injecting a modern feel into his services, alienates the old Calvinists who might otherwise have been willing to overlook his insistence on baptising adults by totally immersing them in water.

Doing Politics

As if he were not already isolated enough by his theology and style of worship, Glass has further deviated from Scottish tradition by becoming politically active. There is a good precedent for political involvement. Calvin after all ran Geneva and John Knox recognised that there was an obligation on the true man of God to reform the state. Neither believed that imposing righteousness on an unregenerate people would actually give those people salvation if they were not part of the elect but nonetheless there was an obligation to make the Word flesh by creating political institutions that were nearer to God's will than those presently existing.[4] In the period when Calvinists were a force in the land they did not hesitate to be politically active and they were prone to see the destiny of social groups, of "the people", in terms of some special relationship with God. They were keen on "covenants" between the people and the civil magistrates that mirrored the covenant between God and the true believers. But the modern world has no place for Calvinists. It is difficult to actually point to the period when Calvinists lost their influence in Scotland but one can readily identify crucial symbolic battles such as those over the desecration of the sabbath. As the world at large came to care less and less what the Calvinists thought about anything, the Calvinists retreated from the world and maintaining their own purity became their major concern. They thus moved back to the position that Luther held which was basically to accept the political world as it stood and concentrate on maintaining conditions for the faithful which would allow them to preserve their righteousness.

This shift demonstrates an interesting point about the connection between religious beliefs and actions (and by extension, about the relationships between any kinds of beliefs and actions). One might suppose that certain sorts of ideology (such as the idea that the Christian has an obligation to promote social righteousness) should always or mostly lead the holders of the belief to act in a certain way (in this case by political involvement) but this is not so. Rather one should view ideologies as wardrobes full of co-ordinated clothes. A certain jacket may go with another, perhaps contrasting, colour of waistcoat to produce a new outfit which still "matches". People may associate a certain course of action with certain beliefs but when the climate changes to make that action impossible they can go back to their ideological wardrobe and shuffle the elements of the ideology to justify a new course of action. Thus the Reformed Presbyterians, who were the most forceful advocates of the need for the Church to have an input to the state now have a policy of abstaining from the state. They will not vote, take political office or serve on juries. They justify this retreat from the political world by pointing to their original covenant with the secular power (in those days the monarchy). The covenant said that the Church had a duty to actively support "the civil magistrate" and that the civil magistrate has reciprocal duty to support "the true religion" by suppressing heresies.[5] Obviously no modern government is interested in suppressing heresies. The Reformed Presbyterians insist that they are right to withhold their side of the bargain and thus what began as a policy of active involvement in the world at large has been turned into a justification for pietistic retreat from the world.

Jack Glass is a rare animal in the modern world: a Calvinist who continues to denounce actively the sins of the modern world (rather than just grumbling about them to the community of the faithful). He is vocal in his attacks on the failings of the secular world and tries to achieve some sort of political platform. He is an even rarer animal in the Scottish context where there is no recent tradition of ministers in politics. In part this is a result of the legal position of the Church of Scotland. Like ministers of the Church of England, those of the Kirk are banned from holding seats in parliament because they are officials of the "state" church. But for the most part, it is a reflection of the fact that the religion of the Kirk has not been a political issue, even in the indirect fashion of the supporters of that religion being under some sort of threat, for a very long time. Thus, while Presbyterian clergymen in Ulster can call on a long tradition to justify their presence in political parties, Glass appears as an anomaly.

Rome and the IRA

Jack Glass's first public protests concerned fairly narrowly religious matters. They were mostly directed at actions by representatives of Protestant churches that could be seen as evidence of a desire for *rapprochement* with Rome. These early protests were usually in the company of Ian Paisley. Glass had heard of Paisley as a "dynamic gospel preacher long before he was a well known public figure"; "I was holding six monthly evangelistic conferences and I invited him over. I was very impressed by him". In March 1966, Glass travelled to Rome with Paisley, other members of Paisley's Free Presbyterian Church of Ulster, and Brian Green, the minister of a Strict Baptist congregation in Hounslow. Paisley and one of his ministers were recognised and turned back at the airport, but Glass and the others got through to make their protest against Archbishop Ramsay's meeting with the Pope.

The Civil Rights Movement in Ulster and the crisis in the Stormont government that followed it added a new dimension to Glass's public life. In January 1969 he announced the formation of his Twentieth Century Reformation Movement, which he described as being "something like the Ulster Constitution Defence Committee — a political organisation influenced by religion".[6] The UCDC was one of the forerunners to Paisley's Democratic Unionist Party. Through 1969 and 1970 Glass was to be found speaking on platforms in Ulster and Scotland in opposition to "papal aggression" and his association with Paisley deepened to the point where journalists talked about Glass as Paisley's man in Scotland. Although he was increasingly involved in the Ulster crisis, he still found time to oppose manifestations of Romeward trends and with eighteen others (mostly ministers in Paisley's FPC) he was charged with disturbing the peace in Westminster Abbey during one such protest.

Paisley's first appearance in electoral politics was to stand against Terence O'Neill, the Prime Minister who offended conservative Protestants in Ulster with his attempts to make the state acceptable to Catholics. In 1969 Paisley (and Michael Farrell, who was, with Bernadette Devlin, one of the founders of the People's Democracy Party) challenged O'Neill and took so many conservative Unionist votes that O'Neill barely scraped home. The following year O'Neill retired and Paisley won the seat at the by-election. That was in April. In June there was a British general election and Jack Glass and Brian Green decided to follow Paisley's lead and contest elections. Brian Green was wiped out in London but Glass, although coming nowhere near winning, managed to come close to the Scottish Nationalist Party candidate in the basically working-class seat of Bridgeton in Glasgow. Bridgeton had been a socialist stronghold since the early thirties when Maxton used to hold it comfortably against the challenges of the Grand Master of the Orange Order, and the Labour candidate was extremely comfortably returned:

General Election 1970: Bridgeton

Labour	11,056
Conservative	3,081
SNP	1,550
Jack Glass	1,180

Separating from Paisley

In 1965, Glass, Green and Paisley had united in an organisation designed to "promote the formation of Separatist Churches holding the Reformed Faith, throughout the United Kingdom".[7] In so doing, they signed a statement of faith that was not only militantly Protestant but also clearly Calvinist. In one paragraph it listed the doctrines of grace: those five points usually known as "TULIP" after the acronym formed from the first letter of the five phrases.[8] Sometime around late 1970, Glass separated from Ian Paisley. The reason for the split was Paisley's association with the American fundamentalist Bob Jones University. Although very conservative, Bob Jones Jnr. and Bob Jones III (son and grandson of the founder) were not Calvinists and had expelled a couple of students from their campus for teaching what they called "hyper-Calvinism". Glass asked Paisley to renounce his association with the Jones family and when he failed to do so, Glass publicly announced his separation from Paisley and Green. From that point on, Glass had been vocal in his attacks on Paisley, once calling him "Mr Facing Both Ways".[9]

Thus in 1973 and 1974 one finds Glass campaigning for the loyalist cause under the banner of Vanguard Scotland, which was a support movement for William Craig's Vanguard Party in Ulster.

Glass has also been vocal in his attacks on other Protestant organisations. His view of the Orange Order is especially jaundiced. Glass was never a full member though he was associated with the Juniors. His father resigned from the Order because of its abandonment of temperance principles.

Taking the full sweep of the Orange Order's history, temperance was not so much the norm as a temporary characteristic. In the eighteenth and early nineteenth century, members of the Order were well-known for their consumption of alcohol. It was only in the second half of the nineteenth century, when total abstinence became common in the Presbyterian churches, that the Lodges began to frown upon drink. But even many of those who accepted temperance principles were prepared to accept drinking in the Lodges as an alternative to members drinking in "secular" public houses where they would not be influenced by the moderating behaviour of decent citizens.[10] John Hope's campaign in Scotland had, with other factors, brought about a reduction in boozing among working-class Protestants and for a short time around the turn of the century, many Lodges were either temperance Lodges or, if not totally dry, at least fairly arid. Already by the thirties, however, one finds Alexander Ratcliffe condemning Orangemen for their drunkeness and Jack Glass's father left the Order because temperance was ceasing to be something that was common even in the rhetoric, let alone in the reality. The problem became even more acute for Glass because of two further changes; the growth of Orange clubs and the introduction of Sunday licences.

In an attempt to dissociate the Order from its image of serious drunken rowdyism, the Irish Grand Lodge had in the nineteenth-century made it a point of regulation that no publicans were to hold office in the Order without special permission from the Grand Lodge, and similarly, no private Lodge meetings were to be held in public houses.[11] The same principles obtained in Scotland. But the fact was that most Orangemen consumed alcohol and they tended to drink in particular pubs and clubs so that even though there was no formal connection between these places and the Loyal Orange Institution, outsiders regarded them as "Orange" establishments. As David Bryce, the Grand Secretary put it:

> There were problems of discipline in these places and because they were known locally as Orange clubs — it was Orange people and people who were sympathetic to the Orange Order who were members of them. Once you began to get problems with discipline and with the running of them — a lot of people had no business experience — then some people thought it would be better to try and get some control of them. So they started a Union of Social Clubs. The Union then advised the clubs how to handle the business aspects.

So existing clubs were accepted into association with the Loyal Orange Institution. In the sixties a lot of new social clubs were opened. Starting a club gave private lodges a new source of finance and the breweries were keen to offer loans at low rates of interest for the expansion of Orange premises. The result was that many Orange halls became licensed and they could, and did, serve alcohol on the sabbath. Thus, they managed to offend two of Glass's principles — temperance and sabbatarianism — simultaneously.

Conservative Protestants have always found Roman Catholic attitudes to the sabbath offensive. In one sermon Glass inserted the following aside on the Catholic Sunday:

> They're keeping the Lord's *half*-day. They keep the Lord's Day in the morning. Celebrate the Mass and then enjoy the pleasure of sin for the rest of the day. Now it's yer Orangemen, yer Protestants, and their social clubs, drinking away the Lord's Day.[12]

Glass quite rightly sees his disagreements with Orangemen about alcohol and keeping the sabbath as stemming from a much more basic difference of religious beliefs. Protestant ministers who are active in the Order might be willing to offer the rather feeble proposition that most Orangemen are "bible loving even if they are not bible reading",[13] but, as the following passage from a sermon shows, Glass is scathing about the average Orangeman's religiosity:

> Notice there are no queues waiting to get in this morning when you arrived. Because the glory of the Lord has disappeared from Scotland. Our heritage has gone because of our sins and wickedness . . . This afternoon they'll be glued to their television screens. I can't see one Orangeman this morning in this church and yet a few weeks from now they'll be marching through the streets to defend their faith. What faith?[14]

The lack of fit between the Order's use of the Bible in its rituals and the amount of actual Bible reading done by its members is a frequent Glass target:

> I wonder how many Protestants read the Bible. They carry it on the Orange walk in cellophane at the front. I think it stays in cellophane. It's to keep the rain out, and to keep the Orangemen out as well! Real Protestants are Bible students who love the Word of God. It's appalling if you don't have a Bible. Protestants come to church with the Bible. Don't bring the *Dandy Annual* or the *Beano*. We don't preach from that or from anything else. You bring your Bible. It's amazing the Protestants who come to church and don't have a Bible. I don't know

what they expect to hear: the greyhound results?[15]

Glass opposes the Orange Order because it is willing to demonstrate and make public protests but does not have the right religion. He equally opposes the religious Protestant organisations which have the correct theology but are not willing to demonstrate. There has for a long time been a good deal of ill-feeling between Glass and the Scottish Reformation Society (the Protestant organisation that James Begg helped found and which the John Hope Trust still helps fund). Ratcliffe and the SRS argued about the dignity of public protests, and now Glass and the SRS rehearse the same argument. In the approach to the Pope's visit to Scotland, the SRS proposed that the occasion be used to educate Protestants:

> To many the occasion will be yet another opportunity to parade with their NO POPE HERE banners. If this is their way of protest, then they will follow that course but isn't it sad that so often those who have the largest banners and shout the loudest, just do not know WHY THEY ARE PROTESTING AT ALL? Opinions and protests are pretty pointless unless they are informed and accurate.[16]

Although the target of the SRS attack might have been the Orange Order rather than Jack Glass, Glass took it as being aimed at him and, reprinting it in his *Scottish Protestant View,* added:

> Notice the name at the top of this newsletter, it is Rev A. Sinclair Horne. This is the man who refused to sign our petition to keep the Pope out of Britain, and who appeared with the Roman Catholic Cardinal Gray at an ecumenical service during the Queen's visit to Glasgow. Praise God our biblical protest is an informed and reformed protest and not a deformed protest like Horne's.[17]

The Cause of Separation

Explaining why people did things is extremely difficult, so much so that many social scientists argue that we cannot do it and that we should either confine ourselves to the description of what people do, or to the explanation of something else, such as the supposed features of an abstract social system. Either of these courses seems pointless;

explanation of human action may be extremely difficult but it is comparably interesting and rewarding. So why did Glass separate from Paisley, the Orange Order, the Scottish Reformation Society and everyone else? We can consider that question in two parts. The first concerns the occasion for the split and the reasons given by Glass. In all cases, the splits came about because no one had exactly the right combination of beliefs and attitudes for Glass. I have already detailed the way in which Glass's product differs from that offered by most of the other churches. With some he further differed in that they did not share his perspective on how politics and religion ought to mix. He then disagreed with those Protestants who shared his view of politics because they did not hold his religious beliefs and values. Consequently, if Glass is going to remain wedded to the notion that he must make public his disagreements with all those who do not share (in very fine detail) his beliefs and attitudes, then he is going to do a lot of separation.

But clearly there is a further source of motivation. One can distinguish between separating from other people because of actual and particular disagreements, and "separation" as a way of life, a mode of operating in the world that becomes attractive in its own right. I do not want to make too much of this point (partly because the evidence for it is difficult to obtain and partly because it is not too important) but it does seem that Glass shares Ratcliffe, Paisley and Cormack's problems in accepting others as equals. All of the people I have interviewed who know both Glass and Paisley well volunteered the proposition that the two would have split anyway, even if the Bob Jones University expulsions had not caused Glass to question Paisley's Calvinism. Some other occasion for separation would have been found. Both men are leaders and both are independent entrepreneurs. As one man who knew both put it: "Ian and Jack both need to run their own shows. Neither can take being told what to do". As I argued in chapter four, this basic psychology fits perfectly with the social structure of independent conservative Protestantism; each man his own interpreter of the Word and each man convinced that his interpretation is God's interpretation. To say this is not to belittle the motivation of Glass and Paisley but only to recognise that organisations get the leaders who are psychologically and ideologically suited to the style of the organisation. Bureaucratic organisations get leaders who are good bureaucrats. Independent Protestants churches are formed around dynamic leaders who select themselves (or more precisely, feel that

God has selected them) and hence whose self-image is considerably more positive than is that of most other people. The same personality features that make them able to build from scratch, with no certification from a large church organisation and with no status that comes simply from stepping into a position, a following, make them impossible collaborators.

Glass's justification for constant separation is that it is necessary to maintain the purity of the witness. The truth must be preserved and preached. That is the first problem. This could be done and one could still associate with people who do not preach the truth but there would remain a danger of secondary contamination. The world at large might fail to see that you are different to this other person if you are seen to keep his company. Thus one needs to keep separate from those in error, even though one is not in error oneself, because to fail to do so threatens the clarity of one's witness. Thus Glass cannot join in an anti-abortion protest with a Catholic priest even though they share the same position on that issue because people who see the joint protest might assume that Glass and the papist were in agreement about other things!

Glass has been willing to moderate this extremist position in the case of political protests. On things religious one must keep separate but, if one is going to practise politics then one has to be prepared to work with some people who are not thoroughly "born again". Thus he has been prepared to let the Apprentice Boys of Derry have their annual service in his church, even though they are no more religious than the Orangemen Glass so often criticises. This is not to suggest that Glass is consciously hypocritical or deliberately inconsistent (which is what his Orange critics say of him) but it is to make the point that separation raises problems that are almost incapable of solution this side of moving the faithful to an island. Those small sects which almost totally isolate themselves from their surroundings can consistently maintain their doctrine of separation but those, like Glass's church which wish to combine doctrinal purity with some active presence in the world, are faced with a constant series of difficult choices about associations. Simple dichotomies between "religious" and "secular" matters cannot work when it is precisely religious beliefs that provide the motivation for the politics in the first place and when a lot of the politics, especially those connected with Ulster and "papal aggression", is politics played out in the name of religious belief. Does one turn down the assistance of the Apprentice Boys of Derry because they are not "real" Protestants when that assistance might help stem the tide of what is seen as very real papal aggression?

In practice Glass has changed and one can see the hint of a firm direction of change rather than simple wavering. In the early seventies, he frequently led marches and demonstrations of Protestants in response to government initiatives in Ulster (and sometimes in response to the absence of such initiatives). He was linked with William Craig's Vanguard movement (which was one of the homes of right-wing unionists when the Unionist Party was still in its power-sharing disarray) and he spoke on platforms with Glen Barr, one of the intellectuals and politicians associated with the paramilitary UDA. But in the same period, he turned down invitations that might have connected him with the Orange Order.

The trend is one of a gradual abandonment of "big" politics and of activities that associate him with others in favour of individual acts of protest. I will try and argue that this has a number of sources which interact: the initial failures of big politics, the increasing "stability" in Ulster, the increasing lack of interest in Ulster, and the increasing realisation that conventional politics, in the sense of petitions, demonstrations, and election campaigns will make no impression on a Scotland and Britain knee-deep in sin. The end result is a dependence on miracles and an abandonment of serious politics.

The Failure of Electoral Politics

Ratcliffe and Cormack failed both to enter Westminster and to maintain a strong and consistent representation in municipal politics. The Protestants of Liverpool had slightly more success[18] but by far and away the best model for conservative Protestants entering British politics is that provided by Ian Paisley. He began his career by ending that of a Prime Minister and from that point on he has built his party so that it can now claim to speak for about half of the Unionist voters in Ulster. In the first direct elections to the parliament of the European Community Ian Paisley gained far more first preference votes than any other candidate and more than the two Official Unionists together.[19] In the 1981 local government elections the Democratic Unionist Party won 142 seats; only nine behind the Official Unionists.[20] The DUP now has three Westminster MPs. And, what is not made clear in those figures, Paisley has created such a strong personal following in his own constituency that one cannot imagine anyone ever winning the seat from him.[21]

Glass could hardly offer a greater contrast. His Twentieth Century Reformation Movement has never grown beyond the limits of his own three congregations and a handful of supporters in Ulster and England. He polled fewer votes in Bridgeton than Cormack did in Leith in 1946 and his two subsequent elections have been no more successful. He did not contest another seat until 1982 when he used the occasion of a media-ridden by-election at Hillhead, Glasgow, to stand on a "Protestant Crusade Against the Papal Visit" ticket. The media was in Hillhead because one of the founders of the Social Democrat Party, the Right Honourable Roy Jenkins, was contesting the seat after just narrowly failing, against all predictions, to win a by-election in Warrington. The newly-formed Social Democratic Party was riding high in the polls and the campaign was sure to get a great deal of coverage. Despite being the only candidate who actually resided in the constituency, Glass could not reach four figures:

Westminster By-election March 1982; Glasgow Hillhead

Roy Jenkins (SDP/Lib Alliance)	10,106
Gerald Malone (Conservative)	8,068
David Wiseman (Labour)	7,846
George Leslie (Scot. Nationalist)	3,416
Jack Glass (Prot. Crusade . . .)	388
Roy H. Jenkins	282
Nicolette Carlaw (Ecology)	178
Bill Boaks (Public Safety . . .)	5

The figure of barely over 1.2% of the total vote put Glass firmly in the "lunatics and no-hopes" category. The election was contested for the publicity rather than with any hope of winning but nonetheless it was contested seriously and one can assume that it represents the full extent of Glass's support in what is, admittedly, an unlikely constituency, taking in as it does the bourgeois area of Glasgow which contains the University and the BBC. A better test of electoral popularity occurred a few months later in the local government elections when Glass contested the Bellahouston Mosspark ward, which took in the park that had been used for the Pope's Glasgow Mass. If there was any body of working-class anti-catholic support, then this election should have exposed it.

Local Government Elections June 1982; Bellahouston Mosspark

Labour	3,306
Conservative	1,909
Social Democrat	1,705
Scot. Nationalist	566
Jack Glass	534

Glass had eased his percentage up to 6.6% but he was still doing nothing to suggest that any dent could be made on the Labour Party's stranglehold over Glasgow and central Scotland politics.

It was not only elections that were having little obvious success; even the largest demonstrations seemed to have little pay-off. The Westminster government's scheme for a power-sharing executive in Ulster was not defeated by the petitions and protests in the west coast of Scotland but by the Protestant workers' strike in Ulster. The analytical point I want to make at this stage is that people change their minds about courses of action when they see the results. Paisley was willing to work with some distictly "unsaved" groups of people; such collaborations paid off and led to success, which could be used to justify the basic pragmatism. In the absence of success there was no good reason for Glass to compromise his separatist witness by working with the Orange Order or anyone else.

A further element in the last decade has been the increasing "stability" in Ulster. It might seem strange to use the term "stability" to describe a place where political assassination is still common and where IRA hunger strikers have died to make a point; where a dying hunger striker can be elected to Westminster; and where millions of pounds worth of property is regularly destroyed by bombs, but the late seventies did see stability in two senses. In the first place, the violence did decline. Less people died in those years than in the early part of the troubles. But more important than "reality" is people's perceptions and it is the case that the sense of panic which many Protestants felt in the early seventies has subsided, partly because they can look back and see that they still exist, that the world continues to turn and that for all of fifteen years of a concentrated IRA campaign, they have not yet been railroaded into a united Ireland. It is a terrible observation but a true one nonetheless that people become tired of crises. Most people involved in Protestant organisations in Scotland (including those who themselves have strong Ulster connections, such as David Cassells,

who will be discussed in the next chapter) believe that the Scots have
become gradually less and less interested in Ulster. This is partly due
to the gradual erosion over the course of the century of family ties but
it also owes a lot to the sheer tedium of a conflict that has run for
fifteen years. People who are in their twenties now were not even
reading newspapers when the present troubles in Ulster began. It is a
full decade since Glass led his biggest demonstrations in support of
Ulster Protestants. People have become both accustomed and tired,
and with that, the impact of such demonstrations and protests has
diminished.

Playing to the Gallery

The *Scottish Protestant View* for January 1981 contains copies of the
press cuttings which reported the protest highlights for 1980.[22] In that
year, Jack Glass was typically active in promoting his views on a wide
variety of issues. In January he picketed a Church of Scotland church
which was celebrating the start of Christian Unity week with an
invitation to Roman Catholic Archbishop Thomas Winning. In
February, he picketed a licensing viewing of Monty Python's film *The
Life of Brian* and told councillors: "If you pass this film you are
crucifying Christ again". They did. By nine votes to four they gave it an
"X" certificate. In April, Glass protested outside a meeting being
addressed by Bernadette Devlin, one of the founders of People's
Democracy and more recently an active supporter of the republican
prisoners' protests and hunger strike. A number of protestors chanted
outside the hall: "Devlin is a killer and IRA murderess". The following
week, Glass and his supporters were to be found outside the Glasgow
City Chambers picketing a civic dinner for the Russian Ambassador.
    One of the protests that received most coverage was the Glass
reaction to Billy Connolly. For anyone who has heard both men
perform, this is an interesting challenge. Both share what is a
distinctly Glaswegian sense of humour and both are masters at the
witty but barbed impromptu aside. One suspects that with only very
minor changes in their biographies, the two men could have been
interchanged. Connolly has written and performed an hilarious sketch
on the Crucifixion which is thoroughly offensive to most conservative
Christians. As Glass puts it: "Connolly had depicted Jesus Christ in a
drunken state and urinating on a Roman soldier on the Cross. He does

this on record and cassette. He is a blasphemer and filth merchant."
When Connolly was invited as the guest of honour to a Variety Club
dinner in the Central Hotel, Glasgow, Glass met him outside and
threw thirty pieces of silver at his feet. The half page report in the
Daily Record inserted an ironic note by adding: "The thirty pieces of
silver would have been appreciated more by Monday's bullion raiders.
Because of a falling market, their £4 million haul has been cut in half".
I will return to the significance of that insertion.

There were three major demonstrations in May. A conservative
pressure group within the Church of Scotland called Concern for the
Kirk had arranged a meeting which was to be addressed by Andrew
Herron, a former Moderator who had, while in office, met the Pope in
1972. Jack Glass and about 40 supporters attended the meeting and
began barracking as soon as the meeting began. Glass as usual picketed
the Kirk's General Assembly, this time because the Archbishop of
Canterbury, Robert Runcie, was to be in attendance. In the same
month, Glass also visited a Roman Catholic children's home to assist a
Protestant father in having his ten-year-old boy withdrawn. The child
had been taken into care by the local authority and placed temporarily
in a Catholic home because of the shortage of places in state
institutions. They insisted that the boy would be transferred if it was
decided to keep him in care for any length of time. The father gave the
boy a Rangers football strip and Glass wrote "No Popery" in the
visitors' book.

An ecumenical rally organised by various supporters of the
charismatic movement was the venue for a picket in June. This time
things became a little heated with some Catholics singing the Irish
National anthem and the Glassites replying with "Onward Christian
Soldiers". The police had to separate the two groups.

In September, Glass and some twenty supporters sailed to the
island of Iona, the home of George McLeod's progressive community,
and there protested against popery. The same month, Glass picketed a
Roman Catholic seminary in Aberdeen to protest about the proposed
papal visit and heckled amateur historian Bill Clarke at Glasgow
airport. Clarke was the archivist who had researched the life of John
Ogilvie and who played a major part in Ogilvie's canonisation.

Glass is very much aware of the need for good press relations and
he is quite conscious of the value of stunts such as the throwing of
thirty pieces of silver. He knows that editors will pay very little
attention to press releases. One only has to compare the coverage

Glass gets with that given to the thoughts and deeds of the Free Church of Scotland to be aware that the stunts work. Reporters will go where Glass goes because they know that he will be good for a nice photograph and a hot quote. But there seems to be a large price paid for this coverage. In the last chapter I made the point about the tone of the press reports on the "wombles" in the Scottish UDA. Skilled reporters are adept at ironicising and satirising the views of those people whose actions they report. For fifteen years, Jack Glass has picketed and protested. He has stood with his banners and slogan waistcoats outside everything from St Peter's in Rome to a travel agent in Helensburgh (the agent was selling package tour weekends to Hamburg's red light district!). What seems clear to me reading the reports is that the tone has become more ironic and the protests are now presented as part of the "rich and varied tapestry" of Scotland's cultural life. The media now treat Glass as a "character"; worth a few paras if nothing else is happening but of no genuine significance.

The social science literature contains a distinction which is useful if not overplayed. We can talk about actions which are *instrumental*, that is, rationally planned to achieve some end, and actions which are *expressive*: engaged in for their own sake, for the fun or pleasure of doing them or as emotional release. Protest movements are often distinguished in these terms. Some are thought to be "sensible" and purposeful because they have realistic aims while others are dismissed as expressions of people's anger or frustration. The problem with the distinction is that it usually has no basis in how the actors think about what they are doing. We might think that camping outside Greenham Common for two years will cause no change in government policy on nuclear weapons but that does not allow us to assume that the people doing just that are not doing rational and instrumental politics. They may well be instrumental but misguided. And anyway, how do we know whether a certain kind of protest is rational and reasonable until it is tried and either does or does not work? It is not a distinction that can be made easily in advance of the actions in question and hence we cannot offer two different kinds of explanations of why people protest: one sort for instrumental protests and one for expressive action.

Nonetheless, there is something valuable in this distinction. When people engage in action, they make calculations about the likelihood of it succeeding. I know that Jack Glass did not expect to win Glasgow Hillhead because I asked him before the election and he told me that his chances were slim "unless there is a miracle". What was certain, even without divine intervention, was a lot of publicity. Hence it makes sense to see the decision to stand in that election in terms of the likely publicity rather than the chances of winning. The reason why Jack Glass spends so much time in public protests is simply that he has no realistic chance of changing things in the ways that really work; by exerting pressure on the right people from the inside or by threatening them with popular sanctions (either in the form of being voted out at elections or by having their product boycotted). Glass's pickets are the protests of someone who is totally powerless. In that sense, they are "merely expressive" but they are only that because the possibility of doing anything instrumental was removed about one hundred years ago.

The Christian's Political Manifesto

Glass is a surprise. Unlike James Begg, the leading anti-catholic figure in the Free Church, of whom no one spoke a good word, Glass is well liked by all of those who have met him. His sense of humour and his ability to make jokes at his own expense suggest a sense of proportion that does not appear in either the man's public behaviour or in the press presentation of that behaviour. Glass actually does seem to combine a hatred for Roman Catholicism (and all other "heresies") with a general sociability and pleasantness towards those who believe in these apostasies.

If the man's personality is a surprise, so are his politics. Most of Glass's public appearances and pronouncements are concerned with a fairly narrow range of issues: Ulster, "papal aggression", moral standards and respect for Protestant symbols. What the contemporary Calvinist thinks about the rest of the world is not obvious. Glass recorded one sermon called *The Christian's Political Manifesto* and I want to spend a little time on the points made there. Like most other Glass sermons, the format is loose.[23] He clearly has a general structure but he feels free to digress and add asides as the spirit moves. He begins by telling the congregation that they should be in favour of hanging and in favour of corporal punishment in schools. They should be against communism but they should also be opposed to racism. "If God was a racialist he'd have only picked the whites for election. God is colour blind." But Glass is against immigration. He believes that each people should stay in its own land. But having started with what sounds like a classic piece of Tory Party apologetics for a covert racism, something that could have come out a National Front pamphlet, Glass surprises by insisting that this means one has to equally well condemn imperialism.

> This works both ways of course. If you're not going to flood Britain with blacks, you can't flood black countries with whites. And so you must be against imperialism of every kind. It's not good shouting about "Russians out of Afganistan" if say for example we invaded some black country. We'd have to shout "Britain out of Tanzania" or something. It works both ways.[24]

Glass has no illusions about British imperialism or the early missionaries' involvement. He quotes Spurgeon's condemnation of the British going into foreign lands and putting a sword at the throats of the natives, offering them the gospel and wondering why this proselytisation was not massively successful. With a fine disregard for the complex inter-relations of modern trade and foreign affairs, Glass offers separate development as the Christian principle. God has put this people here and this people there. Let everybody leave everybody else alone and mind their own business. This is a "little Britain" philosophy curiously at odds with the imperialism and jingoism that informs Orangeism.

Glass is opposed to greedy trade unions and greedy workers who take double time for weekend working and do as little as possible. One should work diligently even if the boss isn't there to watch because God is watching and God is the real boss. But again, Glass has no illusions abut businessmen and managers:

> And after He's spoken to the workers, He speaks to the bosses, Chapter 4, He says "Masters, give unto your servants that which is just", not as little as you can get away with. I remember I worked for a firm and the girls were terribly paid and it was a Christian firm, that was the sad thing about it. Like — I went into the management and said "I'd like a rise" and they said "Uh, no, they live by faith here." He has two cars; the workers were to exercise all the faith. And he brought us in on the Saturday to work in the bookshop and gave us four shillings tea money. You know what he did? Took it back off us on the Monday and said it was a mistake. Oh, it was a great time. A Christian firm. Mind you, they

gave you a calendar at New Year; the ones they couldn't sell."

Glass's God does not take class sides. He expects the workers to work as if they were working for God and the bosses are expected to pay well because they must remember they have a boss in heaven. After a short aside on a man who used to be in the congregation who was always being "led by the Lord" to other people's property and to change his name ("maybe he would have been more honest if he'd been led by the tax man or the social security"), Glass comes back to mean employers:

> Individualism, the rat race, the boss who says "I'll grind my workers into the dust as long as I make big profits". You know all these tea plantations, you know, he's working a seven day week, threepence an hour, you know, and they've got all these big profits, you know. "Poor peasant there, that black man. What would he do with money if he got it?" Give him a chance and we'll see.

As one might expect, Glass is opposed to homosexuality; an opposition that he often presents in terms of the threat of homosexuals to children. He begins by noting that the main Scottish teachers' union, the Educational Institute of Scotland, has just passed a motion agreeing to support any teacher dismissed because he or she was homosexual:

> If your kid's got a homosexual teacher, there's nothing you can do about it as long as he doesn't interfere with your child. That'll not stop him teaching it though. And the dirty old men you used to warn your children about are now in the classroom, teaching your kids. Maybe could be fondling them on the sly. That's the society we live in. Do you know what the Bible says about that? Does the Bible say "Let the gay people have a gay time", does it? They've destroyed that word "gay". You're scared to say you're gay now, aren't you? Now if you say you're having a gay time, someone'll come up to you and say "Are you one too?" (Congregation giggles) "Give me a shot of your nylons." Leviticus 20 and verse 13. You'll see that homosexuality does not get my vote. Homosexuality is a sin. We don't get God saying "Poor little gay men, we'll have to open the church hall and let them have their own little gay church and their gay minister". God says "To death with them"!

Other targets in the sermon are terrorism (which is especially associated with Roman Catholicism because of the Pope's refusal to excommunicate members of the IRA), alcoholism and irreligion. He is also against abortion (but he allows it for the exceptional case, such as when the mother's life may be at risk; there it should be acceptable). If the foetus survives to become a child then it should "be seen and not heard". Glass is very much a believer in traditional notions of discipline and self control; free expression is not part of the Christian's political manifesto.

Some elements of Jack Glass's political thinking are novel; the products of his personal synthesising work, but by and large this is good old-fashioned populism. It is Ratcliffe and Cormack, it is Huey Long in Louisiana and Ian Paisley in Ulster. It combines a desire for a return to those notions of internal control and firm punishment that we think of as Victorian, a desire for a revival of the "Protestant ethic" in work, and a critique of Godless capitalists and "bosses" who sweat their labourers. It is working-class conservatism but it does not naively accept that the past was glorious. Glass has a tendency to suppose that the present culture is "vile and sinful" but he does not romanticise any particular historical period. Glass is not a democrat. His political philosophy is based on the idea that the Bible provides norms for behaviour which should be followed, irrespective what the majority of people might want. And yet when it comes to a choice between democracy and other systems, Glass supports democracy, especially if his opponents can be seen as authoritarian. In his criticisms of the Latin American evangelist Luis Palau, who ran a six-week series of crusade meetings in Glasgow's Kelvin Hall in 1981, Glass was quick to point to Palau's rather dubious friendships with a string of unsavoury Latin American dictators.

In so far as they appeal to anyone, Glass's politics appeal to a very small section of the population. They speak to the "little man" who feels squeezed between the bosses, those élites that Ratcliffe called "the high heid yins" and that Paisley called "the fur coat brigade", and organised labour. Given that Glass has achieved practically no political following, there is not much point in speculating about the class position of those who *might* follow him but understanding his philosophy and seeing what sorts of people it might appeal to does give us some insight into the world as it appears to Glass and the small number of people who do follow him. Their world is one of resentment. They believe that they once owned their world; Scotland was once a reasonably righteous place. Now it is run by atheists and perverts, greedy sinful bosses and greedy sinful workers. They, the true believers, are a small remnant whose inheritance has been stolen from them. They have been sold into bondage. But they are law-abiding. They are loyal, even though by meeting the Pope the Queen has betrayed that loyalty. And they are British, even though the state has betrayed their national identity.

One can put this sense of betrayal into a larger social and historical context. The situation of conservative Protestants in the United States offers an interesting contrast. Their position was eroded by subsequent waves of immigration. The country they once controlled became pluralistic and their values became just one set amongst others as waves of Irish, Italians, Poles and so on arrived with their own languages, cultures and religions. The American fundamentalists' reaction was to establish a distinct set of institutions to preserve their own identity in the locations in which they were strong, a process aided by the size of America and its federal political structure. Different states could have different laws and even separate counties could follow their own interests on many social and behavioural questions. Because they saw the threat coming, the American fundamentalists were able to erect barriers between themselves and the pluralistic world outside. The Scottish conservatives were fooled by the institutional arrangements that preserved a fiction. This fiction was that Scotland (and Britain as a whole) was practically committed to Christianity and to those conservative social and moral values that were the public face of nineteenth-century Protestantism. The Church of Scotland was the state church. The Queen was the head of the established Church of England. The monarch took oaths which stated that Protestantism would be preserved. The Scottish school system was built on the frame of the schools of the Kirk and the Free Church. The result was a complacency on the part of conservative Christians. While Lord Reith was running the BBC there seemed to be no need to set up separate Christian radio and television stations. The conservative Protestants bought the myth of the corporate Christian state and so failed to create the distinct institutions which would have allowed them to preserve their identity and interests. They thought the world they lived in was their world and they did not realise the extent to which it had become secularised until it was too late to do anything about it. The result is a sense of grievance and of betrayal.

The Need for Revival

All conservative Protestants believe that ultimately the only solution to social and political problems is a new wave of righteousness, a revival. But for Jack Glass and the Twentieth Century Reformation Movement that belief is a necessity. To return to the contrast with Ian Paisley and the Democratic Unionist Party in Ulster, how does one explain their different fortunes? The answer is in that interaction between environment and ideology which I suggested at the end of chapter two while talking about Ratcliffe's later years. Paisley has been more successful for two interlocking reasons; his context is more promising and he is more pragmatic. The context will be returned to in the final section of this book but here it is enough to note that Ulster Protestants have always been under threat. While the intensity of that threat has varied the basic threat has always remained because it rests on arithmetic. The Protestants were a distinct minority. It was thus always possible to tell plausible "papal aggression" stories to Ulster Protestants. There was a tradition of mixing religion, ethnic identity and politics which made ministers in politics normal. Glass, in Scotland in the 1960s, was spreading his seed on the stony ground, not because his aim was poor but because most of the ground was stony. This meant that his initiatives met with little success. In the absence of political success, there was no good reason for pragmatic compromise. Far from it; sticking desperately to the most extreme "pure" position was really the only course of action that could be justified. Compromise that failed, pragmatism that met with no success, would have been indefensible. There is no rhetoric that could have legitimated it. Failure can be explained and justified provided one is sticking to the "old paths in perilous times". Then one can say that one rejected popularity, rejected the shallow support of men, in order to do God's work. One might suppose that every cause, be it a social, political or religious movement desires success, wants to become popular, but this is to overlook the sense of superiority that can be gained from being part of a small elect, a *cognoscenti*. Anybody can be popular; anyone can appeal to the masses but it requires a special dedication to maintain the true faith, to keep up a pure witness. There is a rhetoric that makes sense of unpopularity by positing it as proof of doctrinal rectitude.[25]

In the absence of widespread support, Glass has to fall back on the rhetoric of purity and rigour:

Someone's got to be really keen to be a member of our church with the press image I've got. To be a member of our church brings opposition upon them. Now, look back at the early days of Paisleyism. It was the same there. Things have changed now because Paisley is quite a popular figure in Ulster.

Glass sees Paisley's success as having been achieved at the cost of "selling out". His own failure is proof that he has not sold out. I would not want to argue with Glass's own story about why he has remained isolated from the obvious sources of support such as the Orange Order and the other groups that represent working-class Protestants in Scotland. What I would want is to add the observations that people's beliefs change and that his actions do not stem *only* from his beliefs but are also related to the social contexts in which he has to act. If Scotland had been a more promising environment for militant Protestantism, it is likely that Glass would have moderated his principle of separation. That the principle was not moderated (and if anything it has been extended and deepened) owes at least something to there being no good reason in hope of success to moderate. If we leave out the miracle of a religious revival, it seems impossible that Scotland will ever turn to Glass in the way that it turned to John Knox.

9

The Anti-Christ in Scotland

IT seems fitting to begin this last chapter by returning to the point where the book began. Since the Reformation, Scotland *had been* a Protestant country. The arrival of large numbers of the Irish was also the arrival of a large number of Roman Catholics. Over the course of the nineteenth century the legal obstacles to the full participation of Catholics in the state were removed. Whether this was "bowing to papal aggression" or giving all the citizens equal rights irrespective of their religious beliefs is not my concern. What is important is that those laws which were symbolic of Protestant ascendancy were gradually removed. But the Protestant character of Scotland was also being eroded by those people who were abandoning the Protestant churches.

Adult Members as % of adult population of Scotland: 1901-1977[1]

	1901	1931	1951	1966	1977
Church of Scotland	46	41	37	36	28
Episcopal Church of Scotland	2	2	2	2	1
Roman Catholic Church	10	12	13	13	14

As the table shows, the proportion of Roman Catholics steadily increased but this increase was not at the expense of the largest Protestant Church — the Church of Scotland — which was managing to decline fairly steadily on its own. Church membership figures are always suspect. Different churches use different notions of what counts as a member and show differing degrees of diligence in collecting and updating such figures but the broad trends that such statistics show can be accepted as realistic representations of the

reality on the ground. The four main Presbyterian Churches — the
Kirk, the Free Church, the United Free Church and the Free
Presbyterians — had a total of 1,174,600 adult members in 1900.[2] This
grew to a peak in 1956 of 1,372,600 but then began to decline sharply
so that by 1980 there were only 994,000 adult members. We can
express this change by saying that the Churches in 1980 were only
85% of what they were at the start of the century. But this crude
observation disguises important regional differences. The two smaller
conservative Churches — the Free Church and the Free Presbyterian
Church — were strongest in the highlands and this geographical
isolation has allowed them to avoid the worst secularising influences.
They have survived the last twenty-five years in relatively better shape
than the Church of Scotland and the United Free Church, both of
which are strongest in the lowland parts of Scotland: those parts in
which Roman Catholics settled. Taking those two Churches alone one
has a greater decline. They are only 71% of what they were when the
twentieth century opened and in that time the population has grown
to be about 115% of what it had been.

The decline in the membership of the major Protestant Churches
was matched by a fall in the size and influence of the clergy. The
Church of Scotland still retains a "Church and Nation" committee and
offers opinions on weighty economic and social matters but such
opinions are not taken seriously by the Westminster government or
the Scottish Office. Although local ministers had considerable
influence on school boards in the early part of the century this too
waned as the rationalising interests of the centre came to predominate
over local values in educational policy. In every sense Scotland has
become incorporated into the British economy and culture. As an
example of economic incorporation one might note the change in
ownership of the main employers in the Vale of Leven.[3] In the last half
of the nineteenth century there were four principal firms in the Vale,
all in the printing, dyeing and bleaching business, employing a total of
about six thousand workers. The owners and managers of the firms
lived in the area and were intimately involved in the religious, political
and cultural life of the Vale. By 1952 only some 1,700 people were
working in the local textile industry (about two-thirds of them
women) and most of the work force were employed by "branch
factories" of large national and multi-national companies. About 2,000
out of a local working population of about 12,000 people worked on
the modern Strathleven industrial estate and three-quarters of them

were employed by two American firms: Burroughs and Westclox. This was just a local example of what was happening all over Scotland. In 1939 there were just five American firms in Scotland. By 1975 this number had risen to 169. In such a context of incorporation it would have been extremely difficult to maintain a distinctly Scottish culture and although the legal and educational systems retain a certain peculiarity there came to be little that distinguished the metropolitan parts of Scotland from England.

Religious beliefs are most easily preserved when they are held by all the members of a society; when they are simply part of the shared taken-for-granted world in which people live. They are also more likely to be preserved when they form part of one social group's identity *vis-a-vis* some other group. In this sense, identity tends to be oppositional. People define themselves by their differences from some other identifiable group. Since the Union of the Crowns, the Presbyterian Churches have played a major part in the preservation of a distinctly Scottish identity and similarly the desire of a lot of people to maintain a Scottish identity has helped preserve the Presbyterian Churches. Thus the gradual incorporation of Scotland into British culture and society has also seen the decline of the Churches.

There are other reasons why religion declined in the modern world; reasons which are common to all industrial societies.[4] Explaining the decline of religion need not, however, delay us here. The important point is simply that the main organisational expressions of Protestantism in Scotland — the Presbyterian Churches — were in decline in the lowlands and their decline had little or nothing to do with the presence and growth of Roman Catholicism. Arguing the case would take another book but there seems little doubt that most militant Protestants misunderstood the connection between increasing recognition of the rights of Catholics and the decline of Protestantism. They saw the gradual erosion of the legal restrictions on Roman Catholics as the *cause* of a corresponding decline in the power and authority of Protestantism. Far from it. As the same people occasionally recognised when they chastised "nominal" Protestants for not doing enough to protect the faith of the fathers, it was precisely because religion *per se* (and hence, in the Scots case, Presbyterianism) was becoming less important that people felt that Roman Catholics should be accorded every right possessed by Protestant citizens.

The end of the Protestant ascendancy in Scotland allowed the Roman Catholic Church to restore its full range of organisational forms and symbols, and, for a time, to expand. But there is a positive consequence of persecution. Nothing preserves a group's identity so much as being a hard-done-by minority. As the Scottish Catholics came to be accepted many of the reasons for maintaining their religion were lost. Acceptance paved the way for assimilation. The maintenance of a separate school system has done a lot to retard the process but there is evidence of "leakage", as Roman Catholics term membership loss.

"Leakage" of Roman Catholics (in thousands): 1951-76[5]

	Catholic Population (estimated)	Baptism	Deaths (estimated)	Migration	Net Loss
1951	750				
		543	244	94	130
1976	825				

If we take the 1951 adult Catholic population and add to it the number of baptisms we have the maximum number of Catholics there could have been in 1976 if there had been no in-flow of Catholics from another country. From this total we take away those who have died and the net migration figure (the excess of people leaving over people coming in) and we have an expected total of 955,000 Roman Catholics in Scotland. So something in the order of 130,000 Catholics have fallen away from the faith. Guessing about the likely direction of bias in the estimate suggests that the actual figure is considerably higher than this, but even this figure is 16% of the Catholic population.

Loss of "bodies in the shop" is not the only problem the Catholic Church faces. The last twenty years has seen considerable changes in the way that Scottish Catholics view their own faith and church. They have become far more questioning and far less traditional. For example, it is obvious from the fall in the size of the average Catholic family that Scottish Catholics are either practising sexual abstinence with new enthusiasm or using contraceptives despite the Church's clear teaching on that subject.

The import of this introduction can be briefly summarised. In this century Scottish Roman Catholics have become firmly established as an accepted part of the Scottish people. The Church is now one Church among others in a religiously *pluralistic* culture. Since the war there has been an increase in "leakage" and a considerable erosion of the Church's authority over its members. These two things combined to produce an obvious need for flag-waving. Some large-scale public event was called for both to demonstrate the re-establishment of the Church and to revive the commitment of the Church's members. Something that could serve as symbol of presence and as a tonic was required. The election to the papal throne of a youngish non-Italian who liked travelling provided the answer: a papal visit to Scotland!

The Natives' Initial Reactions

The reactions of the Protestant Churches to the announcement of a possible visit matched their general attitudes to ecumenical relations. The main Churches were active in the British Council and World Council of Churches and they generally welcomed the visit. In particular the Church of Scotland, whose response set the tone for the general public reaction, made friendly noises, although certain pressure groups within the Church, such as the National Church Association, were opposed. In the view of most of the Kirk, the visit was to be welcomed as another step towards establishing good neighbour ties with the Scottish Catholics, and even those who could not be enthusiastic about the arrival of the man described by the Westminster Confession as the "anti-christ", accepted that the Scottish Catholics were entitled to a pastoral visit from the head of their Church. This was perfectly in line with the Kirk's policy for the last twenty years, which was that officials and representatives of the Kirk should show the normal courtesies to the officials and representatives of other Christian bodies, even though they may disagree with some or most of the teachings of those bodies. A year before the papal visit I was in Aberdeen to talk to William Still, one of the most respected conservative voices in the Kirk, and he expressed little concern over the possibility of the Kirk having some sort of reception for the Pope. He was much more concerned about the issue of ordaining women!

The smaller and more conservative churches such as the Free Church and the Free Presbyterian Church were opposed to a papal visit but they insisted that any opposition should be peaceful and passive and distanced themselves from popular Protestant organisations such as the Orange Order. They tried to adopt a positive approach, suggesting that the visit should be used for educational purposes as an opportunity to remind Protestants of what it is they believe rather than a time to demonstrate against what Catholics believe. It was this position of "non-militant" opposition that was advocated by A. Sinclair Horne, the secretary of the Scottish Reformation Society and described by Jack Glass as a "deformed protest".

The Orange Order was firmly opposed to the visit, which it argued was "unconstitutional". Concern about the safety of the British "constitution" was amplified by press speculation that Prince Charles might be intending to marry a Roman Catholic princess from one of the European monarchies. The Order rejected the claims of the Catholic hierarchy that a papal visit was a pastoral event and insisted that such a visit was "political" and as such had to be prevented.

Wars and Rumours of Wars

One of the features of the Protestant reaction was the use of what seemed very much like veiled threats. At one of the Orange Walks in July 1981, David Bryce, the Grand Secretary of the Scottish Orange Order, referred to the recent attempt on the Pope's life and coupled it to the trouble liable to be caused by a visit to Scotland:

> If he cannot be protected within the walls of the Vatican, the most Roman Catholic place in the world, then there is no chance of adequate protection being provided in Scotland which is overwhelmingly Protestant and where a large section of the population is hostile to the visit.[6]

Other Protestant leaders voiced similar sentiments. In his *18 Reasons Against the Papal Visit,* Jack Glass said:

> The Pope is a controversial figure and therefore a troublemaker. We ban other troublemakers from this country, then why not the Pope? The riots of Toxteth could be like a picnic compared to the resentment and riots the papal visit could cause. If this self-styled champion of peace has any concern for the tranquility of Britain, he will stay at home, but perhaps he wants to cause trouble in this Protestant country. I wonder if the Home Secretary will ban the papal visit in the interest of public order as he has banned other processions and visits. The visit of this man could cause another Ulster type situation here — the

polarising Pole should stay away.[7]

No Protestants were actually willing to say that *they* would use violence to stop the visit but many were keen to suggest that *someone else* might use force. When asked the inevitable questions about sectarian violence, most leading Protestants condemned it and made it clear that they did not support it, but insisted that it was a real possibility and that, to be on the safe side, the visit should be banned.

The other common feature of the responses of Protestant leaders was to offer grossly inflated figures for the number of people who would actively oppose the visit. To give an example, David Cassells (of whom more later), in his meeting to discuss marches and plans for demonstrations with the Chief Constable of the Strathclyde Police, confidently predicted that 65,000 Protestants would converge on George Square in the centre of Glasgow for a protest meeting on the evening of the Pope's visit to the city.[8]

The basis for these statistics was the supposed membership of the organisations whose officials expressed opposition. Shortly after the visit was announced, David Samuels, an Anglican priest who is General Secretary of the Protestant Reformation Society presented a petition to the Prime Minister objecting to the visit. This petition was supported by a variety of Protestant associations claiming a total membership of 120,000 supporters. A spokesman for all the British Orange Orders added the weight of his supposed membership of 200,000 to this petition.[9]

An excursion into Protestant organisations

Two organisations which have not yet been discussed appear in the lists of those opposed to the papal visit: the Scottish Constitution Defence Committee and the Scottish Loyalists.

The SCDC displays its influences in its name, which is derived from the Ulster Constitution Defence Committee, one of the many organisations which Paisley ran before he formed the Democratic Unionist Party. The SCDC was formed in Glasgow by Pastor David Cassells.[10] Cassells is an Ulsterman from a Baptist background who had served in the Royal Ulster Constabulary before feeling called to the ministry. He studied at the Bible Training Institute in Glasgow and while there became assistant evangelist at the Tent Hall. The Tent

Hall was a curious survival from the days of the Moody and Sankey mission of 1882. It was the evangelistic arm of one of those city mission organisations which, like the Salvation Army, combine evangelism with practical social work. The original idea had been that those who were "saved" through its meetings should leave and become good members of existing Protestant churches but they did not want to and it developed its own congregation. From the first Cassells had an uneasy relationship with the board of businessmen and representatives of the main denominations that ran the Glasgow United Evangelical Association (as the whole mission was formally known). When the senior evangelist left, Cassells was not immediately offered the job. He thinks he was about 20th on the list. But he was eventually invited to take over and he stayed for two years before the tensions between his conservative theology and the liberal evangelicalism of most of the board (displayed, for example, in their support for the Billy Graham type of mass evangelism) became too great and Cassells took most of the Tent Hall fellowship off to form the Jock Troup Memorial Church. The dispute with the GUEA board was not just about theology, of course. There was the problem of Cassells' connections with Ian Paisley. It is not true that Ian Paisley's wife is a close relative of Cassells, although they do share the same name and come from the same part of Ulster and are thus probably related in some distant way. The bond between Cassells and Paisley is one of ideological agreement rather than blood ties. Since Glass "separated" from Paisley, Cassells has become the Protestant churchman in Glasgow most in sympathy with Paisley's religious teachings, and being an Ulsterman, Cassells also has a personal interest in the politics of the Ulster crisis. Furthermore, to express the bond in the terms Cassells uses, Ian Paisley is the head of the only conservative Protestant denomination in the United Kingdom that is visibly growing and hence it made sense for Cassells to build links with the Paisley organisation.

It would not, however, be accurate to see the Jock Troup Memorial as simply the Glasgow branch of Paisleyism. Cassells is very much aware of the dangers of being too closely associated with something as controversial and (he hopes) transient as Ulster's present political crisis. Almost all of his members are Scots who have no particular sympathies with Ulster beyond those that come from seeing that crisis in terms of a struggle between the IRA, as the armed expression of the fruits of Roman Catholicism, and Protestantism. To date, the Jock

Troup has not formally been admitted to the Free Presbyterian Church of Ulster, although the Protestants Reformers Church in Liverpool (the successor to Longbottom's church) has been.

Nonetheless, Cassells has acted as "local agent" for Ian Paisley and in forming the Scottish Constitution Defence Committee, he used the model of Paisley's earlier organisation. The SCDC was intended as a co-ordinating committee for the leaders of the various militant Protestant organisations in Scotland and Derek Nielson, a leading figure in the Grand Lodge, is a member. Jack Glass was invited to join but refused on the grounds that it was liable to bring Ulster's problems to Scotland; a view that could be seen as something of a departure from his own position in the early seventies. Unlike Glass, Cassells was an active member of the Orange Order and for a while he was Grand Chaplain.

The Scottish Loyalists are the aggressive youth arm of the Orange Order in the west coast. The group was formed in 1980 by young Orangemen frustrated by the police's willingness to allow the supporters of the Troops Out movement the right to parade in Glasgow. It felt that such marches should be banned and when the Orange Order refused to organise counter marches which would almost certainly have caused violence, the Scottish Loyalists took to the streets and attacked the IRA supporters. Like the UDA a decade earlier (many Scottish Loyalists supporters are also active in the UDA), the Loyalists are a source of considerable embarrassment to the Grand Lodge which wishes to project an image of bourgeois respectability. Attempts were made to expel some leading figures from the Order but it was clear that if such measures were pursued it would cause a major split. The leadership of the Order had to confine itself to making condemnatory noises and to squirming with embarassment when Jake Kirkpatrick, a leading spokesman for the Scottish Loyalists, went on television to talk about their plans to stop pro-IRA marches by physical violence if necessary.[11] It is difficult to put a figure on the support for the SL. It is very much a loose grouping of people willing to get out on the streets when there is something like a pro-IRA demonstration to protest against and as such its membership tends to fluctuate with whatever is happening. Like so many militant Protestant groupings it tends to counter-box. It needs some example of "Roman Catholic aggression" to galvanise its supporters. When things are quiet the organisation declines.

18 Reasons against the Papal Visit

All of the organisations that were opposed to the papal visit published their own list of reasons why it should not go ahead but that produced by Jack Glass as a flyer in the Hillhead by-election covered the same ground as the others. I want to summarise Glass's *18 Reasons* and compare them with the content of nineteen-thirties' anti-catholicism summarised in chapter five.

The first reason is headed "treachery" and refers to the actions of the "Romanisers" in the Protestant Churches, especially Robert Runcie, Archbishop of Canterbury, "whose regret is that he cannot as yet celebrate the Mass in the Roman Church". The second is "headship": "the papal visit will be an insult to Her Majesty the Queen as it will challenge her headship of the Church of England. This usurping Pope claims to be the head of the universal church of Christ". Next Glass attacks "ecumenism": "for years the ecumenist traitors to the Word of God . . . have been trying to introduce a counter-Reformation in this country, now they feel that the papal visit is their hour of triumph and the final nail in the coffin of the Reformation".

Under the heading of "population", Glass points out that the Roman Catholic population of Britain is only four million out of a population of fifty-five million and yet the Pope, if he comes, will receive more publicity "than the Moderator of the Church of Scotland and the Archbishop of Canterbury combined". A good point but one which applies equally well to Glass himself who heads a church of only about two hundred members and yet receives a considerable amount of publicity. "Adoration" is used to suggest that the crowds who greet the Pope seem to be worshipping him rather like Christ. "Politics" come next in the acrostic: "Let no one be fooled by the news that this visit will be a pastoral visit. It will most certainly have all the trappings of a political state visit. It is politics by the back door. The Pope as head of state will receive a state reception from the Queen who assured him of a warm welcome when she visited him in Rome and broke her coronation vow to be a faithful Protestant".

Under the heading of "assassination", Glass argues that he is opposed to political violence but that God allowed the attempt on the Pope's life and that if the church prays enough, God may well do something else to prevent the visit. Like the Orange leaders, Glass does not advocate violence but simply states the possibility "that someone could attempt to assassinate the Pope in Britain because of the resentment his proposed visit will cause".

Other paragraphs argue that the Pope is the spiritual head of the IRA (because he refuses to excommunicate convicted terrorists and because he sent an envoy to the dying hunger striker Bobby Sands) and the head of an organisation that suppresses dissent. There is also the legalistic argument which points to the Williamite Bill of Rights and Act of Settlement and their clear statement that loyalty to the Crown is conditional on the Crown being actively Protestant. The Thirty-Nine Articles of the Church of England and the Church of Scotland's Westminster Confession of Faith identify the Pope as the anti-christ and assert that the Bishop of Rome has no jurisdiction in these lands; therefore the Pope should not be allowed to visit Britain. Perhaps the most vitriolic passage is reserved for the media:

> Your attention has already been drawn to the large number, yes majority, of newsmen who are either ecumenists, Romanists or Marxists, and who hate the Protestant cause, so one should not be surprised to see the Vatican's little man in a white suit puffed by the news media. They will come with their cameras from all over the world to capture on film the Devil's twin. News suppression will only be practised against bible Protestants who oppose the visit. The author of this tract can testify to that already as his comments against the visit have been suppressed in Scotland.

The question of the media's response to "bible Protestants" is an important issue and I will return to it.

Here we have all the features of modern anti-catholicism. There are legalistic references to the British Constitution and its Protestant basis and mention of the conditional nature of Protestant loyalty. Protestants are obliged to be supporters of the constitution but only so long as the Crown does its part by upholding the true religion. There is the idea that liberty and basic political freedoms are uniquely Protestant and must suffer under Roman Catholicism, and there is the unequivocal assertion that terrorism (and in particular the IRA) is uniquely Roman Catholic. What is absent from this list is any claim about sexual perversion or about crime and deviance in general. Glass has occasionally reprinted articles in the *Scottish Protestant View* which report crimes committed by Catholics and in particular by priests but there are no Ratcliffian assertions about the sexual depravity of Catholics. There is a paragraph that lists the failings of Roman theology but if *18 Reasons* is representative of popular anti-catholicism in the nineteen-eighties (and it is similar to the reasons given by the Orange Order for opposing the visit), then its main feature is the emphasis on the supposed links between Rome and, not sexual depravity, but political depravity in the form of terrorism.

The Bias of the Centre

Everybody thinks that the press is against them. Spokesmen for every shade of opinion on every issue feel that they are not being fairly represented in press, radio and television coverage of their activities. One of the rarely remarked advantages of the new video recording technology is that it allows the recording, replaying, slowing down and freezing of television reports for detailed analysis. But to date those taking advantage of this research opportunity have mainly concerned themselves with testing the claims of those on the left-wing of political life who feel hard done by.[12] No one seems to take seriously the claims of those on the right that the media is dominated by leftists and absolutely no one has ever investigated the Glass claim that "the majority of news men are ecumenists, Romanists or Marxists".

There are a number of different things at issue in complaints about bias. Firstly there is the question of the actual content of reports and then there is the separate issue of the motivation for whatever "slant" one might discover in such reports.[13] It may well be that the media do take the values of militant Protestantism less seriously than those of liberal Protestantism and yet this may be explained by factors quite different to those advanced by militant Protestants.

One complaint concerning content of media product on militant Protestantism is simply that there is not enough of it and it is common to find people like Glass arguing that the activities of the Roman Catholic Church get more attention than they deserve on the basis of their percentage of the total population. This may well at times be the case but it probably has little to do with any *animus* towards Protestants. What most people do most of the time is not "news". Only things that are unusual and out of the ordinary are "news". Even if it were possible for people in the media to select items from their surrounding world purely on the basis of their frequency — newspapers as collections of randomly sampled facts — no one would buy the product. If the frequency of an event figures at all in the selection process it does so only to *rule out* the mundane, the routine and the popular. Similarly the fact that a lot of people hold certain views is a very good reason for not often reporting events which are symbolic of those views. In the old hack's motto: "Dog bites man is not news". Ironically Glass's own relationship with the press shows his understanding of the principles of selection. For the leader of an organisation that has fewer members than any large parish church, Glass gets an inordinate amount of press attention; precisely because he is deviant and hence interesting.

One complaint which might be supported by the evidence is that the *reasons* for militant Protestant demonstrations are given scant attention. I can certainly think of occasion on which marches through Glasgow by Scottish Loyalists have been mentioned in one sentence with no report of the purpose of the demonstration and occasions when the same paper has given a couple of column inches to the motives behind a march of Iranian students.[14] But again, this can partly be understood in terms of novelty. Most readers of Glasgow papers know what the Scottish Loyalists stand for; Iranian students are strange and need more explaining.

A particular sub-case of the attention complaint concerns letters to editors. The late Rev George Dale, secretary of the National Church Association, has written of a bias in the Glasgow papers against his opinions.[15] But one can offer as a counter example the frequency with which the letters of William Speirs, an inveterate letter writer since his days with the Scottish Protestant League in the nineteen-thirties, are published in local papers. Obviously we could only discover if the letters of conservative Protestants are heaved into the wastepaper bin more often than those of any other interest group if we surveyed the number of letters received on any particular topic. But again, such complaints show a considerable naivety about the principles used for selection. The selector is not in the business of producing representative samples or of getting at the truth behind any issue. Letters are obviously selected for controversy value ("Let's print two: one for and one against") and for more nebulous considerations of interest: is this letter witty, provoking or does it cast a new light on a subject? If the selector of letters to be published does not think that the readers will be interested or provoked or even entertained by any particular letter, then it will be ditched, even if there is no special *animus* against the opinions aired in the letter.

The most plausible bias claims are those that deal with, not attention, but "frame". I introduced this in the preceding chapter when I discussed the way in which Jack Glass tends to be portrayed as an eccentric. What most often infuriates militant Protestants is the tone in which the reports are framed and the choice of words used in the text. Clearly something not particularly subtle is being added to the sentence "400 Protestants marched through Glasgow" if one rewrites it as "400 Protestant extremists marched through Glasgow". Attention may be given to the reasons for the protest but the words used may imply that no one in their right mind would take such reasons seriously. One can recognise the idea of "framing" but there are serious problems in demonstrating that any particular "frame" is actually intended. I have used the term "militant" a number of times to differentiate those who actively protest (or who support active protest) from those who hold "Protestant" beliefs but hold them in such a way as to suggest that they do not mind others holding quite different beliefs. I think such a usage can be defended as a simple and economic way to make that differentiation. I would also defend it by arguing that until the term became associated with the general opprobrium that is attached to the extreme (that word again) left of the Labour Party, in the formation "Militant Tendency", many of those I label as militants would have been only too happy to claim the term. The "church militant" was once something that its supporters were proud of. All words carry an enormous amount of symbolic and conceptual baggage in addition to their core meaning. While analysts have always to try to avoid terms which carry undesired implications, there is no neutral language. For this reason it is always difficult to demonstrate that the use of a term which we feel has certain connotations was actually designed to suggest those connotations to the readers or listeners. Proving "bias" in the selection of words to describe people and actions is thus an extremely difficult enterprise.

Where it is sometimes easier to identify value-judgements in reports is in the use of contrasts and comparisons. Members of the Scottish Loyalists get extremely annoyed at the way in which the press report their counter-demonstrations to Troops Out marches as if the two groups and the two sets of values being represented were similar. It is certainly the case that the Scottish journalists I have spoken to about sectarianism tend to see the two sides as comparable. They do not see the world from the value-position of the Scottish Loyalists, which is that they are supporters of the British constitution and thus legitimate while supporters of the Irish Republican movement are disloyal traitors.

To return to the Glass example, the report of his thirty-pieces-of-silver demonstration which added that they would have been of use to the silver bullion robbers whose haul had just dropped in value because of changes in the price of silver, is very clearly adding a facetious note to the story. By making a joke and attaching that joke to something which for the actor was an intensely serious business, the reporter was "framing" the story in a way that Glass would have found offensive.

Is there any evidence for a deliberate policy in elements of the Scottish media to undermine conservative Protestantism? There certainly was such a policy in the nineteen-thirties and the *Daily Record* made no bones about its opposition to Alexander Ratcliffe's League in the council elections. The editor stated that he would only accept correspondence that promoted Protestant-Catholic co-operation and published leaders arguing against voting on religious lines.

One of the few clear contemporary example of such an editorial policy was given in a rather unguarded letter from Dr Nelson Gray, the executive producer of Scottish Television's religious programmes, to a Glass supporter who had asked why Glass had not been invited to speak on *Late Call*, the late evening "sermonette" series. Gray replied:

> I have to inform you that the policy of Scottish Television is to foster the ecumenical spirit in Scotland and I am sure you will agree that, in principle, Pastor Glass is opposed to this development on Biblical grounds.[16]

It is probably the case that everyone involved in religious broadcasting is in varying degrees eager to "foster the ecumenical spirit", if only because such broadcasting has to appeal to the mass audience and thus will always tend to the centre or lowest common denominator. Gray differs from his colleagues only in his open admission that such a view is "policy". Glass published Gray's letter in the *Scottish Protestant View* and a number of people, including a journalist who was not a member of any of Glass's churches, protested. The result was a complete about-face and an invitation to Glass to appear in an STV programme.

Another example of editorial policy resulting from considerations of audience could be found in the short-lived *Sunday Standard*. The

Standard was an attempt by the Outram Group, which publishes the *Glasgow Herald*, to produce a quality Sunday paper: a Scottish rival to the *Sunday Times* and *Observer*. The *Standard* almost invariably ignored militant Protestant Orange stories because it was appealing to the non-sectarian bourgeoisie. The *Sunday Post* also ignores such stories but then the *Post* is not regarded as a newspaper of "record".

I raise the question of media bias for two reasons. Firstly, there is some evidence of a bias against militant Protestants in the Scottish media but I think it usually stems from a desire to appeal to a large readership rather than from theological or political conviction. And those considerations sometimes *assist* militant Protestants in that their activities may be "newsworthy" even though they are extemely unrepresentative. However, the price paid for being "newsworthy" is that militant Protestantism may be reported within a debunking or irreverent "frame". The second reason for raising the issue is that a good deal of what we know (and almost all of what future generations will know) of the papal visit and the reactions to it rests on the media coverage. Hence an awareness of what interests inform that coverage is essential.

The Press and the Papal Visit

The news coverage of the Protestant reaction to the intended papal visit has a number of features, few of which could be immediately attributed to anti-protestant bias. In the early stages, reporters gave a good deal of coverage to the Protestant objections, obviously in an attempt to make the visit "controversial" and hence interesting. Ironically, this coverage had the consequence of leading to the eventual embarrassment of the Protestant protest because it massively exaggerated the scale of the potential reaction and its possible militancy. The press seemed to encourage representatives of Protestant organisations to make extravagant claims. A writer in a supposedly "quality" Sunday paper said: "the contingent of Loyalist Volunteers being mobilised in Northern Ireland is expected to try to cross to the mainland over the next two months to join the ranks of Protestant militants determined to disrupt the visit".[17] Note the selection of words and their presentation. The loyalists are "Volunteers" with a capital "V" which implies that they are armed and organised in a militia along the lines of the old Ulster Volunteer Force.

They are not "getting ready" but are being "mobilised"; again a military metaphor. And they are going to *"try* to cross" to the mainland, as if there were any obstacles to them making such a journey. Again, the suggestion is that these people are either actual or potential criminals who could and should be stopped by the Prevention of Terrorism Act (the only law which would allow them to be banned from the mainland). Similar language, this time in its normal habitat, the tabloid, was used to inflate a small fire, started outside the door of a Catholic church in Liverpool, into a "blaze".[18] And any reporter worth his byline seemed able to find some Protestant leader willing to add a few noughts to the total of his committed supporters.[19]

Anyone who has tried to use newspaper reports in serious research is aware of the inflationary nature of reporting. All fires, no matter how small, are "blazes" and "infernos". Every minor discomfort is a "horror". Initial reports of threats tend to be exaggerated and then when the event in question happens, it is usually devalued so that there is a new angle for the second round of reports: the "flop". So plans for a demonstration usually talk of "mass protests" and cities being brought to a halt, while the reports of the actual demonstration (unless they can amplify the event even further) will talk of disappointing turnouts. The point about this is that it is normal journalistic practice and does not derive from any particular *animus* against Protestants. In fact, the same device was used in the reports of the turn-out for the papal mass in Manchester. Initial reports talked of expected throngs and later reports talked of disappointing attendances.[20]

As for the tone of the reports, it is difficult to find any obvious evidence of anti-protestantism. In most cases, again in order to generate a "story" rather than because of great sympathy for the anti-papal visit lobby, the reporters were happy to quote the juiciest parts of the statements from the Protestants. These were sometimes "framed" in such a way as to suggest that anyone holding such beliefs must be a dinosaur but a surprising number of reports did not even do that.

An observation I offer as speculation (because I have not done the very detailed comparative research that would be needed to demonstrate this point) concerns the differences between Scottish and English papers. My impression is that the English papers gave more time to the Protestant protests, presumably because such things could be presented as part of the "quaintness" of the Scots. The Scottish papers did not seem so keen to amplify the dangers of a Protestant backlash.

But apart from that thought, my impression of the media coverage of the anticipated Protestant reaction is that it showed no great evidence of an anti-protestant bias; the sensationalist interest in promoting the papal visit as controversial was paramount. That such an interest led to the eventual embarrassment of the Protestants can hardly be blamed on the reporters who were willing to accept (and perhaps encourage) the wilder claims of the spokesman for the Protestant organisations.

The Beast in Scotland

Pope John Paul II arrived in Britain on Friday the 28th May, 1982. Until almost the last moment there were doubts about the visit. Britain seemed about to enter a war with Argentina, a predominantly Catholic country, and many people felt that a papal visit would be seen as support for Britain in that conflict. However, if nothing else, financial considerations would have made the visit very difficult to cancel. What the *Guardian* sub-editor with his usual sense of humour called "prodigal sums" had been spent on the arrangements and although a successful tour would have made a large hole in the Church's finances, a cancelled tour would have been a disaster.[21]

When he arrived at Victoria Station in London, the Pope was met by a small group of Protestant demonstrators who heckled from a distance. The protest was peaceful but a number of ministers of Ian Paisley's Free Presbyterian Church were arrested and kept on remand for the duration of the papal visit. This seems to have been part of deliberate police policy and is an ironic consequence of all those unguarded statements about potential violence and assassination threats that the Protest leaders had been making for a year. Whether the police actually thought there would be serious trouble is doubtful but they were taking no chances and throughout the tour, demonstrators were very firmly suppressed.

After two days in London, the tour moved north through Coventry to Liverpool. If there was going to be trouble, it would show here in the city that rivalled Glasgow for sectarianism. A few months earlier, a group of about 40 Orangemen had heckled the Archbishop of Canterbury, Robert Runcie, in Liverpool Cathedral. There was no repetition of that protest. The police pushed the two groups of protesters led by Glass and Paisley into the Toxteth area, well away from the Pope's route.

On Monday the 31st May the Pope arrived at Turnhouse in Edinburgh, and after a rally at the Murrayfield rugby ground he went to the Mound to meet the Moderator of the Church of Scotland and other church leaders. To a conservative Protestant no location could have been more galling. The meeting took place in the forecourt of New College, the Church of Scotland's theological hall (which had previously belonged to the Free Church), next to the hall where the General Assembly meets, and directly under the statue of John Knox, the leader of the Reformation in Scotland. Among the crowds outside there were between one and two hundred demonstrators. Again, the police response was heavy-handed. One of Glass's supporters was assaulted by a policeman when he tried to unfurl a banner and four people were arrested and charged with disturbing the peace. The reports the following day were the usual mixture of inaccuracy and innuendo. The *Glasgow Herald* said: "Protestants extremists, among them the Rev Ian Paisley tried to push their way through the police barriers as the Pope passed in his Popemobile. The group numbered about 100, many had Ulster accents, and some rolled up pamphlets to hurl at the Popemobile".[22] The use of "hurl" rather than "throw" is a choice piece of tabloid-speak and shows a considerable ignorance of the projectile qualities of rolled pamphlets. The protest was, in fact, well behaved, if noisy.

Inside the gates of New College, the Pope was receiving a less than enthusiastic welcome from the Moderator of the Church of Scotland. One person who was present at the greeting noted that while the words were reasonably warm, talking about the Pope as a brother in Christ, the tone in which they were delivered was that of the mean host who displays his annoyance at his guest's appearance by asking: "You'll have had your tea, then?"

The next day the show moved to Glasgow. In the morning Glass led a march of between 700 and 800 Apprentice Boys and Scottish Loyalists from Govan to the city centre. In the afternoon the Scottish Loyalists marched again and about 200 protesters, led by Glass and Paisley, demonstrated outside Bellahouston Park where the Pope was celebrating mass. This demonstration was good humoured and there were no arrests.

The culmination of the Protestant demonstrations should have been the rally in George Square in the evening. It was this event that David Cassells had expected to be attended by 65,000. The actual turnout was not much more than 1,000 and many of those people were the young bloods of the Scottish Loyalists. Some of them were drunk, having spent the time between their various demonstrations during the day in nearby pubs. Their disaffection with the Orange leadership was demonstrated by heckling their Grand Master, Thomas Orr. They also heckled the secretary of the Scottish Reformation Society, and would only listen to Ian Paisley.

Thus for all the sound and fury of the previous year, with its petitions and protest marches, the anti-christ had walked on Scottish soil, celebrated mass, met the leaders of the Scottish Protestant Churches and left without being assassinated, prevented from appearing in public or even being mildly discomfited by militant Protestants.

Aftermath

The first reaction of many Protestants was to find contingencies which could explain the poor turn-out for the protests. Police brutality was one of the first mentioned and certainly the policing of the event was forceful. Media bias was also blamed. The Falkland crisis also made the lists as a reason. Some protest organisers felt that the opposition had been growing nicely and had then petered out in the month before the visit because a lot of people thought it would not take place. The momentum once lost could not be recaptured.

But none of these contingencies could blunt the significance of what had taken place. Anti-catholicism is nothing if it is not anti-popery. "No Popery!" was the slogan of the party that took a third of the votes in the Edinburgh elections of 1936. Militant Protestants had always insisted that they had nothing against individual Catholics; it was the system of beliefs and the Church they opposed. Yet here was the anti-christ, the head of that system, passing unmolested and virtually unopposed through Scotland.

How did the militant Protestants react to such a public display of their unpopularity? Almost predictably given the history of factionalism, they argued with each other. Ian Paisley in his *Revivalist* magazine tried to claim all the credit for the protests:

I want to tell you something. The Free Presbyterian Church of Ulster is the only Church that took a bold, strong, militant stand, and my brethren in Scotland and England said to me, before I left, "Brother Ian, where would we have been if we hadn't your help and your support, and the help of your ministers and the help of your Churches? We would have been left". Thank God for the Rev Brian Green who stood with us through thick and thin; Pastor David Cassells who is doing a brilliant job of work in Glasgow, God bless him! Our brother Gordon Ferguson as well, and even our brother Jack Glass buried the hatchet, and said, "Can I join with you too?" I said, "We welcome all who will stand for the Lord". I haven't changed. If he has changed, thank God, I hope he has; but as far as I am concerned all who fight the Lord's battles are welcome to join with us in our stand for God. This little Church despised and hated, thank God, is come to the Kingdom for such a time as this.

There was one thing that made my heart burn with shame, the Free Church College — the Free Kirk of Scotland — Chalmers' Church, they have their College right up on the Mound; they had an ideal site to display a great banner, but their College was shut up and there wasn't one squeak of protest from them. How sad!

I must pay tribute to the Rev Sinclair Horne, who is the leader of the Scottish Reformation Society and a Reformed Presbyterian minister, who stood with us at the Mound and stood with us in St George's Square. Thank God for the remnant testimony that doesn't bow the knee to Baal![23]

Naturally, Jack Glass was not too pleased at being described as having changed and returned to Paisley's fold. The Free Presbyterian Church may have been the largest organisation to demonstrate against the visit but Glass's people were there:

In London we were threatened by the police who were following us and who tried to suppress our protest but God gave us the victory and the protest was made. In London we protested at Victoria Station, Buckingham Palace, and Trafalgar Square but I did not see Paisley at any of these places. It was the Free Presbyterian Church of Ulster minus Paisley who protested at Victoria and we thank God for their stand . . . we also acknowledged the presence of some of the Jock Troup Memorial Church members at the protest but Paisley does not acknowledge any other than his own church making a stand. I

appreciate the part Paisley played in the protests, but let him not lord it
over his brethren and lie for his own self exaltation.[24]

Glass, Paisley, Green and Cassells all agreed that the Orange order had
been a great disappointment. The Order had published a well-
presented booklet called *The Pope cannot be welcomed to Britain
because* . . . and had held some early demonstrations and protests but it
took no part in the demonstrations during the visit. This did not
surprise Glass who read it as proof of what he had always argued; that
the Orange Order was more interested in drinking on Sundays than it
was in religion.

> They were always good for a crowd on an Ulster protest or an anti-IRA
> protest. They flopped when they did anything on religion like their
> marches to the General Assembly but they always told me that if the
> Pope ever came, then they would turn out. Well, the only people who
> were in the front line were people from Paisley's church, my own
> church and the Jock Troup Memorial. You had about 300 born-again
> Bible Protestants and your 80,000 Orangemen were nowhere to be
> seen.

Glass expected this; Cassells was surprised and in his bitterness
accused the Orange Order in Liverpool of having stayed out of the way
so that they could make amends for their earlier heckling of Runcie
and so rehabilitate themselves with the Anglican clergy of Liverpool
Cathedral. If that was their intention, it worked. Shortly after the visit,
the Canon of the Cathedral invited the Liverpool Orangemen to have a
church parade at which he would dedicate their banners.

Shortly after the Pope's visit, I talked to Cassells about his views of
the Orange Order:

> I used to be Grand Chaplain. I left because I was preaching my heart out
> on a Sunday night hoping that people would come to church (and) they
> were sitting sipping pints of beer and half 'uns of whisky in their social
> clubs. Orangeism now has to sit down and ask itself what it is. They are
> not Protestant; certainly not by text book Protestantism. There is no
> form of Christian religion in most forms of Orangeism. If they are
> going to say that they are a quasi-political body on behalf of Loyalism or
> non-Romanism but they don't want to be that either so they are social, a
> liking for flute bands, a liking for beer and whisky, a liking for parading

at certain times of the year. The Orange Order says it's got 80,000 members. I think it's got 20,000. They said they were going to stop it and when the visit came they didn't know what to do.

The divisions were complete. The two highland Churches had refrained from active protests against the papal visit. The major Protestant denominations had welcomed it. Orangeism was itself divided, as it had been earlier by the actions of the UDA and then the Scottish Loyalists, into those concerned to project an image of bourgeois respectability and those who, frustrated by their own lack of influence, just wanted to *stop* the visit; as one UDA man put it: "To go right ahead!" And the militant ministers were now separated from the Order. Glass had spent years attacking the secular Protestantism of the Orangemen — what he called "tribal Protestantism" — and now David Cassells, the last militant Protestant minister of any stature to be associated with the Order, was asking himself fundamental questions about his future relationship with popular Protestantism.

The reaction to the papal visit surprised Glass less than Cassells but both of them offered the same reaction: Scotland was no longer a Protestant country. It had a Protestant history but there was no widespread indigenous Protestantism out there, just waiting for the man and the hour to rise up. There were only two things to be done. Go back to basics and start from scratch building up small congregations of committed born-again believers. And pray for the miracle of revival.

The Collapse of Militant Protestantism

Scotland was superficially similar to Ulster in its potential for religious violence. It contained two populations with different religions and different cultures. At times these populations pursued their politics through opposed parties. Riots against Catholic emancipation and skirmishes at the annual Orange walks have been commonplace. Only fifty years ago, political parties offering a populist anti-catholicism won major victories in local elections in Glasgow and Edinburgh and the "Billy Boys" fought the "Norman Conks" on the streets of Glasgow. Even today the Orange Order can attract about 45,000 walkers for it's 12th of July parades to celebrate the victory of King William over the forces of popery.

Yet in 1982 the anti-christ appeared in Scotland and was welcomed

under the statue of John Knox by the Moderator of the General
Assembly of the Church of Scotland. Less than 3,000 people all told
took part in demonstrations to oppose the visit. How is the decline of
anti-catholicism in Scotland to be explained?

The answer is as complex as the changes that have occurred in the
culture and in the social and economic structure of Scotland in the last
century but it begins with the often ignored division of Scotland into
two quite distinct parts: the highlands and lowlands. The accidents of
geography and geology have produced a time lag of about 150 years
between changes in the accessible lowlands and the remote and
mountainous highlands. Although there are arguments about the
proper use of terms like racial and ethnic conflict, I will describe anti-
catholicism as a species of ethnic conflict and argue that one needs two
quite distinct things for sustained ethnic tension. One needs an
ideology, a set of beliefs that picture the others as devalued in some
way: ignorant, evil, easily led or whatever. But one also needs actual
contact and competition with the others. There is a crucial difference
between theoretical and practical racism.

The religious reformation of the highlands of Scotland came
very late. By the time the people of the north were becoming
converted to evangelical Protestantism, that religion was dying out in
the lowlands and being replaced with a more moderate rationalist
faith. The highlanders had the religious basis for anti-catholicism.
They did, and still do, believe that the Pope is the anti-christ but most
highlanders do not interact with Roman Catholics. The main body of
Catholics came into Scotland as immigrants from Ireland and they
settled in the lowlands. Thus while the highlanders had a theoretical
dislike for Catholicism, they had no practical experience of
competition with any significant numbers of people for whom Roman
Catholicism was a major identifying feature.

The position for the working-class Scots of the lowlands was the
reverse. They had day-to-day competition with Roman Catholics for
employment and housing, for political power and for the superior
status of their culture and its symbols but they did not possess the
religious beliefs which would have given a sustainable legitimate basis
to their conflict. This can be seen very clearly in the complete alien-
ation of working-class Protestants (in this sense meaning no more
than "non-catholics") from the major Protestant Churches. Despite
the odd racist in the Kirk's leadership and the odd church document
that talks about the dilution of good Scottish racial stock by the arrival

of the Irish, anti-catholicism has rarely been more than an intellectual belief for the Church and with the gradual abandonment of old-fashioned Calvinism even this intellectual belief largely disappeared. The limited dispersal of the Irish Catholics meant that relations with Roman Catholics did not figure highly in the priorities of the Churches even when they were sufficiently conservative in their theology to have linked such interaction with negative stereotypes of Catholics. In this century the major Churches have been led by people who have taken the presence of Catholics as a stimulus to ecumenical endeavour rather than an opportunity for a return to a militant Protestant theology.

Thus the Scottish context was always poor ground for a virulent anti-catholicism because the various elements, ideological and practical, that could have combined to produce and sustain such conflict were not combining but were located in discrete geographical areas and social groups. In addition, a number of other features intervened, one of the most important of which was the Scottish bourgeoisie's attachment to the Liberal Party. The rising middle classes who formed the backbone of the Chalmers Free Church in the lowlands were Liberals and although some of them found their way, via Liberal Unionism, into the ranks of the Conservative Party, this attachment prevented the development of a simple division in Scottish politics between the Catholics in the Labour Party and the Protestants and Orangemen in a Conservative Party.[25] There has never been a Protestant party in Scotland in the sense that the Unionists in Ulster are a Protestant Party. Chapters two and three, with their detailed accounts of Ratcliffe's Scottish Protestant League and Cormack's Protestant Action, document the failure of the most successful attempts to create such a party. The division of political loyalty on religious grounds has usually been localised, short-lived and of little significance. Some working-class Protestants still vote Tory but even the activists of Scottish Loyalist grouping of Orangemen have failed to persuade their members not to vote for Roman Catholic Labour candidates. Although strenuous attempts have been made in the last decade to modernise the Scottish Conservatives, they are still dogged by their reputation for being a party of hunting, shooting and fishing landed gentry, perfectly exemplified in the person of Sir Alec Douglas-Home. With such a character, the Scottish Conservatives cannot expect to win the support of working-class Protestants.

In common with most other industrial nations, Britain has become secularised and the churches have become the preserves of the middle classes. Thus the churches are unlikely to produce ministers who have any great sympathy for the anti-catholicism which they see as being, like Orangeism, a reactionary working-class phenomenon. Even when the ministry does recruit from the working class, the training procedures with four years at university and three years of theological college will socialise candidates out of their Orange backgrounds and into the polite culture of the bourgeoisie. This difference in class backgrounds is poignantly exaggerated by the fact that it is generally only the most radical and most liberal ministers (such as those of the Iona Community) who are willing to work in the poor urban parishes which are the homes of Orangeism. An example is Alistair Osborne, who accepted the job of forming a team ministry for the thoroughly depressed and deprived area of Ferguslie Park in Paisley.[26] This is one of the places that had a strong UDA cell in the early seventies and is typical of the urban areas in which Orangeism is strong. Osborne was a radical socialist who has no sympathy whatever for anti-catholicism and who early on in his ministry made it clear that he would not have an Orange church parade to his church. Another slum parish, this time in Edinburgh, was pastored by an American Presbyterian who had no knowledge of Orangeism or militant anti-catholicism and who manages to write about his years in the parish without ever mentioning (probably because he did not know) that his parishioners included many people who expressed their anti-catholicism in attacks on Catholics.[27]

And when the Orange Order did find two ministers who were prepared to be active in the Lodges, the result was tension and finally open conflict, with one of the ministers disappearing, reportedly because of an affair with a married woman and the other being charged with defrauding the Order. Some of the conflict in this case was a result of the personalities of these ministers and of that particular generation of Orange leaders but a good deal of it was simply the practical tension that resulted from the division with which I started this summary: the separation of religious ideology and practical conflict. Those who saw their Protestantism as an evangelical religion were always at odds with those whose Protestantism was largely a matter of not having been born a Catholic. Had the culture as a whole remained more religious, this division would not have become so acute. In a largely secular environment, it could not be glossed over and issues such as drinking alcohol and rowdyism became reasons for those who wished to preserve a religious Protestantism divorcing themselves from the Orange Order and the other expressions of fraternal Protestantism. Although the problems of the successive editors of the *Vigilant* — Alan Hasson and Maurice Brown — were unique to these individuals, their impact on the Order stemmed from the fact that it was so unpopular with the clergy that it did not have a large pool of talented and able clerics from which to choose its leaders and yet it was keen to promote clerics to positions of leadership. It was thus always reliant on one or two individuals and thus vulnerable to their character faults.

These are all problems that came from the social locations of certain beliefs and attitudes. There were also problems that resulted from the nature of Protestantism itself. In Chapter four, I argued that the combination within evangelical Protestantism of the basically democratic belief in the "priesthood of all believers" and the idea that it was crucial to know the "truth" produces endless squabbles about who has actually got the truth. For that reason, conservative Protestantism is especially prone to factionalism and schism. Protestant leaders are constantly "separating" and denouncing each other as compromisers and Romanisers. Every Protestant organisation is " the only true Protestant organisation" and impotence exaggerates this tendency. Compromise and coalition would have been encouraged by a degree of success that suggested that greater success might be achieved if Protestants buried their differences, if only on a limited and strategic basis. But unpopularity meant that such success receded and with it any value in compromise. Purity became the major goal and each group argued with each other group about its own unique possession of the truth.

A number of the above observations depend on secularisation. That is, they concern problems that arose because of the general decline in the importance of Protestantism for Scotland as a whole and for individual Scots. This itself needs explaining, otherwise one falls into the circular argument of saying that there is less religious conflict in Scotland than in Ulster because religion is less important in Scotland. One has to explain why people were prepared to abandon their religious beliefs. This is quite straightforward and can be done by making use of Coser's rather obvious thoughts on group conflict.[28]

When two groups are in conflict and they use certain of each other's characteristics to justify that conflict, then it becomes important to members of the groups to maintain those characteristics.

Ulster has not beome secularised to the same extent as the rest of Britain because religion is crucial to both sides in maintaining their identity and justifying their continued conflict. This is not to say that the civil war in Ulster is a "religious" war but only to say that, as long as religious affiliation is a discriminator of the two sides, then there are strong personal and social pressures to maintain the religious identity. Had Roman Catholics been perceived by most Scots as potent threats to their culture and society, then one can expect that secularisation would not have been as widespread. People would have had an important reason to maintain the faith. But most Scots did not feel themselves threatened by Roman Catholicism. That in turn can be explained by going back to the initial observation about the divided nature of Scotland. Those people who actually felt themselves in competition with the Irish Roman Catholic immigrants were also those people furthest away from the traditions and teachings of the Protestant Churches. In addition, the Irish were readily assimilated into Scottish society. They arrived at a time when the economy was growing. As they became established they continued to maintain some ethnic separation by having their own schools and some social institutions but they also became involved in the secular Labour movement.

The concentration of Roman Catholics has already been mentioned. Only in the Inverclyde, Glasgow, Monklands, Motherwell and Hamilton districts do Catholics form more than 25% of the population. In Dumfries and Galloway it is less than 6%. In Perth and Kinross, Orkney, Shetland, Kirkcaldy, Dunfermline, Kyle and Carrick, the Borders, Central, and Argyll and Bute, Catholics form less than 10% of the population.[29] And those figures are for the late 1970s; concentration was greater before the last war. Thus not only is the percentage of Roman Catholics in Scotland considerably less than it is in Ulster but they are more highly concentrated in small geographical areas. Scots, unlike the Ulster Protestants, did not feel themselves surrounded and pushed into a corner by a hostile population which either outnumbered them (if they looked at Ireland as a whole) or which was at least large enough to pose a significant threat (if they took Ulster as their reference).

A final point about Scottish Catholics, so obvious that it is often missed; for all the waving of tricolours at Celtic football games, Scottish Catholics are not trying to move Scotland into a new political unit. Since the Union of the Crowns, Scotland has been in an "alien" state and, as the failure of even the demand for devolution, let alone outright nationalism, has shown, most Scots are quite content in the United Kingdom. In the absence of a neighbouring Catholic state into which Scotland might be moved by the machinations of wily Catholics, the best claim militant Protestants can make is that Roman Catholicism is subverting the Protestant constitution of the United Kingdom, but in a culture that is largely secularised such a claim falls on profoundly deaf ears.

One might suppose that the present Ulster crisis would have led to a revival of anti-catholicism and in some ways it did. It gave new life to the old chestnuts about Catholics being treacherous and evil. It gave militant Protestants a political issue which they could take on to the streets. It led to the formation of small paramilitary units. But the main impact was to discredit militant Protestantism. Rightly or wrongly, most people read the Ulster crisis as "the sort of thing that happens when people mix religion and politics". The result was a considerable determination to prevent such a thing happening in Scotland. The various élite groups which were in a position to lead opinion acted in concert to discredit sectarianism. The Church of Scotland became firmly opposed to Orangeism. The media played a part in damping down sectarian violence by either under-reporting it or by "framing" it as the work of hoodlums who would have been engaged in violence and criminality even if Ulster did not provide them with a pretext.

Just a Boys' Game

Anti-catholicism in Scotland is no longer a force. Even the independent ministers such as Glass and Cassells now recognise that there is no bedrock of militant Protestantism out there waiting to be tapped. Both of them now talk about their work in terms of building up their congregations from scratch, of converting people and organising Christian education. They see themselves in much the same way as all minorities see themselves in a pluralist society: just one small subculture in a society knee-deep in small subcultures. If Protestantism survives, it will be in a "ghetto", in small isolated communities, separated from the main culture either because of geographical features (as in the case of the highlands and islands) or because a group of people have chosen to build their own social institutions to preserve their faith and identity. There is no large widespread anti-catholicism just waiting for the right sort of leader. Scotland is no longer a country in which the culture is informed by strongly held Protestant principles. In some urban areas, young Protestants and Catholics still fight but even this violence is considerably less than it was in the days of the "Billy Boys" and the "Norman Conks". It is just a boys' game. And isolated in the geographical peripheries, older people still believe that the Pope is the antichrist and that the health of a society depends on keeping the Lord's day. But most Scots are not part of either of these cultures. They see the young bloods of the Scottish Loyalist movement as unprincipled thugs; they see the highland Calvinists as quaint oddities. Most Scots live in a secular society.

Footnotes

Chapter One

1. S. Urban, "Account of Scotland and its inhabitants", *The Gentleman's Magazine*, Vol. 24, August 1854, p. 417.

2. For a good general history of the Christian Church in Scotland, see A.L. Drummond and J. Bulloch, *The Scottish Church 1688-1843* (Edinburgh: St. Andrews Press, 1973) and J.H.S. Burleigh, *A Church History of Scotland* (London: Oxford University Press, 1960).

3. John Kennedy, *The Days of the Fathers in Ross-shire* (Inverness: Christian Focus Publications, 1979), p. 25.

4. Sir David Stewart of Garth, *Sketches of the Character, Manners and Present State of the Highlanders of Scotland etc.* (Edinburgh: Archibald Constable, 1822), p. 57.

5. John McInnes, *The Evangelical Movement in the Highlands of Scotland 1688-1800* (Aberdeen: The University Press, 1951), p. 26.

6. John Macculloch, *The Highlands and Western Islands of Scotland (in 4 volumes)* (London: Longman, Hurst, Rees, Orme, Brown and Green, 1824), Volume 4, pp. 388-97.

7. McInnes, op.cit., pp. 215-261, discusses Scottish and highland education. See also D.J. Withrington, "The SPCK and highland schools in the mid-eighteenth century" *(Scottish Historical Review,* 41, 132, Oct. 1962), pp. 89-99.

8. Quoted in Margaret M. McKay (ed.), *The Revd John Walker's Report on the Hebrides of 1764 and 1771* (Edinburgh: John Donald, 1980), p. 6.

9. Ibid., p. 19.

10. R.H. Campbell, *Scotland Since 1707* (Oxford: Basil Blackwell, 1965), p. 253.

11. Quoted in McKay, op.cit., p. 6.

12. Among the many accounts of the highland enclosures, three good recent ones are James Hunter, *The Making of the Crofting Community* (Edinburgh: John Donald 1978); Eric Richards, *A History of the Highland Clearances* (London: Croom Helm, 1982); and J.A. Bumstead, *The People's Clearance* (Edinburgh: Edinburgh University Press, 1982).

13. On kelping, see A.J. Youngson, *After the Forty-Five: the economic impact on the Scottish Highlands* (Edinburgh: Edinburgh University Press, 1973), pp. 138-9 and Macculloch, op.cit., Vol. 3, pp. 151-5.

14. Richards, op.cit., p. 318.

15. For an account of the Kildonan riot, see Kenneth J. Logue, *Popular Disturbances in Scotland 1780-1815* (Edinburgh: John Donald, 1979), pp. 64-72.

16. On cargo cults, see Kennelm Burridge, *New Heaven New Earth: a study of millenarian activity* (Oxford: Basil Blackwell, 1971) and *Mambu: a Melanesian millennium* (London: Methuen, 1960); Peter Lawrence, *Road Belong Cargo* (Manchester: Manchester University Press, 1964) and Peter Worsley, *The Trumpet Shall Sound: a study of cargo cult in Melanesia* (London: MacGibbon and Kee, 1957).

17. Stewart, op.cit., p. 130.

18. Hunter, op.cit., p. 101.

19. Ibid., p. 25.

20. McInnes, op.cit., p. 107.

21. McKay, op.cit., p. 4.

22. Ibid.

23. Ibid., p. 3.

24. On the clergy of Caithness, see Alexander Auld, *Ministers and Men of the Far North* (Wick: W. Rae).

25. Norman Macfarlane, *The Men of the Lews* (Stornoway: The Gazette Office, 1924), p. 245.

26. Kennedy, op.cit., p. 29.

27. Alex. Macrae, *Revivals in the Highlands* (Stirling: Aeneas MacKay, 1907), p. 3.

28. Macfarlane, op.cit.

29. McInnes, op.cit., p. 212.

30. Macfarlane, op.cit., p. 250.

31. McInnes, op.cit., pp. 215-219.

32. Macfarlane, op.cit., p. 158.

33. Ibid., p. 28.

34. Ibid., pp. 148-9.

35. Ibid., p. 163.

36. Kennedy, op.cit., p. 84.

37. Macfarlane, op.cit., pp. 12-18.

38. Ibid., p. 33.

39. "Investigator", "Puritanism in the Highlands", *Quarterly Review,* Vol. 89, 1851, p. 314.

40. Kennedy, op.cit., pp. 78-9.

41. McInnes, op.cit., pp. 90-91, discusses the highlander's alternative to dissent.

42. The causes of the revival are discussed at length in Steve Bruce, "Social Change and Collective Behaviour: the religious revival in 18th Century Ross-shire", *British Journal of Sociology*, Vol. 34, 1983, pp. 554-572.

43. For a detailed analysis of the Disruption in Aberdeen and the sorts of people who supported the Free Church, see A.A. MacLaren, *Religion and Social Class: the Disruption Years in Aberdeen* (London: Routledge Kegan Paul, 1974).

44. There were also small rumps left behind at each reunion. A number of highland congregations left the Free Church in 1892 to protest at slackening of confessional standards and formed the Free Presbyterian Church. There were in the lowlands about 3,000 people in the Original Secession Church and a small number of people continued in the Reformed Presbyterian Church (the

Cameronians or Covenanters) after the bulk joined the Free Church in 1876.

45. Cited in Charles A. Pigott, *A Geography of Religion in Scotland* (Edinburgh University: Ph.D. thesis, 1979), p. 63.

46. John Macculloch, op.cit., Vol. 3, pp. 24-25.

47. These and subsequent figures on Irish migration and settlement come from James Handley, *The Irish in Scotland* (Cork: Cork University Press, 1945). This section draws heavily on Handley's work.

48. Ibid., p. 90.

49. Ibid., p. 289.

50. James Handley, *The Irish in Modern Scotland* (Cork: Cork University Press, 1947), p. 108.

51. Ian A. Muirhead, "Catholic Emancipation; Scottish reactions in 1829", *Innes Review*, 1973, p. 26.

52. Ibid., p. 26.

53. Ibid., p. 39.

54. Ibid., p. 33.

55. Ibid., p. 41.

56. Thomas Smith, *Memoirs of Revd James Begg* (Edinburgh: John Gemmell, 1885), p. 55.

57. Ibid., pp. 50-51.

58. Ibid., p. 70.

59. Ibid., p. 169.

60. Ibid., p. 194.

61. James A. Wylie, *Disruption Worthies: a memorial of 1843* (Edinburgh: Thomas C. Jack, 1881). What separated the Free Church from the other Presbyterian Churches was of far more concern than Roman Catholics to the average Free Church minister. And of non-Presbyterian religions, the Jews were more interesting to Free Churchmen than were Catholics. There were two reasons for this. Firstly, the Scots Presbyterians have always had a fondness for the Old Testament and for thinking of their own fate in terms of "covenants". Hence a certain sympathy for the Jews. There was also a more immediate interest. A number of schools of biblical prophecy in America were popularising the idea that the end of the world would follow a return of the Jews to Israel and would remove all the Christians and leave the Jews to spread the Christian message around the rest of the world. Hence converting the Jews to the true faith became, for those who followed this trend in millenerianism, compelling.

62. Donald Carswell, quoted by Handley, op.cit., 1947, p. 100.

63. Ibid., p. 103.

64. Smith, op.cit., pp. 133-5.

65. Handley, op.cit., 1947, p. 104.

66. David Jamie, *John Hope: Philanthropist and Reformer* (Edinburgh: The Hope Trust, 1907), p. 13.

67. Ibid., p. 102.

68. Ibid., p. 119.

69. Ibid., p. 130.

70. Ibid., p. 251.

71. Andrew L. Drummond and James Bulloch, *The Church in Victorian Scotland 1843-1874* (Edinburgh: St. Andrew Press, 1975), p. 77.

72. J.B. Primmer, *Life of Pastor Jacob Primmer* (Edinburgh: Wm. Bishop; London: J.A. Kensit, 1916) p. 6.

73. Ibid., p. 18.

74. Ibid., p. 29.

Chapter Two

1. *Protestant Advocate*, 1(1), 1922, p. 2. Very little has been written on the SPL. One of the few students of religion and politics in Scotland — Tom Gallagher — gives a basic account of the SPL but confuses it with Cormack's Protestant Action Society (the subject of the next chapter). See T. Gallagher, "Scotland, Britain and Conflict in Ireland", pp. 53-72 in T. Alexander and A. O'Day, *Terrorism in Ireland* (London: Croom Helm, 1984).

2. Alexander Ratcliffe, *The Truth About Section 18 of the Education (Scotland) Act*, p. 13. Bibliographical details of Ratcliffe's pamphlets are given at the end of this section.

3. *Protestant Advocate*, 3(7), July 1925, p. 2.

4. James M. Brisby was another militant Protestant who campaigned on the education issue. He was an Ulsterman who settled in Glasgow around the turn of the century and founded his own evangelical church. From 1910 he edited and printed his own *Scottish Protestant Review*, a monthly that ran features on Protestant church history and the evils of popery. In 1914 he helped promote, and acted as chaplain to, the Glasgow companies of the Ulster Volunteer Force. Although he was popular enough to win election to the Glasgow School Board (usually coming second to the United Free Church minister James Barr who was later socialist MP for Motherwell) he was left impotent by the domination of the Board by the official candidates of the main churches. In May 1911 of 22 members of the Board, five were official Kirk representatives, five were official Catholic Church members, three were UFC representatives, there were five non-official UFC people. On occasions Brisby might be supported by the UFC members because, as "independents", they shared a common interest in opposing the main church blocks but the UFC was well on its way to becoming a liberal church and hence was not too interested in Brisby's anti-popery campaigns.

5. Quoted in *Protestant Advocate*, 2(7), July 1924, p. 1.

6. *Protestant Advocate*, 3(7), July 1925, p. 1.

7. *Protestant Advocate*, 2(9), September/October 1923, p. 78.

8. Ibid.

9. *Protestant Advocate,* April/May 1927, p. 125.

10. *Stirling Journal and Advertiser*, 23rd May 1929.

11. Ibid., 30th May, 1929.

12. Ibid.

13. *Protestant Advocate*, January 1927, p. 1.

14. On populism see Margaret Canovan, *Populism* (London: Junction Books, 1981).

15. Percy Sillitoe, *Cloak Without Dagger* (London: Cassell, 1955). Harry McShane, a leading organiser in various left-wing movements in Glasgow at this time, held a similarly low opinion of the morals of the councillors — *No Mean Fighter* (London: Pluto Press, 1978) — and such views were sufficiently widespread to be attributed to the characters of the fictionalised story of Glasgow gangs in the twenties; A. McArthur and K. Long, *No Mean City* (London: Corgi, 1964).

16. *Protestant Vanguard*, 6th December 1933.

17. On Davison's speech and its repercussions, see Michael Farrell, *The Orange State*, London: Pluto Press, 1981, pp. 136-7.

18. *Protestant Vanguard*, 13th September 1933, pp. 1-2.

19. *Protestant Vanguard*, 27th September 1933, p. 1.

20. *Protestant Vanguard*, 27th July 1935, p. 7.

21. In fact, Ratcliffe had trouble finding this number of candidates. One whom I interviewed said that, although he was committed to SPL principles, he had been very reluctant to go forward because he was not an experienced speaker and had considerable business commitments. Only with great difficulty did Ratcliffe persuade him that it was his duty to stand.

22. See Canovan, op.cit. and J.B. Alcock, "Populism: a brief bibliography", *Sociology*, 1971, 5(3), pp. 371-87. On Paisleyism, see David Taylor, *The Lord's Battle: an ethnographic and social study of Paisleyism in Northern Ireland* (unpublished Ph.D. thesis, The Queen's University of Belfast, 1983) and Clifford Smyth, *The Ulster Democratic Unionist Party: a case study in political and religious convergence* (unpublished Ph.D. thesis, The Queen's University of Belfast, 1984).

23. Alexander Ratcliffe, *Parliamentary Debate on the Prayer Book Measure 1927*, p. iv.

24. *Daily Record*, 6th November 1933.

25. *Protestant Vanguard*, 27th June 1933, p. 7.

26. Ibid., 30th May 1933, p. 5.

27. The exchanges with Young are published in the *Protestant Vanguard*, 20th February 1935.

28. J. Boyle, "The Belfast Protestant Association and the Independent Orange Order", *Irish Historical Studies*, 13, 1962-3.

29. *Protestant Vanguard*, 6th September 1933.

30. Alexander and Mrs Ratcliffe, *My Week in Gaol*, p. 3.

31. *Protestant Vanguard*, 1st November 1933, p. 9.

32. *My Week in Gaol*, p. 5.

33. For a discussion of routinisation and institutionalisation in social movements, see John Wilson, *Introduction to Social Movements* (New York: Basic Books, 1973).

34. M. Dilworth, "Religious Orders in Scotland, 1878-1978" in David McRoberts, *Modern Scottish Catholicism 1878-1978* (Glasgow: Burns, 1979), pp. 92-110.

35. This material can be found in Alexander Ratcliffe's *The Life of a Carmelite Nun* and Edith O'Gorman's *Convent Life Unveiled*, both of which were published by

the League. On the nature and role of degradation ceremonies in certain kinds of institutions, see Erving Goffman, *Asylums* (Harmondsworth, Middx: Penguin, 1968).

36. *Edinburgh Evening News*, 13th July 1935.

37. *Protestant Advocate*, 7 (5), p. 69.

38. *Protestant Vanguard*, 27th December 1933, p. 7.

39. Ibid., 23rd January 1935, p. 7.

40. Ibid., 27th January 1933, p. 1.

41. *Protestant Advocate*, September/October 1923, pp. 71-72.

42. *Protestant Vanguard*, 24th January 1934, p. 5.

43. Ibid., 7th March 1934, p. 4.

44. Ibid., 6th February 1935, p. 7.

45. See Steve Bruce, *One Nation Under God: some observations on the new Christian right in America* (The Queen's University of Belfast: Social Studies Department, 1984).

46. *Protestant Vanguard*, 30th September 1939, p. 2.

47. Ibid., June 1940, p. 2.

48. Ibid., 28th October 1939, p. 2.

49. Ibid., 11th November 1939, p. 5. Ratcliffe's views on Germany, Jews and the War were expounded at length in *The Root Cause of Anti-Semitism, The Truth About Religion in Germany, The Truth About the Jews, Are We Fighting For Democracy?, Mr Churchill on Trial, Truth About the Christian Church and War, Hitler and the Roman Catholic Church*, and *Something New About the Jew*. It has to be said that had Britain not been at war with Germany, Ratcliffe's conversion to anti-semitism would have not have been such a bad idea. Although it has hardly been documented it is clear from the recollections of Glasgow people of that generation that there was a good deal of generalised, if weak, anti-Jewish feeling in the city.

Chapter Three

1. I would like to thank J. Macdonald Morris and J.G. Maclean, the secretary and vice-president of Protestant Action for their assistance in contacting PA members and collecting documentary material.

2. For example, A.N. Clarke's *Contact*, London: Pan, 1983.

3. PAS membership form, c. 1932.

4. There is some confusion about when James Marr entered the council. He did not stand at the main elections in 1935 but was in place by the end of that year which suggests there was a by-election.

5. PAS election manifesto, 1935, p. 3.

6. This account comes from a copy of a letter dated "Guy Fawkes Day 1935" from an unknown American to Dr Anderson of the American Christian Alliance in New York. The reference to Wm. Trainer is a mistake and almost certainly refers to

J.G. Trainer, a PA Councillor and Church of Scotland minister without a charge.

7. Compton Mackenzie, *Catholicism and Scotland* (London: Routledge, 1936), pp. 170-72.

8. *Protestant Action*, new series, 2 (2), 1938, p. 1.

9. *Edinburgh Evening Dispatch*, reprinted in *Protestant Vanguard*, 27th March 1935, p. 5.

10. *Protestant Vanguard*, 8th November 1933, p. 10.

11. *Daily Express*, 21st January 1938.

12. On the Klan in America, see John Mecklin Moffat, *The Ku Klux Klan: a study of the American mind* (New York: Russell and Russell, 1963).

13. *Protestant Action*, new series, 2 (4), p. 6.

14. Ibid., p. 5.

15. This quotation and details of the case come from a lengthy statement made by Renfrew to John Cormack and recorded by a stenographer, and from the various legal documents.

16. A PA activist suggested that this was more a result of Prescott's congregation pressing him to distance himself from PA than a change of principle on his part, but (and the same can be said about others, in particular George Horne, who stood as independents later) abandoning the party label while claiming that one has not changed suggests a lack of commitment to the party.

17. Alexander Ratcliffe said this of Hoover when he ran against the Roman Catholic Democratic Presidential candidate, Al Smith; *Protestant Advocate*, 6 (4), December 1928, p. 48.

18. *Protestant Vanguard*, 29th June 1935, p. 5.

19. Ibid., August 1939, p. 5.

20. Michael A. Poole, "Religious residential segregation in urban Northern Ireland", pp. 281-308 in F.W. Boal and J.N.H. Douglas, *Integration and Division: geographical perspectives on the Northern Ireland problem* (London: Academic Press, 1982).

21. *Daily Express*, 20th January 1969.

Chapter Four

1. *Protestant Vanguard*, August 1937, p. 3.

2. Ibid., 27th September 1933, p. 5.

3. There is some doubt about the status of John Meacher, a close associate of Ratcliffe when the League was in Edinburgh and later the Edinburgh Secretary of the League. In 1932 Meacher was listed as a member of the council of the Edinburgh Protestant Society which was an anti-Ratcliffe group. However, in later years Ratcliffe referred to Meacher as a loyal League supporter without mentioning this rift.

4. *Protestant Vanguard*, April 1937, p. 7.

5. Ibid.

6. *Protestant Action*, new series, 13th November 1938, p. 10.

7. *Ulster Protestant*, September 1958.

8. *Vigilant*, December 1958, p. 12.

9. Steve Bruce, *Firm in the Faith: the survival of conservative Protestantism* (Aldershot: Gower Publishing, 1984), Chapter 7.

10. James Thomas Findlay, *The Secession in the North: the story of an Old Seceder Presbytery, 1688-1897* (Aberdeen: Lewis Smith and Son, 1898); John McKerrow, *History of the Secession Church* (Edinburgh and Glasgow: A. Fullerton and Co., 1841).

11. Roy Wallis, "A theory of propensity to schism", Ch. 10 in his *Salvation and Protest: studies of social and religious movements* (London: Frances Pinter, 1979).

12. This schema was first published as "Identifying conservative Protestantism", *Sociological Analysis*, 44 (1), 1983, pp. 65-70. I am grateful to the editor and publishers for permission to reuse this material.

13. The terms "sectarian" and "denominational" are here used in the sense given to them by Wallis' development of the work of Bryan R. Wilson. See Roy Wallis (ed.) *Sectarianism* (London: Peter Owen, 1975); Bryan R. Wilson, *Sects and Society* (London: Heinemann, 1961); *Patterns of Sectarianism* (London: Heinemann, 1967); and *Religious Sects* (London: World University Library, 1970).

14. This feature of liberal Protestantism is discussed in greater detail in "A sociological account of liberal Protestantism", *Religious Studies 20*, pp. 401-15.

15. See various contributions to Wilson, op.cit., 1967.

16. See Bryan R. Wilson, "The Exclusive Brethren: a case study in the evolution of a sectarian ideology", pp. 321- in his *Patterns of Sectarianism*, op.cit., 1967.

17. Doug and Helen Parker, *The Secret Sect* (Pendle Hill, NSW, Australia: the Parkers, 1982).

18. David Taylor, op. cit, footnote 22, Ch. 2.

19. Robert Wallace, "Church tendencies in Scotland" in Sir Alexander Grant, *Recess Studies* (Edinburgh: Edmonston and Douglas, 1870).

20. The figures are derived from John Highet, *The Churches in Scotland Today* (Glasgow: Jackson, Son and Co., 1950); *The Scottish Churches* (London: Skeffington, 1960); and R. Currie, A. Gilbert and L. Horsley, *Churches and Churchgoers: patterns of church growth and decline in the British Isles since 1700* (London: Oxford University Press, 1977).

21. John Wilson, *Introduction to Social Movements* (New York: Basic Books, 1973).

Chapter Five

1. Martyn Lloyd-Jones, *Roman Catholicism* (London: Epworth Press, n.d.), p. 11.

2. Ibid., p. 7.

3. Tony Gray, *The Orange Order* (London: Bodley Head, 1972), pp. 43-51.

4. S.M. Lipset and E. Raab, *The Politics of Unreason: right-wing extremism in America, 1790-1977* (Chicago: University of Chicago Press, 1978), Ch. 3.

5. On the relationship between D.R.C.'s and Afrikanerdom, see Ken Jubber, "The prodigal church: South Africa's Dutch Reformed Church and the country's apartheid race policy", *Social Compass*, forthcoming; W.A. de Klerk, *The Puritans in Africa: the story of Afrikanerdom* (Harmondsworth, Middx: Penguin, 1975); and F.A. van Jaarsveld, *The Awakening of Afrikaner Nationalism* (Cape Town: Human and Rousseau, 1961).

6. *The Jesuit Conspiracy: the secret plan of the Order detected and revealed by the Abbate Leone, trans. from the French* (London: Chapman and Hall, 1886). This book was a classic source frequently used by Ratcliffe, Walter Allen and other "controversialists".

7. Max Weber, *The Protestant Ethic and the Spirit of Capitalism*, (trans. T. Parsons) (London: George Allen and Unwin, 1976) has an excellent account of the development of inner worldly asceticism. See also Gianfranco Poggi, *Calvinism and the Capitalist Spirit: Max Weber's Protestant Ethic* (London: Macmillan, 1984) and Gordon Marshall, *In Search of the Spirit of Capitalism* (London: Hutchison, 1982).

8. It should not be supposed that Roman Catholicism itself has such a mechanical model for clearing away sin. Catholics would insist that confession and penance be accompanied by a genuine change of heart but their critics tend to see only the external mechanical elements.

9. *Manifesto of the Scottish Protestant Alliance or Reasons for an Enlarged Basis of Union and Action for the Overthrow of Popery in Every Form* (Edinburgh: Scottish Protestant Alliance, 1854).

10. J.B. Primmer, *Life of Pastor Jacob Primmer* (Edinburgh: Wm Bishop and London: J.A. Kensit, 1916), pp. 142-8.

11. Alexander Ratcliffe, *The Jailed Nun*, p. 2.

12. Harold Garfinkel, "Conditions of successful degradation ceremonies", *American Journal of Sociology*, 61, March 1956, pp. 420-24.

13. In Alexander Ratcliffe, *The Horrors of Convent Life*, p. 6.

14. Alexander Ratcliffe, *The Life of a Carmelite Nun*.

15. B.L. Quinn in Alexander Ratcliffe, *Why Priests Don't Marry*, p. 4.

16. Ibid., p. 6.

17. Alexander Ratcliffe, *Rome, Marriage and Divorce*, p. 4.

18. Alexander Ratcliffe, *The Abominable Confessional*, p. 6.

19. Ibid., p. 19.

20. Alexander Ratcliffe, *The Priest's Immoral Questions to Women in the Confessional*, p. 2.

21. G.W. Target, *Evangelism Inc.*, (London: Allen Lane, 1968), p. 154.

22. *Protestant Vanguard*, 2nd October 1935, p. 6.

23. *The Confessional Unmasked showing the Depravity of the Romish Priesthood, the Iniquity of the Confessional and the Questions put to Females in Confessions* (London: Protestant Electoral Union, c. 1865), p. 56.

24. *Protestant Advocate*, 1 (1), September 1922, p. 8.

25. *Protestant Vanguard*, 27th February 1935. Ratcliffe's detailed argument about Catholicism causing crime is in his pamphlet, *Roman Catholics and Crime*.

26. For a detailed analysis of the relationship between the initial commission of "potentially criminal acts" and crime statistics, see Steven Box, *Deviance, Reality and Society* (London: Holt, Rinehart and Winston, 1976), Ch. 3.

27. Anon. "Puritanism in the Highlands: The Men", *Quarterly Review*, 89, 1851, p. 311. A more sociological version of this section appears as "Puritan perverts: notes on accusation", *Sociological Review*, forthcoming.

28. On the separists, see Thomas Brown, *Annals of the Disruption*, (Edinburgh: MacNiven and Wallace, 1893), p. 677.

29. Bernard Weisberger, *Gathered at the River* (Boston: Little Brown, 1958).

30. S.D. Clarke, *Church and Sect in Canada* (Toronto: University of Toronto Press, 1948), p. 210.

31. Doug and Helen Parker, *The Secret Sect* (Pendle Hill, NSW, Australia: the Parkers, 1982), p.61.

32. A.P. Hampshire and J. Beckford, "Religious sects and the concept of deviance", *British Journal of Sociology*, 34 (2), June 1983, pp. 215.

33. Alexander Ratcliffe, *The Priest's Immoral Questions to Women*, p. 2.

34. *Daily Mail*, 6th November 1964.

35. A. Eister, *Drawing Room Conversion* (Durham, NC: Duke University Press, 1950).

36. Max Weber, op.cit., p. 106.

37. I reported this case for BBC Northern Ireland's *More A Way of Life* television programme, 20th February 1983.

38. Cormack's views on women councillors are given in an interview with the *Daily Express*, 31st May 1962. One source thinks that Cormack was speaking tongue-in-cheek.

39. This unusual interpretation was achieved by arguing that the statements usually attributed to Paul should be read as Paul citing positions with which he disagreed!

40. R. Strachey (ed.), *Religious Fanaticism: extracts from the papers of Hannah Pearsall Smith* (London: Faber and Gwyer, 1928).

41. H.R.F. Ebaugh, *Out of the Cloister: a study of organizational dilemmas* (Austin, Texas: University of Texas Press, 1977).

Chapter Six

1. Hereward Senior, *Orangeism in Ireland and Britain, 1795-1835* (London: Routledge Kegan Paul, 1966).

2. Tony Gray, *The Orange Order* (London: Bodley Head, 1972), p. 111.

3. David A. Roberts, "The Orange Order in Ireland: a religious institution?", *British Journal of Sociology*, 22, 1971, pp. 269-282.

4. John F. Harbinson, *The Ulster Unionist Party, 1882-1973* (Belfast: Blackstaff Press, 1973).

5. David A. Roberts, *The Orange Movement in Ireland, 1816-1916; a study in the sociology of religion and politics* (University of London: Ph.D. thesis, 1974), p. 29.

6. *Scottish Loyalist View*, n.d., between November 1983 and January 1984, p. 3. I offer this as an extreme example. As a counter, it should be noted that the UVF paper, *Orange Cross* (No. 98), condemned the petrol bombing of two young Catholics with the words: "Shame on you, you have disgraced the name Protestant".

7. On the original covenant, see J.H.S. Burleigh, *A Church History of Scotland* (London: Oxford University Press, 1960), pp. 210-232. The Ulster Unionist Covenant is discussed in most histories of modern Ireland.

8. Roddy Gallacher, "The Vale of Leven, 1914-75: changes in working class organisation and action", pp. 186-211 in Tony Dickson, *Capital and Class in Scotland* (Edinburgh: John Donald, 1982).

9. *Vigilant*, I (5), p. 9.

10. *Vigilant*, I (9), p. 1.

11. Ibid.

12. Militant Protestantism was a small world. The Secretary of the Vigilance Committee and the man who encouraged Hasson to become involved was James Russell, once Vice-President of Cormack's Protestant Action. Hasson's ally in this campaign was Dr Leslie Hope, the Glasgow minister who had helped Ratcliffe in his first few years in Glasgow before turning against him. For press coverage of the "B-I-P" plan and the debates, see *Sunday Post*, 26th May 1957, and *Daily Express*, 9th April 1958.

13. *Vigilant*, IV (5), p. 1.

14. Grand Orange Lodge of Ireland to A.G. Hasson, 21st August 1959.

15. Iain McGregor, *The Holy Terrier* (Edinburgh: typescript, no date).

16. The demonstration was fully reported in the *Belfast Telegraph*, 13th and 14th July 1959, and the *Belfast Newsletter* and the *Northern Whig*, 14th July. The quotations are from the *Whig* account but they are almost identical to those in the other accounts.

17. *Open Record, May 1960, In Causa John Adams and Others Against The Reverend Alan Guthron (sic) Hasson, MA, BD, STM, and Others*, Court of Session, Scotland.

18. Mann Judd Gordon and Co. (Chartered Accountants), *The Grand Orange Lodge of Scotland; Report on Investigation, October 1960*, p. 8.

19. *Daily Record*, 30th October 1963.

20. *The Times*, 15th July 1971. I should make it clear that I in no way challenge any of these legal decisions or wish to imply that Hasson was guilty. I simply report the conflicting views and the reasons people gave for those views.

21. This is an exact copy of the minutes of the meeting found in the papers of the late John Adam. I am very grateful to Adam's daughter and his son-in-law, Dr Clifford Smyth, for access to this material. To what extent these records are accurate is, of course, an open question. I have asked the Rev J.D. Maclean if they represent the substance of his speech. He said he could not recall but he repeated the claim that Hasson was being blackmailed by his half-brother and his mother.

22. *Winnipeg Free Press*, June 1963, reprinted in *Vigilant*, IX (8), June/August 1963, p. 3. See also *Scottish Daily Express*, 14th March 1963.

23. The hostel case was reported in the *Edinburgh Evening News*, 17th and 18th November 1982, and the verdict is reported in the *Scotsman*, 2nd December 1982.

24. Ian Henderson, *Scotland: Kirk and People* (London: Lutterworth Press, 1969), pp. 44-48 on Macleod and the Iona Community. For Hasson's comments on the Iona Community, see *Daily Express*, 10th June 1957.

25. Arthur Jones was reinstated by the General Assembly May 1984.

26. *Glasgow Herald*, 26th April 1979.

27. A good example of hysterical over-reporting is Ian Sutherland's "Doing the Orange Walk", *New Society*, 9th July 1981, pp. 49-50, which says that the proliferation of the various small paramilitary groups" indicates a climate highly conductive to their growth" and that "Protestant extremism in Scotland remains a potent force, openly condoned by sections of the respectable establishment". Both views could only be plausible to those with no acquaintance with Scottish Protestantism.

28. The extent and impact of government planning on Scotland is discussed by Christopher Harvie, *Scotland and Nationalism: Scottish society and politics, 1707-1977* (London: George Allen and Unwin, 1977), Ch. 5.

29. *Glasgow Herald*, 21st May 1973.

Chapter Seven

1. Michael Farrell, *Arming the Protestants; the formation of the Ulster Special Constabulary and the Royal Ulster Constabulary 1920-27* (Dingle, Co. Kerry: Brandon Books, 1983).

2. David Boulton, *The UVF* (Dublin: Torc Books, 1973).

3. Arthur Aughey and Colin McIlheney, "The Ulster Defence Association: paramilitaries and politics", *Conflict Quarterly*, II (2), Fall 1981, pp. 32-45. See also Sarah Nelson, *Ulster's Uncertain Defenders: Loyalists and the Northern Ireland conflict* (Belfast: Appletree Press, 1984).

4. The UDA has also tried to develop a political party arguing for an independent Ulster. Initially the New Ulster Political Research Group, this became the Ulster Loyalist Democratic Party. It has contested a number of elections and polled badly. The UVF had a short flirtation with electoral politics in the 1974 General election when its candidate polled badly. A difficulty in calculating the extent to which the UDA is still involved in the killing of Catholics is the proliferation of "fronts". The Ulster Freedom Fighters who have been involved in a large number of killings are widely reckoned to be UDA men, just as the Protestant Action Force and the Red Hand Commando are taken to be UVF fronts. For a summary of all the paramilitary groups and their allegiances see David McKittrick, "Orange Underworld", *Irish Times*, 10th January 1977, p. 10.

5. *Daily Record*, 12th June 1973.

6. *Daily Express*, 22nd December 1973.

7. *Daily Express*, 4th June 1974.

8. *Daily Record*, 17th June 1977; *Glasgow Herald*, 17th June 1977.
9. *Daily Express*, 6th November 1973.
10. BBC Scotland *Current Account*. Interview, 21st September 1976, transcript, p. 1.
11. Ibid., pp. 2-3.
12. Ibid., p. 9.
13. *Scotsman*, 13th December 1976.
14. *Scotsman*, 20th December 1976.
15. This is a transcript of a recorded conversation. I have "edited" the original in the sense of inserting punctuation and presenting some of the words in their English spelling rather than attempting a phonetically accurate transcription. Those dialect words that will readily be understood I have represented in their dialect form; the rest I have anglicised.
16. *Glasgow Herald*, 31st May and 5th June 1979; *Scotsman*, 31st May and 7th June 1979. The appeals were reported in the *Daily Record* and the *Scotsman*, 6th March 1980.
17. *Glasgow Herald*, 5th June 1979.
18. *Scotsman*, 31st May 1979.
19. *Daily Record*, 19th February and 2nd June 1979; *Scotsman*, 11th, 19th, 31st May and 8th June 1979; *Glasgow Herald*, 6th June 1979.
20. *Scotsman*, 23rd June 1979.
21. *Scotsman*, 13th June 1979.
22. *Daily Record*, 31st July 1979.
23. *Daily Record*, 13th and 19th November 1982; *Scotsman*, 10th and 19th November 1979; *Glasgow Herald*, 19th November 1982.
24. *Scotsman*, 31st May 1979.
25. A resolution of the Free Presbyterian Church Presbytery condemning the Government's failure to provide security and calling on members to defend themselves was read to all congregations on Sunday 26th February 1984.
26. James Patrick, *A Glasgow Gang Observed* (London: Eyre Methuen, 1973). For an account of the gangs of an earlier period — the Protestant Billy boys and the Catholic "Norman Conks" who were active in the early thirties — see Percy Sillitoe, *Cloak Without Dagger* (London: Cassell and Co., 1955).
27. Patrick, op.cit., p. 40.

Chapter Eight

1. BBC Sound Archives, *World at One*, LP 34523.
2. In addition to the cited documents, this chapter draws heavily on five interviews with Pastor Glass between 1980 and 1984. The mistake about Glass's father seems to stem from D. McKittrick, "The Scottish Pastor who mimics Paisley", *Irish Times*, 20th March 1982.
3. *Articles of Faith and Constitution of the Zion Sovereign Grace Evangelistic Baptist Church, n.d.*

4. For an excellent account of early Protestant politics, see Michael Waltzer, *The Revolution of the Saints: a study in the origins of radical politics* (Harvard: Harvard University Press, 1965).

5. For a statement of the Reformed Presbyterian position, see the papers in *Tercentenary of the National Covenant of Scotland, 1638-1938: Memorial Convention of the Three Reformed Presbyterian Churches of Scotland, Ireland and America* (Edinburgh, Glasgow and London: Blackie and Son, 1939) and *Testimony of the Reformed Presbyterian Church of Ireland, Vol. II* (Belfast: Synod of RP Church, 1939).

6. *Glasgow Herald*, 10th January 1969.

7. Insert on Paisley in *Scottish Protestant View*, 1976, p. 4.

8. "TULIP" comes from the first letters of the following phrases: Total depravity of the sinner, Unconditional election, Limited atonement, Irresistible grace, Perseverance of the saints.

9. Insert in *Scottish Protestant View*, 1976, p. 6.

10. The case is well argued by William Archer in 1853. See David A. Roberts, *The Orange Movement in Ulster, 1886-1916: a study in the sociology of religion and politics* (London University, Ph.D. thesis, 1974), p. 242.

11. Roberts, op.cit., pp. 242-248.

12. Jack Glass, *The Pope's Blessing*, recorded sermon.

13. Rev Martyn Smith, quoted in David Taylor, *The Lord's Battle: an ethnographic and social study of Paisleyism in Northern Ireland* (unpublished Ph.D. thesis, The Queen's University of Belfast, 1983), p. 35.

14. Jack Glass, *The Pope's Blessing*, recorded sermon.

15. Jack Glass, *The Charismatic Movement*, recorded sermon.

16. *Scottish Reformation Society Newsletter*, 1980, p. 3.

17. *Scottish Protestant View*, 12 (4).

18. P.J. Waller, *Democracy and Sectarianism: a political and social history of Liverpool, 1868-1939* (Liverpool: Liverpool University Press, 1981).

19. In the 1979 elections 572,239 valid votes were cast. The first four candidates on the first count were Ian Paisley (170,688), John Hume (140,622), John Taylor (68,185) and Harry West (56,984). Paisley increased his personal standing in the 1984 EEC elections when he gained 230,251 first preference votes. John Hume had 151,399 and John Taylor, standing as the single Official Unionist candidate on this occasion, gained 147,169 votes. For a summary of election results from 1968-79, see W.D. Flackes, *Northern Ireland: a political directory, 1968-79* (Dublin: Gill and Macmillan, 1980).

20. S. Elliot and T.J. Smith, *Northern Ireland: the district council elections of 1981* (Belfast: The Queen's University of Belfast, 1981).

21. Paisley took the North Antrim seat at Westminster in the 1970 General Election with 41% of the vote. In the two elections of 1974, he gained a massive 64% and 73% of the vote. This was inflated by the UUUC decision to support one anti-powersharing candidate in each constituency but even when opposed by an Official Unionist, as in 1979 and 1983, Paisley still took 52% and 54% of the vote; in each case polling twice as well as his nearest rival.

22. Jack Glass very often fills the *Scottish Protestant View* with cuttings from secular

papers which report his activities. This section is based on that material in *SPV* 12 (3).

23. The format of Glass's sermons is very often stylistic rather than logical. *The Christian's Political Manifesto* is constructed as a series of observations on points beginning with the various letters in the title. It is framed on an acrostic, a similar technique being used for *18 Reasons Against the Papal Visit*.

24. This and all other quotations in this section come from the sermon *A Christian's Political Manifesto*.

25. On political sects, see Roger O'Toole, "Sectarianism in Politics: case studies of Maoists and De Leonists", pp. 162-189 in Roy Wallis, *Sectarianism* (London: Peter Owen, 1976). On sectarianism generally, see Bryan Wilson, *Religious Sects: a sociological study* (London: Weidenfeld & Nicolson, 1970).

Chapter Nine

1. James Darragh, "The Catholic population of Scotland, 1878-1977" in David McRoberts, *Modern Scottish Catholicism, 1878-1978* (Glasgow: Burns, 1979).

2. These figures were compiled from the variety of sources listed in Steve Bruce, "The persistence of religion: conservative Protestantism in the United Kingdom", *Sociological Review*, 31 (3), 1983, pp. 453-470.

3. See footnote 8, Chapter 6.

4. For detailed presentations of the various secularisation themes and the empirical material that supports them, see Bryan Wilson, *Religion in Sociological Perspective* (London: Oxford University Press, 1983); David Martin, *A General Theory of Secularization*, (Oxford: Basil Blackwell, 1978) and Peter L. Berger, *The Heretical Imperative* (London: Collins, 1980).

5. This table is adapted from D. McRoberts, op.cit., p. 241.

6. *Scotsman*, 13th July 1981.

7. Jack Glass, *18 Reasons Against The Papal Visit*.

8. *Daily Record*, 5th April 1982.

9. *Guardian*, 2nd September 1980.

10. The SCDC was launched with a press conference at the North British Hotel in Glasgow on the 7th August 1980. Dr. Paisley addressed its first public meeting in the City halls the next evening.

11. Ulster Television, *Counterpoint*, 19th February 1981.

12. See, for example, the Glasgow University Media Group, *Bad News* (London: RKP, 1976).

13. The theoretical and methodological problems associated with the "discovering" of hidden agendas, underlying "real" meanings and so on are discussed by W. Sharrock and D. Anderson, "The persistent evasion of technical problems in media studies", *Sociology*, 16 (1), pp. 108-15.

14. The experience of one freelance journalist who files a variety of political stories with the Scottish press suggests considerable under-reporting of Orange events. Unfortunately, I cannot be more specific without ruining his chances of selling further stories.

15. George Dale, the secretary of the National Church Association, in a private communication in July 1983, listed various occasions on which he had tried to correct misleading newspaper stories with letters to the editor and not been published. The claims are also made in *Bulwark*, May/June 1983.
16. The Gray letter of January 1983 was reprinted in the *Scottish Protestant View*, March 1983.
17. *Observer*, 4th April 1982.
18. *Belfast Telegraph*, 10th May 1982.
19. For example, "65,000 Orangemen may parade through Glasgow", *Daily Record*, 5th April 1982.
20. *Guardian*, 1st June 1982, headline p. 4. "Missing 800,000 upset Manchester Close Calculations".
21. *Guardian*, 27th May 1982.
22. *Glasgow Herald*, 1st June 1982.
23. *Revivalist*, July/August 1982.
24. Jack Glass, mimeo.
25. For general material on the influence of religion on voting in Scotland, see Ian Budge and D.W. Urwin, *Scottish Political Behaviour: a case study in British homogeneity* (London: Longmans, 1966) and John Kellas, *The Scottish Political System* (Cambridge: Cambridge University Press, 2nd edition, 1975).
26. *Focus on Ferguslie: a report on the St. Ninian's Team Ministry 1974-1980* gives a detailed account of Ferguslie Park and Osborne's work. I am grateful to Alistair Osborne for a long interview which gave me considerable insight into Orangeism and the Kirk.
27. W.J. Christman, *The Christman File* (Edinburgh: St. Andrew Press, 1978).
28. See Georg Simmel, *On Individuality and Social Forms* (Chicago: Chicago University Press, 1971), pp. 70-95; and Lewis A. Coser, *The Functions of Social Conflict* (London: RKP, 1965).

Bibliographical Appendix

Scottish Protestant League

Alexander Ratcliffe was a prolific pamphleteer. The following is a list of his publications that I have found or have found mentioned. There were probably others that have not come to light. All were published by Ratcliffe himself in Edinburgh until 1931 and then from Glasgow. Almost all of them were entirely his own composition. Some were essentially reprints and in those cases the author is given in brackets.

The "Wake Up Scotland" Series Scottish Protestant League (most composed between 1924 and 1929)

1   The Horrors of Convent Life
2   The Life of a Carmelite Nun
3   Parliamentary Debate on the Prayer Book Measure of 1927
4   Evolution: Hell with the Lid off
5   The Horrible Lives of the Popes of Rome
6   The Great Duffy-Ratcliffe Debate of the 1918 Education Act
7   (title unknown)
8   An Exposure of the Margaret Sinclair Fiasco
9   Purgatory: Rome's Semi-Hell
10 Are Romanists Allowed to Read the Bible?
11 Roman Catholics and Crime
12 Why Priests Don't Wed (B.L. Quinn)
12a The Priest's Immoral Questions to Women
13 Rome, Marriage and Divorce
14 The Abominable Confessional
15 (title unknown)
16 (title unknown)
17 Liguori the Filthy
18 Debate: Should Mr Campbell be put out of the Episcopal Church in Scotland?

Early assorted publications (c. 1922-1935)

All About Him: a profile of Alexander Ratcliffe
My Week in Gaol (Mrs Ratcliffe)
Was the Church of Rome the First Church?
Pope Joan (the female Pope) and her Baby
The State of the Blessed Dead
Convent Life Unveiled (Edith O'Gorman)
Escape from Convent and Conversion (Edith O'Gorman)
In a Nudist Camp ("Eyewitness")

Commonsense War Pamphlets (c. 1941)

1   Are We Fighting for Democracy?
2   Mr Churchill on Trial

British Protestant League Truth Series (c. 1942-43)

1   The Truth about the Christian Church and War
2   The Truth about Religion in Germany
3   The Truth about Hitler and the Roman Catholic Church
4   The Truth about the Jews
5   The Truth about Jesus being a Jew
6   The Truth about Women Preachers
7   The Truth about Conversion
8   The Truth about Democracy

Later assorted publications (1943-46)

The Salvation Army: its Jewish origin, methods and tyranny
The Root Cause of Anti-Semitism

Ratcliffe's firt periodical was launched in September 1922 as a bi-monthly: *Protestant Advocate*. The first volume had eight issues and the second volume began as a monthly in January 1924. Hence the third volume begins in January 1925. In July 1926 the *Advocate* went back to being a bi-monthly so that volume 4 only had 9 issues in 1926, a tenth for January/February 1927 and so on until 4 (12) in June/July 1927, when Ratcliffe went back to monthly production with a volume 5. The monthly pattern lasted through all of volume 5 and most of volume 6. The May/June 1929 issue took the *Advocate* back to bi-monthly but the volume was continued for 12 issues which meant that (just to mke the researcher's life easy) volume 7 begins in January of 1930. Volume 7 was erratic, sometimes monthly, sometimes bi-monthly ending with the twelfth issue in July 1931. By then Ratcliffe had moved to Glasgow. The periodical was re-launched there as the fortnightly *Vanguard* and a tabloid newspaper format replaced the quarto magazine size. The *Vanguard* continued to be produced until Ratcliffe's death although there were one or two gaps when he was ill and the frequency and size fluctuated. A complete set of the *Protestant Advocate* is available in the British Museum periodicals library. There is a set of *Vanguard* until 1941 in the Mitchell Library, Glasgow.

Protestant Action

John Cormack's movement produced a monthly periodical called *Protestant Action*. I have been unable to find any copies of the first series, which was produced some time between 1934 and 1937. I have copies of a "new series" of *Protestant Action* that must have begun as a fortnightly in August 1937 and which continued until some time in 1939.

The Orange Order

The *Vigilant* was launched as a monthly magazine in March 1955. It continued in that format until May 1968 when, with 14 (3), it was changed to tabloid newspaper size and bi-monthly publication. At the end of 1973, the *Vigilant* was replaced by a monthly magazine called the *Orange Torch* which still appears.

Index